What readers are saying about *Augmen* *Practical Guide*

All in all, this is an excellent book that will appeal to a lot of people, especially students and beginners. There is a really nice flow from one section to the other and lots of code examples. This kind of system would be fantastic to have in schools to introduce kids to a whole wide variety of topics, from basic computer programming, matrix math, pinhole cameras, game programming, simple artificial intelligence, and interacting with cameras to a whole range of other topics.

> ► **Steven Ness**
> Programmer, Sness Consulting

This book enables anyone with basic programming skills to create augmented reality applications quickly and easily. It uses a novel tag-based system for creating augmented reality applications. This book describes both how to use this system, which is called ARTag, and how to create the virtual content using the OpenGL graphics system.

> ► **Dr. Gerhard Roth**
> Adjunct Research Professor, University of Ottawa and
> Carleton University

Augmented reality is at the crossroads between computer graphics and computer vision. This new technology will enable a wealth of possibilities in many domains—engineering and especially entertainment—blending together reality with fiction. AR is a new field, and ARTag is a solid and flexible tool that will make your AR ideas come alive faster than you can say "AR." The first half of his book takes you all the way through the relevant aspects of computer graphics theory. The second half teaches you to deliver the goods. This pioneer work is your best crack today at what will be commonplace tomorrow.

> ► **Christian Langis**
> Systems Developer

Augmented Reality

A Practical Guide

Augmented Reality
A Practical Guide

Stephen Cawood

Mark Fiala Ph.D.

The Pragmatic Bookshelf
Raleigh, North Carolina   Dallas, Texas

Many of the designations used by manufacturers and sellers to distinguish their products are claimed as trademarks. Where those designations appear in this book, and The Pragmatic Programmers, LLC was aware of a trademark claim, the designations have been printed in initial capital letters or in all capitals. The Pragmatic Starter Kit, The Pragmatic Programmer, Pragmatic Programming, Pragmatic Bookshelf and the linking g device are trademarks of The Pragmatic Programmers, LLC.

Every precaution was taken in the preparation of this book. However, the publisher assumes no responsibility for errors or omissions, or for damages that may result from the use of information (including program listings) contained herein.

Our Pragmatic courses, workshops, and other products can help you and your team create better software and have more fun. For more information, as well as the latest Pragmatic titles, please visit us at

http://www.pragprog.com

ISBN-10: 1-934356-03-4

ISBN-13: 978-1-934356-03-6

Printed on acid-free paper with 50% recycled, 15% post-consumer content.

First printing, January 2008

Version: 2007-12-19

Contents

## Chapter 1

About Augmented Reality

1.1 What Is Augmented Reality?

Wouldn't it be cool to walk around a level of your favorite video game and battle life-size game characters? For decades, video game developers have yearned to make their games more immersive, and when you consider the difference between Spacewar and Halo, it's obvious that a great deal of progress has been made. However, the typical video game is still played with the gamer sitting statically on a couch while staring at a screen.

Video games don't have to be so passive. Although the Nintendo Wii has helped turn video games into aerobic workouts, games don't even need to be played indoors. Freeing gamers from their living rooms is just one application of the burgeoning technology called *augmented reality* (AR).

The ambitious goal of AR is to create the sensation that virtual objects are present in the real world. To achieve the effect, software combines *virtual reality* (VR) elements with the real world. Obviously, AR is most effective when virtual elements are added in real time. Because of this, AR commonly involves augmenting 2D or 3D objects to a real-time digital video image. The simplest example of visual AR is overlaying a 2D image on digital video. However, it is also possible to add 3D objects—they can be rendered so that they appear to belong to a scene containing real 3D objects. Generally speaking, adding a 3D object to real-time video makes for a more impressive demonstration of AR technology.

When virtual objects are added to a scene, it is known as *visual AR*. By definition, AR elements are not visible to the naked eye, so visual AR relies upon some sort of display. This display can be as simple as a computer monitor or a television, or it could be something more advanced—such as a see-through eyepiece on a *head-mounted display* (HMD). New options are becoming available as many AR researchers are focusing their efforts on interfaces such as handheld devices, webcams, and more advanced HMDs.

This book introduces and explains AR to software hobbyists. It gives you all the information you will need to quickly start developing your own AR applications, and the final two chapters show you how to create your own AR video game. To get you up and running as fast as possible, sample code and compiled versions of the samples are provided. Furthermore, to make the examples as accessible as possible, code is provided in C++, and one sample is ported to C#. The compiled samples include versions for Linux, Mac OS X, and Windows. Want to dig deeper? You will also find detailed explanations of AR technology—even the math will be explained.

Using AR, it is possible to achieve a level of immersion that is beyond what most people associate with video games. However, this is not the only application of AR technology. Granted, few people these days have access to the HMDs that allow for truly immersive experiences, but it is possible to create AR applications using readily available hardware. In this book, we will show you how to create your own AR applications using nothing more than a PC and a USB 2.0 webcam.

1.2 The Origins

In 1968, Ivan Sutherland created a working prototype of what is widely considered to be the first VR system and the first AR system. Although it used simple wire-frame graphics, the project was the genesis of AR. Sutherland wrote about his work in a Harvard University paper entitled "A Head-Mounted Three-Dimensional Display" (http://www.aec.at/en/archiv_files/19902/E1990b_123.pdf). Sutherland's system required that the user wear a cumbersome HMD that was so heavy it had to be suspended from the ceiling. Based on this, the device was nicknamed the Sword of Damocles.

Sutherland recognized that his interface was limited, so he continued to work on better systems. A few years after his first VR system, Sutherland wrote a paper called "The Ultimate Display." Sutherland's dream interface was described in this paper, and to any Star Trek fan his description would conjure up images of the famous holodeck.

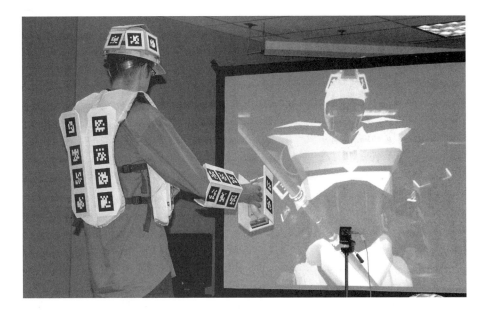

Figure 1.1: A LARGE MAGIC MIRROR

He wrote, "The ultimate display would, of course, be a room within which the computer can control the existence of matter. A chair displayed in such a room would be good enough to sit in. Handcuffs displayed in such a room would be confining, and a bullet displayed in such a room would be fatal. With appropriate programming such a display could literally be the Wonderland into which Alice walked" (http://www.informatik.umu.se/~jwworth/TheUltimateDisplay.pdf).

1.3 Magic Lens vs. Magic Mirror

The two common paradigms for AR are the *magic mirror* and the *magic lens*. The magic mirror technique involves putting a computer monitor, or a television, behind the area that is being captured by an AR video camera. The display is the *mirror*, and it often displays the augmentations via real-time video. If you have a large display (for example, a projection screen), you can stand in front of a magic mirror and enjoy some full-scale augmentation (see Figure 1.1). For example, you might be a hockey goalie blocking shots from virtual shooters.

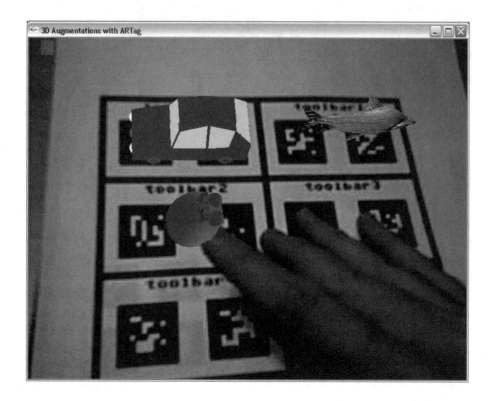

Figure 1.2: THE MAGIC LENS PERSPECTIVE

The magic lens viewpoint is a completely different approach. Rather than offering the user a mirror to look at, the magic lens allows the user to *see through* to an image of the real world with added AR elements (see Figure 1.2). In this setup, the user has some sort of display in front of him; it could be as simple as a standard computer monitor or as complex as an HMD. In this book, the magic lens approach will be used for most of the examples.

1.4 Marker vs. Markerless AR

As you'll learn in Chapter 3, AR systems generally require some indication of where exactly they should augment a digital image. This is most commonly accomplished with *AR markers*. Various markers have been tried—everything from light-emitting diodes (LEDs) to a person's hand. But the simplest form of marker is a unique pattern that is visible to

Figure 1.3: A 3D AR FISH ON A MARKER PATTERN

the AR camera and can be identified in the AR system software. These patterns are physically added to the real world. In Figure 1.3, the fish is a virtual 3D object, and the pattern below contains marker tags. The marker tags are used to determine the viewpoint of the real camera so that the virtual fish can be rendered appropriately.

To demonstrate AR technology, this book will use the ARTag marker system (http://www.artag.net). ARTag was developed by Dr. Mark Fiala, coauthor of this book and a researcher at the National Research Council of Canada (NRC) (http://www.iit-iti.nrc-cnrc.gc.ca/r-d/cv-vi_e.html). ARTag is a digitally generated and scientifically verified fiducial marker system for AR (see Figure 1.4, on the next page). *Fiducial* means the markers are used as a trusted reference.

ARTag is a computer vision software system that uses markers to align real and virtual cameras. ARTag recognizes special black-and-white square markers, finds the pose, and then sets the modelview matrix

Figure 1.4: ARTAG FIDUCIAL MARKERS

so that subsequent rendering operations appear relative to the array and, therefore, relative to the real 3D world. In other words, the ARTag markers allow the software to calculate where to insert virtual elements so that they appear properly in the augmented image.

To use ARTag, marker patterns are printed and then placed where the user would like virtual elements to appear. ARTag has a *software development kit* (SDK) that includes a library of markers, the computer vision software to find them in images, and some code to help load and display 3D models. You will be learning more about how ARTag works later in the book. In fact, you'll probably find more information than you could ever want about AR markers.

Adding AR markers can be as simple as printing a marker pattern and then placing the printout in the field of a webcam image that's running through AR software. When the markers are recognized by AR software, the computer is able to determine the position and angle of the marker. The software can then use this information to extrapolate the correct position and orientation of a virtual object. When this computation is complete, the software overlays the virtual object on top of the original camera image, and the augmented version is shown to the user. If the AR software renders the object correctly, it will appear to be part of the real-world scene. Since the orientation is also calculated, the virtual object can be adjusted as the marker is moved around in 3D space.

It is possible, however, to create an AR effect without using markers; this is known as *markerless AR* and is ideal since it does not require the forethought of adding markers to a scene. A tracking system can instead track the position of LEDs, or reflective balls, with special equipment for placing virtual elements in a digital image. Such systems are often seen in university VR labs. Markerless tracking, however, is understood in the AR community to mean not adding anything to the environment. Instead, "natural" features such as the corner of a window or a distinctive painting on a wall would be used.

In the future, markerless AR will probably turn out to be the preferred method of AR. However, markerless AR has not yet advanced to the point where it's possible to provide a simple way for the public to use the technology, and markerless systems that perform as well as marker-based, or LED-based, systems are not yet available. For this reason, this book will use an AR marker system.

1.5   Examples of Applied AR

AR is rapidly gaining popularity, but it is still a fledgling technology. Most of the current applications are academic, but there are some commercial products on the market. These applications include everything from factory floor design to storytelling. Based on the wide breadth of these uses, it's clear that AR has a promising future. The next section highlights some examples of contemporary AR projects.

ARQuake

ARQuake (http://wearables.unisa.edu.au/arquake) is a virtual reality game using the game engine from id Software's classic first-person shooter, Quake. The game is an excellent example of how AR can be used to immerse a person within an augmented environment. ARQuake gamers are able to freely move around the physical space used for each level (see Figure 1.5, on the following page). To all those gamers who have been told to "go play outside," the ARQuake system may be the answer to their digital dreams.

ARQuake began in 1998 as a project at the University of South Australia. The original team members included Dr. Bruce Thomas, Dr. Wayne Piekarski, Benjamin Close, John Donoghue, John Squires, and Phil De Bondi. Over the years, it has been featured in many news stories and academic papers. Today, the project is still going and is currently maintained by Piekarski, Close, and Thomas.

To display the AR elements, track the player, and control the game, AR-Quake uses an HMD, a notebook computer, a head tracker, and a GPS system. To create the illusion of Quake monsters attacking the player, ARQuake adds virtual monsters to the player's viewpoint through the HMD. As the player moves his head, the game calculates which virtual monsters should appear in his HMD display.

ARQuake inspired commercially available AR game systems such as a_rage—the Augmented Reality Active Game Engine. The a_rage engine

Figure 1.5: AN ARQUAKE VIRTUAL MONSTER

is still in its infancy, but games based on it have been featured at trade shows such as the Electronic Entertainment Expo (E3).

Looking toward the future, the company that makes a_rage held a contest to create a concept for its gaming hardware. The winning design is a sleeker version of the current ARQuake hardware (see Figure 1.6, on the next page). The days of cumbersome AR hardware are numbered.

BBC jam Storyboooks for Kids

In the past four years, the Creative Research and Development team (CR&D)—in the New Media division of the BBC—has funded a number of projects meant to explore the potential of AR. In 2006, roughly 500 people registered and took part in the first public trial.

This trial was run with *BBC jam*, which is a new online learning service developed to complement the school curriculums across the United Kingdom (http://www.bbc.co.uk/jam). The stated aim of the BBC jam trial was to use AR to create interactive stories suitable for children aged five

Figure 1.6: A_RAGE CONCEPT HARDWARE

to seven. Three AR *storypacks* were offered for download. They were designed to be used with a standard PC and a USB webcam. Using the storypacks, young readers could use AR to explore and interact with scenes in a 3D *virtual pop-up book* (see Figure 1.7, on the following page). The jam AR storypacks employ a specially designed on-screen interface, narration, linked HTML help pages, and specially designed story scene printouts.

The jam project was evaluated by external researchers from London Knowledge Lab, and the CR&D team is now planning a second round of trials for other age groups and other subjects. Other AR activity within CR&D includes work with secondary-school teachers and pupils to develop interactive science visualizations in a user-centered and collaborative design process.

The Invisible Train

The Invisible Train (http://studierstube.icg.tu-graz.ac.at/invisible_train/) is a handheld multiplayer AR game developed by Daniel Wagner, Thomas Pintaric, and Dieter Schmalstieg at the Vienna University of Technology. In the game, the railroad is represented by a miniature wooden track, but the trains are entirely virtual (see Figure 1.8, on page 11).

Figure 1.7: BBC JAM CHARACTERS MAKE IT HOME.

The goal of the Invisible Train game is for players to avoid crashing their trains into one another. The participants use personal digital assistants (PDAs) to view the virtual trains, control train speed, and change the position of railroad switches. Cameras on the PDAs are used to capture the table and view the virtual trains as they move around the track. Using PDAs in this manner is an example of the magic lens metaphor for AR.

Although it would be possible to use HMDs with this game, the creators thought PDAs would be better for their application. For example, PDAs are far less cumbersome, and they are also much cheaper. Furthermore, the players don't have to worry about adjusting to any sort of unusual hardware—they simply point the PDA toward the track, and they can see the virtual trains on the PDA's screen.

The Invisible Train game has won numerous awards and has been showcased at conferences such as SIGGRAPH 2004, Ars Electronica

Figure 1.8: THE INVISIBLE TRAIN GAME (IMAGE COURTESY OF VIENNA UNIVERSITY OF TECHNOLOGY)

2004, IEEE Virtual Reality 2005, and Wired NextFest 2005. The AR marker system originally used for the Invisible Train was replaced by one inspired by ARTag—the marker system that will be discussed in great detail in this book.

AR Polygonal Modeling

AR polygonal modeling (ARpm) is a project by Peter Fiala at Purdue University. Using ARpm, the popular Autodesk 3D Studio Max (3DSMax) modeling software is converted into an augmented reality application. A user wears an HMD and works on a 3D object that appears to sit on the table in front of her. The usual working scene of 3D objects and the grids, labels, and other user interface items appear as virtual objects above an array of markers. Instead of the usual pull-down menus to access the 3DSMax tools, the menus are associated with tangible objects (*toolbar* marker arrays). The object shown in Figure 1.9, on the following page, was created entirely using the ARpm system.

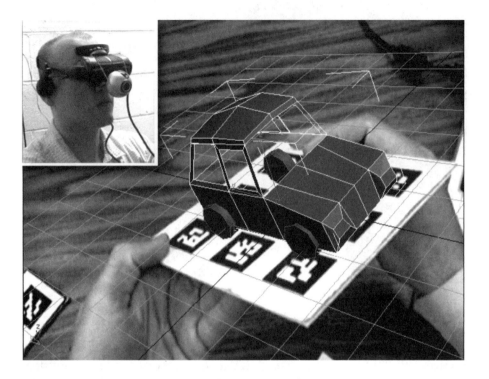

Figure 1.9: THE ARpm SYSTEM

The user operates ARpm with the following items: an HMD with a camera affixed (for video see-through AR), a 3D mouse, a 12" by 12" base array of markers and a stack of 2" by 4" cards. Each card has a small array of markers. The 3D mouse is not a specialized piece of hardware; it is a conventional wireless mouse attached to a rigid array of markers. In 3DSMax there are orthographic and perspective view panes (sections of the window) that can be resized. ARpm enlarges the perspective pane and mixes it with the video image to present it to the HMD. Through the HMD, the user can see the 3D object being created, and the standard grid lines appear to exist on top of the base array on the table in front of her. In 3DSMax, the actions of the mouse and mouse clicks depend on what mode the user is in. For example, there are modes such as "modifier," "sphere creation," and "vertex movement." Usually, in 3DSMax, one switches between modes by using hotkeys or pull-down menus. In ARpm, the user changes these modes by clicking her mouse in front of an icon hovering above each of the *toolbar* cards. The user can physically arrange the cards on her desktop, and thus she can place the controls where they are most convenient.

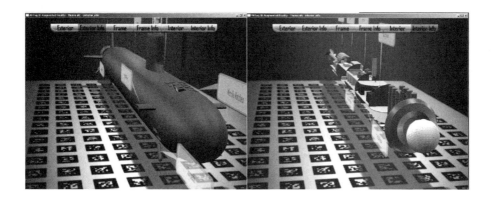

Figure 1.10: TWO DIFFERENT VIEWS OF A VIRTUAL SUB

National Research Council of Canada Examples

AR technology can be used for a wide range of applications. The following sections include some AR examples that help present its potential for nongaming purposes. These programs are currently being tested by the NRC. By experimenting with various sorts of programs, researchers can explore potential applications of AR technology. You can download videos of some of these samples from http://www.artag.net/videos.html.

AR Submarine Views

This AR application shows various 3D submarine models. By using a mouse—or in this case, a table stylus—a user can switch between various views of the submarine. For example, the user can first look at an exterior view and then select Interior Info to see a detailed model of the inner components of the sub (see Figure 1.10).

This sort of application can be used as a powerful educational tool. You can imagine that this technology would be invaluable to anyone who needs to learn the inner workings of a machine. A similar sort of AR framework is used for the next two NRC examples.

Historical Education Example

In the submarine example, the user's viewpoint moved through space and allowed you to look at different slices of the sub. In this historical education example, you are able to move through time and see how a region might change.

Figure 1.11: A CASTLE CIRCA 1450 AD

Specifically, you can see the same settlement as it was in different eras. The user can move around the table and see the various historical views from any angle.

You may begin with an early Celtic settlement (circa 500 BC), but with one click, you can progress 1,200 years to a wooden palisade (circa 700 AD). Another click takes you to about 1450 AD, when a castle is established at the same location (see Figure 1.11). Finally, a modern settlement is shown—complete with parking lot and fast food.

This sort of display is usually found in museums—using physical models. However, with AR, considerable space can be saved; for example, an entire museum's worth of displays could be presented on one table.

Architectural Demo Example

Not every demonstration has to be for educational purposes. A third example uses the same framework to show how an architectural firm

Figure 1.12: ARCHITECTURAL MOCK-UPS

might create mock-ups of various building designs for a client. Using this demonstration, the client can clearly see how each proposed high-rise would fit in with the existing structures. Amongst the options are Reasonable and Deluxe (see Figure 1.12). The final option is, comically, labeled Unreasonable.

Mobile AR

Technology Review (http://www.technologyreview.com) recently forecast that mobile AR will be one of the ten hottest technologies of 2008. This is based on the reasonable prediction that AR will appear more and more on handheld devices, especially camera cell phones. Not only are cameras becoming standard on cell phones, but they are also increasingly powerful. And everyone will have them; according to an article on Ars Technica (http://arstechnica.com/news.ars/post/20050720-5116.html), "Sales of cell phones will exceed 1 billion handsets each year in 2009, becoming the most common consumer electronics device in the world."

Figure 1.13: AR ON A CELL PHONE

What this means is that mobile handheld devices will have capabilities that make them ideal for AR. A visual AR platform needs at minimum a video input, a computer, and a display screen, but it can have increased potential with the addition of a network connection and other goodies such as a GPS receiver and orientation sensor. The Gizmondo was a short-lived handheld gaming console that had all of these; some high-end cell phones will soon have all these features.

One of the newest trials at the NRC is cell phone and PDA implementations of AR functionality. See Figure 1.13; it shows a cell phone running the same 3d_augmentations program that is used as a sample for this book.

Chapter 2

Getting AR Running

You just have to experience AR firsthand to fully appreciate it. In this chapter, you'll start by getting AR running on your system. You'll also find detailed explanations of the demos that are in the ARTag SDK—even a few that were created specifically for you. Once you have tried some of the demos, you can move on to the sample code projects and then maybe even create your own AR programs.

2.1 Augmented Reality Setup

Running the AR demos should be relatively easy, and assuming that you already have a USB 2.0 webcam, it won't cost you a penny. You won't need to do any coding or compiling; compiled versions are provided for you in the code\GetARRunning\ folder of the book's download or from the ARTag website (http://www.artag.net). You can run these compiled demos without downloading the full ARTag SDK, but if you want to create AR programs, then you will need to download the full SDK (the link is available on http://www.artag.net). ARTag is provided free for academic purposes. If you want to use it in a commercial product, you will need to license it from the National Research Council of Canada (http://www.nrc-cnrc.gc.ca).

Let's get started.

1. Set up your webcam.

   The first step is to ensure that your USB 2.0 webcam is working properly. To test your camera, you could use any number of software programs. Most likely, your camera came with software, and using this software will probably be the easiest way for you to test that it's working properly. Once you have verified that your camera is able to display real-time video, move on to step 2.

Note: A USB 2.0 webcam is recommended, although the programs have been tested with some USB 1.0 cameras (specifically the Intel CS 110, CS 120, and Intel Pro webcams).

2. Print out a *base0* ARTag marker pattern.

The example software provided with this book will search your webcam's digital image for ARTag markers, so you had best provide some of them. Adding markers to the image is simple—just print a marker pattern, and place it in front of the camera. If you plan on trying these exercises more than once, you may want to mount the printed markers onto some cardboard so that they're easier to hold and less likely to get destroyed by the cat.

For the first demo, you will use the marker pattern base0.gif. You will find this image in the code\src\ARTag patterns\ directory. Make sure the ARTag markers are big enough that they appear at least 20–30 pixels wide—when the pattern is close enough that you expect the markers to be detected. For example, if your camera's video image is 640 by 480, try to make the marker width roughly 1/20th of the image. This means a pattern such as *base0* (which is an array of many markers) should take up most of an 8.5" by 11" page. If you use a regular webcam, the markers can usually be detected if they're at least a 1/2" wide. The larger the markers, the less you'll have to fiddle with the focus for them to be detected. In some cases, the marker patterns may be corrupted when printing them or resizing them in the image software you use to load and print the markers. You can check this visually since the corrupted pixels are usually gray; ARTag markers are black and white.

Also keep in mind that markers will perform better when they are flat, so you may want to mount some of them. If you're going to print the markers on anything permanent or something more expensive than a simple letter-sized page, be sure to try them on regular paper first.

If you aren't in the mood to do any printing, you could use a hard-copy version of Figure 2.1, on the next page. The pattern should ideally take up almost all of an 8.5" by 11" page. If you're reading this book in PDF form, sorry, you'll have to print the page.

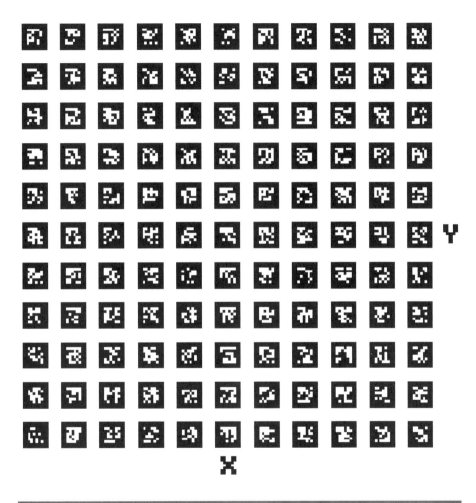

Figure 2.1: THE *base0* ARTAG TEST PATTERN—TRY THIS IMAGE WITH THE BASIC_ARTAG_OPENGL DEMO

3. Run the basic_artag_opengl demo software.

Now that you have all the required elements, it is time to put them to use. Connect your webcam, and run the basic_artag_opengl command-line demo. You will find two compiled versions of this demo in code\GetARRunning\basic_artag_opengl_compiled. If you do not have a Point Grey Research Dragonfly camera, then use the USB version.

When you run the demo, you will see command-line output such as this:

```
Camera started with resolution=320x240 version: ARTag Rev2h:
Windows OpenGL version
double artag_camera_fx,artag_camera_fy,artag_camera_cx,
artag_camera_cy=1100.000000,1100.000000,0.000000,0.000000
reading coordframe file panel_set.cf
Loaded array file panel_set.cf
```

4. Place the ARTag pattern in view of the camera.

At this point, you are running the basic_artag_opengl demo. You should see a live video image from your webcam. The last step is to simply place the *base0* ARTag marker pattern in view of the camera. When the AR software recognizes the pattern, you will see an ARTag texture augmented to the camera image (see Figure 2.2, on the facing page).

Remember that the ARTag software is trying to find the ARTag markers. If you don't have sufficient lighting, or the markers are obscured or too small, they will not be found. You should also avoid having gridlike structures or a background with lots of polygonal objects, which will save time since ARTag won't search them to see whether they are valid markers.

Once you have this demo working, try pressing the spacebar to toggle the view from magic lens to magic mirror. You may find the magic mirror effect more convincing if you place the marker pattern in front of your screen. This way, you will see the augmented image in your computer monitor, and the monitor will seem more like an actual mirror.

Congratulations, you have AR running in your home! Try to move the marker around; turn it, twist it, and see what happens.

Figure 2.2: THE BASIC_ARTAG_OPENGL ARTAG DEMO

2.2 More ARTag Demos

Now that you have AR working, you'll able to play with some of the other ARTag demos. The code\src\ARTag patterns\ directory contains the marker pattern images required to run the rest of the demos (see Figure 2.3, on the next page).

pointer1.gif is used as the virtual pointer in the artag_cad demo. toolbar0_7.gif and panel_140_2047.gif are used in the 3d_augmentations demo. base0.gif is used for basic_artag_opengl and artag_cad, and you should use it if you bring in your own objects for the 3d_augmentations demo. The toolbar marker patterns can be cut out along the black lines, producing eight rectangular toolbars.

Remember that ARTag assumes the markers are on a flat surface, so you'll achieve the best results by mounting them on something flat, or at least putting them on a flat surface.

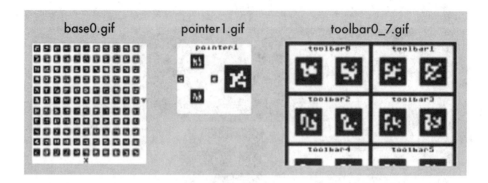

Figure 2.3: ARTAG DEMO PATTERNS

The 3d_augmentations Demo

This command-line program shows 3D models overlaid upon a real-time video image. To run the 3d_augmentations demo (also known as the magic_mirror demo), launch the 3d_magic_mirror program. You can use a few different patters with this demo: toolbar0_7.gif, base0.gif, and panel_140_2047.gif. Remember to print the patterns so that each marker is large enough to be recognized by the AR software (see Figure 2.4, on the facing page). Press the spacebar to switch from the magic lens perspective to the magic mirror perspective.

Each ARTag marker is given a unique ID. In order for the markers to be detected, the software must be looking for the right IDs. In some cases, many ARTag markers are combined into an array pattern. Only the *base0*, *toolbar1*, *toolbar5*, *toolbar6*, and *toolbar7* arrays and ARTag IDs 924 and 1023 are used in the default configuration of this demo. Pattern panel_140_2047.gif shows images of ARTag IDs 924 and 1023.

3D Demo Configuration Changes

To make the 3D augmentation demo more interesting, you may want to substitute in your own 3D models. To do this, all you have to do is change the settings in setup_artag_3d.cfg so that the software loads your model files. In this example, you will change the model references so that chess pieces appear instead of the default models. Once you have made this change, you will be able to move the ARTag markers to play a game of chess with virtual pieces.

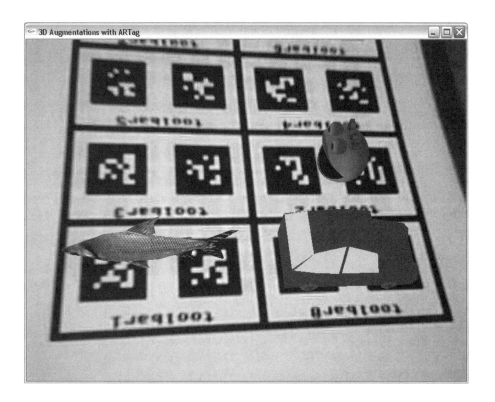

Figure 2.4: THE COOL 3D_AUGMENTATIONS DEMO

Delete, or comment out, the following lines from setup_artag_3d.cfg:

```
//- enter objects below - export OBJ, WRL
//or ASE formats from 3DSMax, etc.
//Create an .mtl material library for .OBJs.

object fish.obj              array base0 center resize
object peters_car.mesh       array toolbar0  center resize
object fish.obj              array toolbar1  center resize
object ms_pacman.obj         array toolbar2  center resize


//above are examples of linking objects to arrays,
//below link objects to individual ARTag markers

//924,1023 from patterns\panel_140_2047.gif
object chihuahua.obj         single 924  center resize
object CanOfAspargus.mesh    single 1023 center resize
```

To use the chess pieces, simply insert the names of the chess models in place of the code you just removed. You will find the altered version in setup_artag_3d.cfg_chess_version.

```
//Link chess pieces to individual marker tags

object Black_Rook.obj        single 1 center resize
object Black_Knight.obj      single 2 center resize
object Black_Bishop.obj      single 3 center resize
object Black_King.obj        single 4 center resize
object Black_Queen.obj       single 5 center resize
object Black_Bishop.obj      single 6 center resize
object Black_Knight.obj      single 7 center resize
object Black_Rook.obj        single 8 center resize
object Black_Pawn.obj        single 9 center resize
object Black_Pawn.obj        single 10 center resize
object Black_Pawn.obj        single 11 center resize
object Black_Pawn.obj        single 12 center resize
object Black_Pawn.obj        single 13 center resize
object Black_Pawn.obj        single 14 center resize
object Black_Pawn.obj        single 15 center resize
object Black_Pawn.obj        single 16 center resize
object White_Rook.obj        single 17 center resize
object White_Knight.obj      single 18 center resize
object White_Bishop.obj      single 19 center resize
object White_King.obj        single 20 center resize
object White_Queen.obj       single 21 center resize
object White_Bishop.obj      single 22 center resize
object White_Knight.obj      single 23 center resize
object White_Rook.obj        single 24 center resize
object White_Pawn.obj        single 25 center resize
object White_Pawn.obj        single 26 center resize
object White_Pawn.obj        single 27 center resize
object White_Pawn.obj        single 28 center resize
object White_Pawn.obj        single 29 center resize
object White_Pawn.obj        single 30 center resize
object White_Pawn.obj        single 31 center resize
object White_Pawn.obj        single 32 center resize
```

When you run the demo again, you'll see that the chess pieces appear instead of the car and the fish (see Figure 2.5, on the next page). If you decide to add your own models, remember that the focal-length parameters may cause your objects to appear squashed or too tall. You will need to measure or guess the parameters to get your models to appear properly. For more information about properly calibrating your camera, refer to Chapter 6.

If you want to play a game of virtual chess, try creating virtual pieces by printing markers for each one. To create the individual marker files,

Figure 2.5: THE ALTERED 3D AR DEMO

run the artag_create_marker.exe application from the code\IntroARProg\ artag_create_marker\ directory. When you run artag_create_marker.exe, you will see instructions for using this application:

```
CREATE_ARTAG_MARKER.C creates a .PGM file from an ARTAG id#
-needs 2 or 3 arguments
-proper format is: CREATE_ARTAG_MARKER 157
                   or: CREATE_ARTAG_MARKER 157 image.pgm
                   or: CREATE_ARTAG_MARKER 157 image.pgm toplabel
-where 157 is an example ID (0-1023)
-if no output image filename (2nd argument) is given, the
image will be written to the default filename artag_create_marker.pgm
-3rd argument causes image to have label above with id
C:\code\IntroARProg\artag_create_marker>
     artag_create_marker.exe 1 artag_marker1.pgm
CREATE_ARTAG_MARKER.C
Wrote artag_marker1.pgm
```

Figure 2.6: CHECK AND MATE!

For example, to create the first marker tag (with no label) in a file called artag_marker1.pgm, enter artag_create_marker.exe 1 artag_marker1.pgm.

For your convenience, markers 1–32 have been included in the directory code\src\ARTag patterns\ARTag markers. They have also been resized to 200% of their original size—this is a good size for a standard chessboard (see Figure 2.6).

One easy way to handle printing a number of markers is to use Paint Shop Pro's Print Layout feature. This feature allows you to add a number of individual image files to the same printed page. Since Paint Shop Pro handles the PGM format natively, you don't need to worry about the markers being distorted during the sizing. In a misguided attempt to extrapolate possible lost data, some image applications will add gray pixels to larger versions of the markers. Remember that the ARTag markers include a white border; without the border, marker detection will not be accurate.

The ARTag CAD Demo

This demo shows how ARTag could be used as a virtual drawing or modeling tool. It is difficult to explain this demo, so you'll probably want to look at Figure 2.7, on the next page, to get an idea of what you're trying to do. By moving around an ARTag marker pattern, you can draw virtual polygons.

To try the artag_cad demo, you will need to print both base0.gif and pointer1.gif. You can get these images in the code\src\ARTag patterns\ folder. If the camera can see both the *base0* array and the pointer, you will have a virtual 3D cursor. With mouse clicks you can create vertical 3D quadrilateral polygons (*quads*)—with their bottoms on the XY plane. The XY plane is determined by the image of the *base0* array.

The first step when running this demo is ensuring that the *base0* array is recognized. You'll know that the patterns have been identified because the demo will add yellow grid lines to the webcam image. Once the *base0* array is working, you should add the pointer1.gif image. If the pointer1.gif image is working properly, you will see a red line with an arrow at the end—this line represents your virtual 3D cursor (see Figure 2.7, on the following page). At first, you may find it difficult to use the virtual cursor, but with some practice, you should get the hang of it.

When creating the polygons, the 3D position is set by the relative position of the pointer1.gif image and the *base0* image. The act of starting or finishing a quad is done with your mouse's left button. In other words, click the left button once to start the polygon, and click again to finish the polygon (see Figure 2.8, on page 29).

You could use a wired mouse with this demo, but it's awkward. One way to simplify the process is to tape a wireless mouse to the *pointer1* array. Then wave it in space to set the 3D position, and click the button to select. This allows you to do everything with one hand. If you decide to try this option, you need to mount this pattern on something rigid like cardboard; otherwise, it will flop around and not provide a stable pointer function.

2.3 Diagnosing Issues with the AR Demos

This section contains some suggestions for what to try when you're having trouble getting the AR demos running on your computer. If you don't find the answer to your question here, try looking in Appendix B.

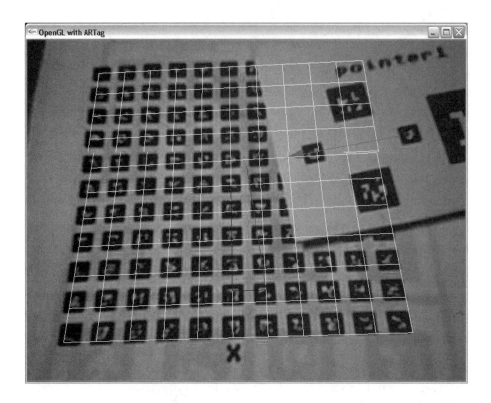

Figure 2.7: ADDING THE VIRTUAL POINTER

- A good place to start your investigation is with OpenGL. The ARTag programs require that OpenGL and GLUT are functioning properly on your computer. opengl_only_test contains code for OpenGL, but no camera input or ARTag code is used, which can help you get OpenGL (with GLUT) working.

  To confirm that you have OpenGL/GLUT working on your system, run the command-line program opengl_only_test.exe (located in \code\GetARRunning\opengl_only_test_compiled). When you run the program, a sample texture will appear in an OpenGL window (see Figure 2.9, on page 30).

- If you think you are having trouble with your camera, confirm that everything else in your system (for example, OpenGL and model loading) works by running image_test.exe. This simple application replaces the camera video input with either a digital image or a 3D model.

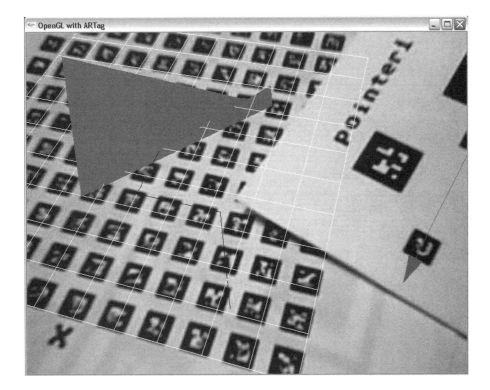

Figure 2.8: CREATING POLYGONS

If you have any issues when running image_test.exe, check the console output for clues to diagnose the problem. For example, you may see the output "Camera started with resolution 0x0," which shows that the camera was not initialized properly.

• If you want to isolate your test to just the ARTag library (and your test image), run artag_console_test.exe. This is a command-line program that doesn't use OpenGL at all. To run this application, type artag_console_test.exe artag_debug_image.pgm. This will run the utility with the artag_debug_image and allow you to test whether ARTag is successfully finding objects. In the default case, ARTag should report "1 object found."

We hope this chapter has provided you with everything you need to know when getting AR running on your machine. If you are experiencing an issue that wasn't discussed in this section, check whether the problem is covered in Appendix B. Now it's on to some coding!

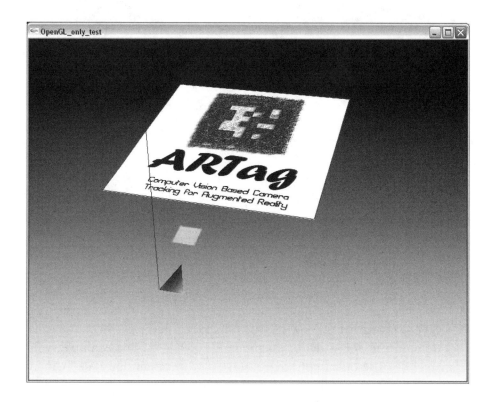

Figure 2.9: RUNNING THE OPENGL_ONLY_TEST PROGRAM

## Chapter 3

Computer Graphics Basics

This chapter will get you under the hood of visual AR by explaining how OpenGL is used to create computer graphics for AR. You will learn about image formation and the pinhole projection model, and you will get an overview of AR math. The chapter starts with fundamental ideas and then progresses in increasing detail. So, you will also learn what a frustrum is, what clipping planes are, and how matrices are used for the image projection and for moving between coordinate systems. It isn't necessary for you to read this entire chapter before you implement your own AR systems. However, you are encouraged to read as much as possible.

3.1 The Pinhole Model

Programmers and artists who create AR applications should always be cognizant of these basic concepts:

- Images on television, computer monitors, PDAs, and other screens are 2D representations of a 3D world. We all know this, but since our minds create a *mental scene* when we see a 2D image, it's important to remember that the image or video is just a 2D array of pixels.

- Computer graphics generally use the *simple pinhole projection* (aka perspective projection) camera model. In this model, light from objects in the environment passes through a single point in space and hits an image plane that is usually flat (see Figure 3.1, on the next page).

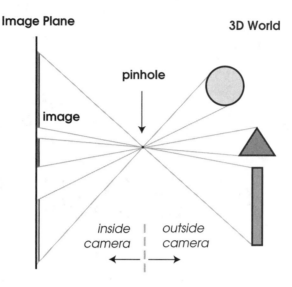

Figure 3.1: IMAGE FORMATION WITH THE PINHOLE MODEL

This first point is obvious, but it's important to distinguish between *regular* 2D images and 3D images—such as RADAR, LIDAR, SONAR, MRI, or CT images. These 3D images are examples of 3D arrays of numbers. There are even line-scan cameras that capture only 1D images. Also, technically speaking, a single photosensor such as a light meter is a 0D sensor. In this book, we are dealing only with the most common type: 2D images.

Inside a computer or digital camera, an image is just a 2D array of numbers. The goal of computer graphics is to create the 2D array such that our minds believe we're looking through a window into a 3D world. Thus, as the artists of the Renaissance understood, you need to obey the geometric rules of image formation if you want to satisfy the *scene building* part of the mind.

You can tell in a moment that a picture doesn't look quite right; the geometry doesn't ring true. Drawing something realistically is difficult for most people, but we all know whether a drawing *looks right*. It took many years of research to figure out the geometry of image formation, yet our subconscious minds have always been able to distinguish between poorly represented geometry and proper geometry. In AR, this extends to believing, or at least finding it plausible, that a computer-rendered object could appear in an image of the real world.

The second fundamental point—pinhole projection—is not as obvious. Unlike real cameras, which have lenses, the virtual cameras used in computer graphics are only pinholes. This wouldn't be practical in the real world, but in CG/AR everything is done with pinhole cameras. If you studied physics in high school, the pinhole model may be familiar, and surprisingly, it doesn't get any more complex for 99% of computer graphics (and AR).

The pinhole is also called the *focal point*, or the center of projection. An image is usually captured on a flat light plate, which is known as the *image plane*. In film cameras, the image plane is photographic film, but for electronic image capture, the image plane is an array of light-sensitive regions in charge-coupled devices (CCDs) or complementary metal oxide semiconductor (CMOS) imagers. Each light-sensitive element on these chips measures light intensity for one image pixel.

A *perspective image* is captured with the pinhole model. Technically speaking, such an image is a perspective projection, or pinhole projection, because the captured scene is drawn from the perspective of a pinhole. The central axis is the direction from the focal point (the pinhole) perpendicular to the image plane. The central axis points in the direction that the camera is *looking*.

In a virtual pinhole camera, in a real pinhole camera (which is not practical for most uses because of its poor light-gathering capability), or in a real camera with lenses, light first passes through the focal point and then strikes the film or image sensor. This means the image formed is upside-down and backward. If we put the image plane right-side-up in front of the focal point, then a line drawn from an object through the focal point will intersect this front right-side-up plane in the same place as if the image plane were upside-down and the same distance behind the focal point. This holds true not only for cameras but for the human eye as well. However, the same geometry still holds if the image plane was in front of the pinhole, and then we don't have to think about inverted images (see Figure 3.2, on the following page).

Artists sometimes use a similar method to create perspective images. The artist sets up a transparent canvas or a canvas that could be easily moved in and out of view. Then, while keeping his head still and looking through one eye, he draws on the canvas where he sees the objects. For example, if he were painting the corner of a stone block, he would look at the block and then move the canvas so that it obscured his view. Without looking away, he would draw the corner on the canvas so it

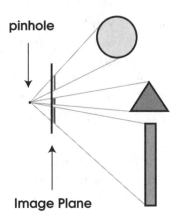

pinhole

Image Plane

Figure 3.2: THE IMAGE PLANE CAN BE CONSIDERED TO BE IN FRONT OF THE PINHOLE.

appeared to be at the same point as the real block. When generating an image for computer graphics, you can imagine a canvas in front of the focal point and the computer squinting before it draws objects on the canvas.

It is possible to build a hobby camera with just a pinhole. However, it wouldn't capture as much light as most people would like. A lens, or set of lenses, serves to capture more light while attempting to obey the pinhole projection model. For a camera to work in the real world, it needs to gather enough light to make an image. Without lenses, pictures would be too dark in all but ideal lighting conditions. Lenses introduce issues such as depth of field and blurriness; however, these effects are usually not considered in computer graphics, especially those generated in real time such as in video games, CAD packages, or AR systems. Sometimes these effects are simulated by applying a blurring operator to images first created with the pinhole method. Objects at different depths are usually rendered separately and blurred before combining them. This gives the effect of different amounts of blur at different depths. This technique is seen in a lot of Japanese animation.

For easier visualization, the image plane can be considered to be in front of the pinhole so that the image is not upside-down.

If you have a circle in 3D space and capture it using pinhole projection, you may get a circle, or you may end up with something that is oval shaped. If the circle is not parallel to the image plane, then it can be represented by an ellipse. If instead you have a straight line in the 3D world, it will always project onto a straight line in the image when you use pinhole projection. *Polygons* are flat regions that have segments of straight lines for edges. A pinhole projection must project the straight lines in the 3D world to straight lines in the image, so polygons will always project to polygons (or lines if the polygon is viewed on an edge). Most real-time computer graphics systems use polygons—which stretch between three or four points at a time.

Projecting Points

The pinhole projection model provides a simple formula for calculating where a point in the world will project on the image plane. This is a simple matter of equivalent triangles (see Figure 3.3, on the next page). Point A in the world projects to point A′ in the image. A is located at a distance z from the camera at a height x, and the image point A′ is located at coordinate u. Using equivalent triangles, we have equation 3.1. You can see (in Figure 3.1, on page 32; Figure 3.2, on the facing page; and Figure 3.3, on the next page) side views of the scene, where the image plane is viewed from a point along the plane (seen "edge on") so that the plane appears only as a line, and the Y-axis points out of the page. The first part of equation 3.1 refers to Figure 3.3, on the next page, where $u = f_x/z$. The same applies to the other dimension, where $v = f_y/z$. In these equations, f is the focal length because it is measured from the pinhole to the image plane.

$$u = \frac{f * x}{z}, v = \frac{f * y}{z} \tag{3.1}$$

POINT IN 3D $(x,\ y,\ z)$ PROJECTS TO IMAGE POINT $(u,\ v)$

The point in the image $(u,\ v)$ and the focal length are measured in pixel coordinates. Typically, the focal lengths of actual lenses are measured in millimeters, but if you know the spacing of pixels in the same units (mm) on the image sensor, then you can convert the length to a distance in pixels.

Note that the size of the image and the image coordinates of a world point grow as the focal length (f) grows. With a larger f, you are more *zoomed in* and the objects are larger, but you have a smaller *field of view* (FOV). With a digital camera, for example, the focal length may be 1,000 pixels as you're zoomed out (maybe looking at an entire building) but becomes 4,000 as you zoom in on a window.

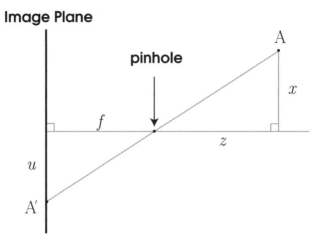

Figure 3.3: MATH FOR PINHOLE PROJECTIONS

But that's not all there is to it. The focal length may not be equal in the X and Y directions. For example, if you have a 4:3 aspect ratio, then you'll need to have separate focal lengths for f_x and f_y. In addition, your image origin is usually the upper-left corner. You don't usually have (0, 0) in the middle of the image (with positive and negative pixel locations). The convention is to start with (0, 0) in the upper left, and therefore you must add an offset ($u0$, $v0$). These new parameters are shown in equation 3.2. The 3D point has the subscript c added to be compatible with later equations. (X_c, Y_c, Z_c) represents the 3D point in camera coordinates.

$$u = \frac{f_x * x_c}{z_c} + u_0, v = \frac{f_y * y_c}{z_c} + v_0 \qquad (3.2)$$

MORE DETAILED PINHOLE MODEL EQUATIONS

This is starting to get into some deep math. For those who are interested in programming computer graphics or AR applications, you should be aware of the following:

- In computer graphics systems, a 3D point is measured relative to a center point by using three perpendicular axes (X, Y, Z). Together, the axes and center point constitute a coordinate system.
- Equation 3.1, on the previous page, assumes the 3D point (x, y, z) is in the camera coordinate system. It's generally necessary to

map coordinates between coordinate systems before you can apply equation 3.1, on page 35. This is true because equation 3.1, on page 35, requires that the numbers refer to coordinates in the camera coordinate system. The 3D point is in object space, not in camera space.

- The projection of a 3D world point to a 2D image point (u, v) (including transferring the coordinates) is usually done in computer graphics using matrices. A single projection matrix encodes the mapping of a 3D world point, in an arbitrary coordinate system, to a 2D image point.
- This projection matrix can be broken down into several matrices, with one for equation 3.1, on page 35, and one or more for transferring between coordinate systems. To save time on numerical calculations, these matrices are combined before drawing an object.

Based on these items, you now know that you need to transfer points between different 3D coordinate systems before you can apply the pinhole model, and you also know that matrices can be used to represent both the pinhole model math (equation 3.1, on page 35) and your transfers between coordinate systems.

3.2 Transferring 3D Points Between Coordinate Systems

Why do you need more than one coordinate system? What's wrong with having everything in the camera coordinate system? Imagine a first-person shooter video game—such as Doom or Halo II—where the virtual camera is moving around in a 3D world. The game uses *world* coordinates to keep track of the virtual camera's focal point and viewing direction. The game consists of stationary polygons (for example, walls, floors, doorways, and buildings) and moving objects (for example, evil and friendly characters). When rendering the stationary scene, you need to transfer the scene polygon vertices from the world coordinate system (which is how they are stored) into the coordinate system for the camera. Only after you have completed the transfer are you then able to apply the pinhole equations.

Note that the word *transfer* is used here to refer to translations and rotations. In graphics jargon, you will hear the term *3D transformation*, but a transformation also includes scaling and shearing operations.

Imagine you want to create an enemy robot for a video game. You will create the 3D model for the robot in its own local object coordinate system. Since both the robot and the player viewpoint will be moving around, rendering this robot requires that you first transfer all points on the robot to world coordinates and then transfer again to camera coordinates before you are able to apply the pinhole model.

If you have moving parts (for example, head, arms, or legs) on this robot model, then you have to perform yet another coordinate system transfer. To render the fingertips on a fully featured humanoid model, you need to transfer between three coordinate systems to reach the hand coordinate system and then between three more to get to the central object coordinate system. You then need one more to transfer to the world coordinate system and an eighth transfer to get to your camera coordinate system. Now you understand why video games are constantly taxing the resources of computers around the world.

How do you transfer between one coordinate system and another? In a simpler world, you could just add or subtract the coordinate system centers. However, that would not take into consideration the effect of rotation. You are, of course, used to game objects being able to rotate in all directions. This complicates the math, but if you represent things with vectors and matrices, it is manageable.

How is one coordinate system defined in terms of another? Take the simple example of a cube that measures ten units on each side. In its own coordinate system, you can define its vertices as (0,0,0); (10,0,0); (10,10,0); . . . up to (10,10,10). Imagine placing the cube model at some oblique angle in a world model. The cube coordinate system's center is located at (10.3, -5.1, 0.44) in the world coordinate system, and the cube is rotated. The cube coordinate system's X-axis is a vector (0.5, -0.866, 0) in the world coordinate system. Likewise, the Y-axis and Z-axis are (0.866, 0.5, 0) and (0, 0, 1), respectively (see Figure 3.4, on the facing page). Each of the vectors representing the cube's axes is unit vectors (length = 1).

If you move along the cube's X-axis by one unit in the positive direction, you've moved 0.5, -0.866, and 0 in the world coordinate system. Thus, you multiply your X component inside the cube coordinate system by this X-axis vector. You keep this result and add to it your Y component, which is multiplied by the Y-axis vector. Then, add your Z component multiplied by the Z-axis vector, and finally add the cube's coordinate system center (10.3, -5.1, 0.44) to get the final coordinate

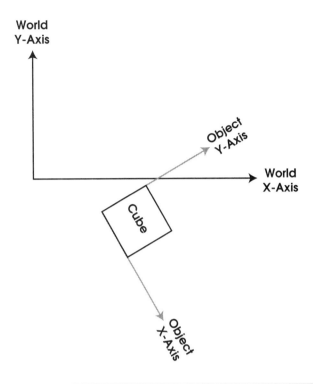

Figure 3.4: OBJECT AND WORLD COORDINATE SYSTEMS: 2D EXAMPLE

system transfer result. Note that since the output is a 3D point, the result is actually three numbers that you're storing in your calculations. In the next chapter, you'll learn how moving between coordinate systems is done with the OpenGL glTranslate(), glRotate(), and glScale() functions.

3.3 Transferring Points Using Matrix Math

Let's see this in some formulae. To convert a point (x, y, z) in object coordinates to (x', y', z') in world coordinates, you need to perform nine multiplications and twelve additions. In equation 3.3, on the next page, you would represent this with standard and matrix notation. Note how the X-, Y-, and Z-axes of the box are represented as columns in the middle of the 3 by 3 matrix. This 3 by 3 matrix is the rotation matrix, and the column vector (10.3, -5.1, 0.44) is the translation vector. Together, the rotation and translation represent the relative pose between the object and the world. Later, you'll see how using a fourth column can make the math much simpler.

$$
\begin{aligned}
x' &= 0.5x & + 0.866y & + 0 + 10.3 \\
y' &= -0.866x & + 0.5y & + 0 - 5.1 \\
z' &= 0 & + 0 & + z + 0.44
\end{aligned}
\qquad
\begin{pmatrix} x' \\ y' \\ z' \end{pmatrix}
=
\begin{pmatrix} 0.5 & 0.866 & 0 \\ -0.866 & 0.5 & 0 \\ 0 & 0 & 1 \end{pmatrix}
\begin{pmatrix} x \\ y \\ z \end{pmatrix}
+
\begin{pmatrix} 10.3 \\ -5.1 \\ 0.44 \end{pmatrix}
$$

$$(3.3)$$

ALGEBRAIC (LEFT) AND MATRIX (RIGHT) REPRESENTATIONS OF 3D POINT TRANSFER FROM OBJECT TO WORLD COORDINATE SYSTEM

So, for each point on the cube—(0, 0, 0); (10, 0, 0); (10, 10, 0); ...— you could perform this transfer and have the cube vertices in world coordinates.

Now let's say you want to do the opposite—convert a point in the world coordinate system to the cube's coordinate system. This process is demonstrated in equation 3.4. Note that the translation vector has changed and the rotation matrix has been transposed—its rows were turned into columns. The upper-left equation shows the simplest form. When going from world to object coordinates, you subtract the translation vector and then perform some multiplications. For those with some linear algebra background, these multiplications can be thought of in terms of dot products between the 3D point and each of the X-, Y-, and Z-axis vectors (you're finding the projection of the 3D point onto these directions).

$$
\begin{aligned}
x' &= 0.5\,(x' - 10.3) & -0.866\,(y' + 5.1) & +0\,(z' - 0.44) \\
y &= 0.866\,(x' - 10.3) & 0.5\,(y' + 5.1) & +0\,(z' - 0.44) \\
z &= 0 & +0 & +1\,(z' - 0.44)
\end{aligned}
$$

$$
\begin{aligned}
x &= 0.5x' & -0.866y' & + & 0 & -10.007 \\
y &= 0.866x' & 0.5y' & + & 0 & -6.369 \\
z &= 0 & +0 & +z' & & -0.44
\end{aligned}
$$

$$
\begin{pmatrix} x \\ y \\ z \end{pmatrix}
=
\begin{pmatrix} 0.5 & -0.866 & 0 \\ 0.866 & 0.5 & 0 \\ 0 & 0 & 1 \end{pmatrix}
\begin{pmatrix} x' \\ y' \\ z' \end{pmatrix}
+
\begin{pmatrix} -10.007 \\ -6.3698 \\ -0.4400 \end{pmatrix}
\qquad (3.4)
$$

INVERSE TRANSFORMATION FROM EQUATION 3.3—COORDINATES ARE TRANSFERRED FROM WORLD TO OBJECT COORDINATES. THREE FORMS OF THIS CALCULATION ARE SHOWN.

When you convert a world point into camera coordinates, you need to do the same operation (depicted in various forms in equation 3.4, on the facing page).

The great benefit of matrices—other than being able to write equations more cleanly—is the ability to combine them. Imagine that you want to render the cube as seen by a camera; you combine the matrix operations into one combination rotation and translation matrix. You also replace numbers with symbols for easier reading (see equation 3.5). You needed to know the pose of the relative poses in the chain: the pose of the object in world coordinates and the camera pose in world coordinates. To do this, you need to construct rotation matrices and translation vectors for each step and then combine them into one rotation matrix and translation vector. You construct the rotation matrices from the X-, Y-, Z-axis vectors, placing them either as rows or as columns in the matrix. This depends upon whether the vectors are in the input or output coordinate system.

The computation savings come when you want to render many points. Imagine that your object was not a simple box with eight vertices but a complex enemy robot model with 5,000 3D vertices. Even if there were many more steps in relative coordinate system changes, you would still perform only 5,000 by 9 multiplications and 5,000 by 12 additions. With our two-stage example, you would perform twice as many calculations if you did them separately (that is, instead of combining matrices and translation vectors). Note that we did not go into the calculation of combination translation vectors. They are created by multiplication with the rotation matrices—in the same manner as the 3D points. Combining matrices provides one combination point transfer operation with one rotation matrix and one translation vector. Let's take a look at some equations for combining matrices.

$$
\begin{pmatrix} x' \\ y' \\ z' \end{pmatrix} = \begin{pmatrix} \cdots \\ \cdots \\ \cdots \end{pmatrix} \begin{pmatrix} x \\ y \\ z \end{pmatrix} + \begin{pmatrix} \cdot \\ \cdot \\ \cdot \end{pmatrix} \tag{3.5}
$$

TRANSFER FROM OBJECT TO WORLD COORDINATES

$$
\begin{pmatrix} x_c \\ x_y \\ z_c \end{pmatrix} = \begin{pmatrix} ,,, \\ ,,, \\ ,,, \end{pmatrix} \begin{pmatrix} x' \\ y' \\ z' \end{pmatrix} + \begin{pmatrix} , \\ , \\ , \end{pmatrix} \tag{3.6}
$$

TRANSFER FROM WORLD TO CAMERA COORDINATES

$$\begin{pmatrix} x_c \\ y_c \\ z_c \end{pmatrix} = \begin{pmatrix} ,,, \\ ,,, \\ ,,, \end{pmatrix}\begin{pmatrix} \cdots \\ \cdots \\ \cdots \end{pmatrix}\begin{pmatrix} x \\ y \\ z \end{pmatrix} + \begin{pmatrix} ,,, \\ ,,, \\ ,,, \end{pmatrix}\begin{pmatrix} \star\star\star \\ \star\star\star \\ \star\star\star \end{pmatrix},$$

$$\begin{pmatrix} x_c \\ y_c \\ z_c \end{pmatrix} = \begin{pmatrix} \star\star\star \\ \star\star\star \\ \star\star\star \end{pmatrix}\begin{pmatrix} x \\ y \\ z \end{pmatrix} + \begin{pmatrix} \diamond \\ \diamond \\ \diamond \end{pmatrix} \tag{3.7}$$

COMBINATION TRANSFER FROM OBJECT TO CAMERA COORDINATES

Every time you add a new coordinate system change, you must put a new rotation matrix on the left, and you must update the translation vector by multiplying it by this rotation matrix. You start farthest away from the camera (in our transfer mapping) and put new matrices on the left as you work closer to the camera. Using your articulated humanoid robot model example, you start with the pose of the finger coordinate system in the hand coordinates, place the hand rotation with respect to the forearm matrix in front, and adjust the translation vector. Next, you include the pose rotation of the forearm in the upper arm. You do this until you place the camera pose in world coordinates rotation matrix in front and adjust the combined translation.

Once you have transferred 3D points to camera coordinates, you need to apply the pinhole equations to get your perspective projection 2D image (see equation 3.1, on page 35). This can also be partially done by using a matrix containing the f_x, f_y, u_0, v_0 pinhole parameters. In equation 3.8, you calculate an intermediate quantity (u', v', w') before applying the two division operations that give you your final image point. The matrix can be added to the left of the chain of matrices that are multiplied together from the coordinate system transfers. So, your final operation is a 3 by 3 matrix (which is not really a rotation matrix anymore since the pinhole equations are added) and a column vector. For each 3D point, you apply the nine multiplications and twelve additions and follow it with two divisions, and you have your image point (u, v) corresponding to the original 3D point back in object coordinates.

$$\begin{pmatrix} u' \\ v' \\ w' \end{pmatrix} = \begin{pmatrix} f_x & 0 & u_o \\ 0 & f_y & v_o \\ 0 & 0 & 1 \end{pmatrix}\begin{pmatrix} x_c \\ y_c \\ z_c \end{pmatrix} \quad u = \frac{u'}{w'} v = \frac{v'}{w'} \tag{3.8}$$

PUTTING EQUATION 3.2, ON PAGE 36, PARTIALLY INTO MATRIX FORM

We hope you have taken some linear algebra and are acquainted with matrices. There isn't space to explain them here, so use your introductory linear algebra textbook to research how to work with matrices.

If you've made it this far, you need to go only one more step and combine the rotation matrices and translation vectors into one large 4 by 4 matrix to be compatible with OpenGL—and most other graphics systems. You can pull the translation component into your matrix by simply including it as a fourth column, but then you also need to include a fourth neutral row to make it a square matrix. Matrices need to be square if you're going to multiply them together. Instead of working with 3D vectors, you work with a 4D vector with the value 1 as the fourth element. This way the translation component is simply multiplied by 1 and added inside the matrix multiplication instead of being added outside as a separate operation (as it was when you had your 3 by 3 rotation matrix and translation vector). The vectors are treated as four elements. The last a or a' provides a number to divide by to return to a standard three-element vector. For example, in equation 3.9, you would divide x', y', and z' all by a' to have a 3D number. This division step is left out until all the 4 by 4 multiplications are performed, since division is a computationally expensive operation.

This simplifies the math—well, at least from the point of view of creating 3D-rendering hardware for a video card—to 4 by 4 matrix multiplications instead of 3 by 3 matrix multiplications and vector additions. For the coordinate system transfers, you can put the rotation in the upper-left corner and the translation vector in the upper-right corner and fill the bottom row with three 0s and a 1. The pinhole projection matrix can also be turned into a 4 by 4 matrix by adding 0s to the left and bottom and a 1 in the bottom right. The benefit of using 4 by 4 matrices is that all operations—except the final two division operations—can be performed by a single hardware or software unit made to efficiently do 4 by 4 matrix multiplication. Although the math may seem more complex, it makes the calculations easier for the machine, so it's easier to create the video card–rendering engine.

$$
\begin{pmatrix} x' \\ y' \\ z' \\ a' \end{pmatrix} = \begin{pmatrix} \dots \\ \dots \\ \dots \\ 0001 \end{pmatrix} \begin{pmatrix} x \\ y \\ z \\ 1 \end{pmatrix}
\tag{3.9}
$$

REWRITING EQUATION 3.5, ON PAGE 41, IN 4 BY 4 MATRIX NOTATION. TRANSFER FROM OBJECT TO WORLD COORDINATES.

$$
\begin{pmatrix} x_c \\ y_c \\ z_c \\ a_c \end{pmatrix} = \begin{pmatrix} ,,,, \\ ,,,, \\ ,,,, \\ 0001 \end{pmatrix} \begin{pmatrix} x' \\ y' \\ z' \\ a' \end{pmatrix} \tag{3.10}
$$

REWRITING EQUATION 3.6, ON PAGE 41, IN 4 BY 4 MATRIX NOTATION. TRANSFER FROM WORLD TO CAMERA COORDINATES.

$$
\begin{pmatrix} x_c \\ y_c \\ z_c \\ a_c \end{pmatrix} = \begin{pmatrix} ,,,, \\ ,,,, \\ ,,,, \\ 0001 \end{pmatrix} \begin{pmatrix} .... \\ .... \\ .... \\ 0001 \end{pmatrix} \begin{pmatrix} x \\ y \\ z \\ 1 \end{pmatrix} , \quad \begin{pmatrix} x_c \\ y_c \\ z_c \\ a_c \end{pmatrix} = \begin{pmatrix} \#\#\#\# \\ \#\#\#\# \\ \#\#\#\# \\ 0001 \end{pmatrix} \begin{pmatrix} x \\ y \\ z \\ 1 \end{pmatrix}
$$

$$\tag{3.11}$$

REWRITING EQUATION 3.7, ON PAGE 42, IN 4 BY 4 MATRIX NOTATION. COMBINATION TRANSFER FROM OBJECT TO CAMERA COORDINATES.

In equation 3.12, equation 3.13, and equation 3.14, you can see three 4 by 4 matrices that can be used for rotation, translation, and scaling of 3D points. You merely multiply them together (but be careful of the order!). Consult graphics textbooks for other matrices that are similar—such as rotations around other axes.

$$
\begin{pmatrix} x' \\ y' \\ z' \\ a' \end{pmatrix} = \begin{pmatrix} 1 & 0 & 0 & d_x \\ 0 & 1 & 0 & d_y \\ 0 & 0 & 1 & d_z \\ 0 & 0 & 0 & 1 \end{pmatrix} \begin{pmatrix} x \\ y \\ z \\ 1 \end{pmatrix} \tag{3.12}
$$

SOME BASIC OPERATIONS PERFORMED WITH 4 BY 4 MATRICES. TRANSLATION BY DX, DY, DZ.

$$
\begin{pmatrix} x' \\ y' \\ z' \\ a' \end{pmatrix} = \begin{pmatrix} \cos(\theta) & -\sin(\theta) & 0 & 0 \\ \sin(\theta) & \cos(\theta) & 0 & 0 \\ 0 & 0 & 1 & 0 \\ 0 & 0 & 0 & 1 \end{pmatrix} \begin{pmatrix} x \\ y \\ z \\ 1 \end{pmatrix} \tag{3.13}
$$

ROTATING COUNTERCLOCKWISE AROUND Z-AXIS BY 0 DEGREES

$$
\begin{pmatrix} x' \\ y' \\ z' \\ a' \end{pmatrix} = \begin{pmatrix} s & 0 & 0 & 0 \\ 0 & s & 0 & 0 \\ 0 & 0 & s & 0 \\ 0 & 0 & 0 & 1 \end{pmatrix} \begin{pmatrix} x \\ y \\ z \\ 1 \end{pmatrix} \tag{3.14}
$$

SCALING (ENLARGING) BY S

3.4 The Rendering Pipeline

Now that you have seen the math for moving points between coordinate systems in a mechanistic process of multiplication by 4 by 4 matrices, you are able to use a relatively simple and elegant *rendering pipeline*.

As an example, imagine you're developing a video game and you have a robot at coordinates (A_x, A_y, A_z). The robot has an orientation *theta*, and it is driving around on a moving platform with location (P_x, P_y, P_z). You want to see this rendered from a viewpoint of a virtual camera with a certain rotation and pose (shown with . symbols for simplicity). The camera has a horizontal and vertical focal length of 1,000 pixels each, and the image center is (320, 240)—which is the middle of your 640 by 480 window. In your program, you are storing and updating the variables $A_x, A_y, A_z, \theta, P_x, P_y,$ and P_z.

Figure 3.5, on the following page, shows the complete calculations for converting an object point (x, y, z) into an image (u, v). A 3D point in object coordinates is transferred through several coordinate systems and has the pinhole model equations applied to project it to a 2D point in the image. Successive 4 by 4 matrices and two divide operations constitute the pipeline.

Starting from the right, you add 4 by 4 matrices to your chain. Since the robot rotates around its own axis, you perform this operation first (put it on the left), and then you translate the robot to (A_x, A_y, A_z), which is relative to the platform. This, in turn, requires another translation of (P_x, P_y, P_z) to bring it into world coordinates. These matrices can be combined using matrix multiplication into one matrix that takes care of all object-to-world coordinate system transfers.

The order listed is the effective order of computations; however, with OpenGL, you start from the "START POINT for OpenGL Projects" point in Figure 3.5, on the next page, and move to the right. You post-multiply a matrix that contains only the "transfer from object to world coordinates" portion. In OpenGL, this is known as the *modelview matrix*.

To give you an idea of what's ahead, the ARTag AR system sets the 4 by 4 viewing matrix (equivalent to the leftmost two matrices in Figure 3.5, on the following page) for the world coordinate system in OpenGL for you when it detects the markers. In your game or application, you need to add your own rotations, translation, and scaling operations. These are the right matrices in Figure 3.5, on the next page, which are labeled *transfer from object to world coordinates*.

$$\begin{pmatrix} u' \\ v' \\ w' \\ 1 \end{pmatrix} = \begin{pmatrix} 1000 & 0 & 320 & 0 \\ 0 & 1000 & 240 & 0 \\ 0 & 0 & 1 & 0 \\ 0 & 0 & 0 & 1 \end{pmatrix} \begin{pmatrix} . & . & . & . \\ . & . & . & . \\ . & . & . & . \\ 0 & 0 & 0 & 1 \end{pmatrix} \begin{pmatrix} 1 & 0 & 0 & P_x \\ 0 & 1 & 0 & P_y \\ 0 & 0 & 1 & P_z \\ 0 & 0 & 0 & 1 \end{pmatrix} \begin{pmatrix} 1 & 0 & 0 & A_x \\ 0 & 1 & 0 & A_y \\ 0 & 0 & 1 & A_z \\ 0 & 0 & 0 & 1 \end{pmatrix} \begin{pmatrix} \cos(\theta) & -\sin(\theta) & 0 & 0 \\ \sin(\theta) & \cos(\theta) & 0 & 0 \\ 0 & 0 & 1 & 0 \\ 0 & 0 & 0 & 1 \end{pmatrix} \begin{pmatrix} x \\ y \\ z \\ 1 \end{pmatrix}$$

Pinhole projection · Transfer from world to camera coordinates · Transfer from object to world coordinates

Viewing matrix

START POINT for OpenGL Projects

$$u = \frac{u'}{w'} \quad v = \frac{v'}{w'}$$

Figure 3.5: FULL RENDERING PIPELINE

This will make your objects appear at different poses within the world. You'll see some examples of this later. For simplicity's sake, one detail has been omitted. The final divide operations are actually performed after you do some polygon clipping operations. Some points will be deleted from your viewable list, and others will be interpolated or created when crossing clipping planes.

Congratulations if you made it this far! Here is a summary of what was covered in this chapter:

- Converting a 3D point to a 2D image point consists of *coordinate system transfer* operations and application of the pinhole model equations. The former, and part of the latter, can be represented in matrix form.
- Every coordinate system transfer can be expressed as a 3 by 3 rotation matrix and a three-element translation vector or a single 4 by 4 matrix.
- OpenGL works with 4 by 4 matrices.
- For each object to be rendered, the coordinate system is transferred several times by multiplying matrices (and vectors in the first method in 2) to produce one 3 by 3 matrix and vector or one 4 by 4 matrix. This 4 by 4 matrix contains all the information including focal length and image center necessary to transfer an object point into a temporary vector. This vector is applied to all points in the object with two final divide operations for each pixel.

You can represent relative poses between coordinates systems in matrix or matrix and vector form. And you can transform a 3D point, or set of points, from an object coordinate system (through several intermediate coordinate systems) into a 2D image point.

Now it's time to move onto the actual creation of pictures. You must consider such issues as the camera FOV, how to draw solid objects, and how to determine which objects are blocking other objects.

There are two main methods for creating a 2D image from a 3D model:

- *Texture mapping*: This method uses the equations from Figure 3.5, on the facing page, that map 3D points into image space and *scan-convert* the polygons to map 3D points into image space and scan-convert the polygons. A z-buffer is used to render close objects overtop of those that are farther away.
- *Ray tracing*: The pose matrices are used in reverse. Lines are drawn out from the pixel positions where they pass through empty space or transparent objects and bounce off solid objects until they reach a light source.

The former is used primarily in video games, and the latter is used for special effects in movies. Texture mapping is much faster and therefore is used in most accelerated graphics hardware, such as in your video card. Since moviemakers don't have to render their effects in real time, they can use the ray tracing method. In this book, you will learn about texture mapping.

3.5 Viewing Frustum and Clipping Planes

The equations and matrices of the previous section are only part of the story. Even if you are rendering only points, you still have to consider points that lie outside the FOV. If you checked the (u, v) coordinates and found that a point lay outside the image borders, then you could simply ignore it. But if a 3D point lay within a mirrored FOV behind the camera, you could not distinguish it from a point in front (after you perform the divisions to create $[u, v]$). Although a camera that can look forward and backward is perhaps intriguing to some, it's not what you want in simulating a real camera, so you have to remove the points behind.

One strategy to accomplish this goal is to first convert all points to camera coordinates and then discard all points with a negative Z_c. You still have to worry about points that lie too close to the $Z_c = 0$ plane—a plane passing through the camera focal point perpendicular to the central axis (that is, parallel to the image plane). You don't want to get a divide-by-zero error condition when you perform the final two divisions for (u, v). Therefore, you could declare a minimum $Z_{c\min}$ value, where

$Z_{c_{\min}}$ is slightly above zero and discard all points where $Z_c < Z_{c_{\min}}$. In 3D space you're putting in a plane $Z_c >= Z_{c_{\min}}$ that acts as a border—points on only one side of it will be kept.

This single plane would do fine for rendering points, but you want to see solid objects. Rendering millions of individual points so they fill in to create solid objects is not efficient, so you must use polygons. Polygons should need no introduction, but just to clarify, they are a *planar* region stretching between three or more points. Three points define a plane, so a three-sided polygon (a triangle) will always be planar, but a four-sided polygon (also known as a *quad*) might not be. For example, take a piece of paper, fold it along a diagonal line from corner to corner, and open the fold partly; you now have four points that make two triangles, and the whole thing is not a planar structure. In computer graphics, you should be careful that quads are indeed planar; otherwise, undesirable rendering effects will occur.

When connecting 3D points with lines or sets of 3D points with planar sections, you have to consider what to do when one of your points is in front of the $Z_c >= Z_{c_{\min}}$ plane and the other is behind. One solution is to cut this line or polygon and give it a new endpoint where it hits the plane. Doing this is known as applying a *clipping plane* (aka a cutting plane).

You will perform the same clipping plane operation four more times to enclose a volume containing all that needs be rendered. With a perspective view from a rectangular window, you can see anything in a pyramidal region of space with the point of the pyramid being our pinhole (focal point), the center of the pyramid being the camera's central axis, and the steepness of the pyramid sides being a function of the focal lengths f_x, f_y. You put a cutting plane along each side of this pyramid with anything outside being removed since it's not visible.

You now have five cutting planes: one parallel to the image plane (perpendicular to the camera central axis) that prevents your camera from seeing points that are behind the camera and getting a divide-by-zero condition and four arranged in a pyramid funnel shape that cut out anything to the left, right, above, or below the FOV.

Graphics systems like to add a sixth cutting plane, one that blocks out anything too far away; this plane represents the base of a pyramid (if the pinhole is the top) and is parallel to the first cutting plane.

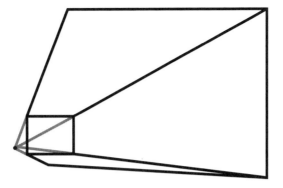

Figure 3.6: VIEWING FRUSTUM FORMED BY SIX PLANES

It has the equation $Z_c <= Z_{c\text{max}}$, and it serves the purpose of defining a maximum distance so that a finite precision can be given to points within the z-buffer. For example, if the z-buffer depth is 16 bits, then all points inside our frustum will be assigned the closest distance to one of 65,536 possible values. Note that these possible values are not equally spaced from the near-to-far cutting plane; they are spaced in increasingly larger steps as you move from near to far.

Now you have an entirely enclosed space defined by six cutting planes; anything inside is visible and will be carried onto the next stage of processing, where it may be rendered ("may be rendered" because something may be in front of it). This space is called the *viewing frustum* (see Figure 3.6).

One way to think about 4 by 4 matrices is that they allow warping of space. You're warping the space inside the pyramidal frustum into that of a cube spanning from x, y, $x = 0 - 1$, and you're clipping using the $x = 0$, $x = 1$, $y = 0$, $y = 1$, $z = 0$, $z = 1$ planes for cutting. But for the purposes of this book, it isn't necessary to strain your brain by unnecessarily delving into projective geometry.

As you can see, it's easy to apply your cutting planes to individual points; if they're inside, you keep them, and if they're outside, you discard them. But what about lines and polygons? This is where the cutting or clipping part of the names of the frustum walls come into play. You have to consider the possibility of dealing with polygons that lie partly inside and partly outside of your frustum. You deal with them by clipping them.

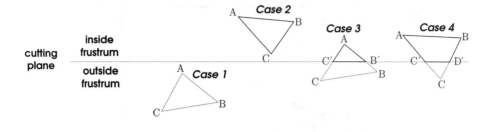

Figure 3.7: FOUR CASES OF CLIPPING A POLYGON AGAINST A CLIPPING PLANE

You apply the following procedure to a list of polygons (with vertex coordinates in the camera coordinate system): clip the set of polygons against the first plane to produce a new set of polygons, and then move onto the second, then the third, and so on. You can do one plane at a time—you'll get the same result whichever order you clip. Figure 3.6, on the preceding page, shows the clipping operation looking edge-on along one of the cutting planes, and Figure 3.7 shows four examples of clipping.

You have several possibilities for each polygon:

- All vertices are outside the plane (case 1 in Figure 3.6, on the preceding page). This case is easy; you just discard the entire polygon.

- All vertices are inside the plane (case 2 in Figure 3.6, on the previous page). This case is also easy; you just keep the whole polygon. In the two remaining cases, some corners are inside, and some are outside.

- In case 3 you replace points B with B′ and replace C with C′. B′ and C′ have interpolated X, Y, Z values as well as color or texture coordinates.

- In case 4, you need to replace C with C′ and add an extra point D′. The number of vertices has increased by one. It is possible to increase a polygon's number of vertices by one for each cutting operation. If you start with a quad (four vertices), in the worst case you could end up with a nine-sided polygon!

As mentioned, you interpolate not only the X, Y, Z values of the vertices but also their color values or texture coordinates.

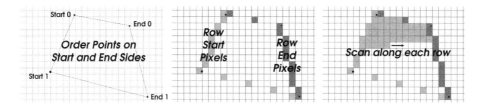

Figure 3.8: SCAN-LINE CONVERSION STEPS FOR A POLYGON

Now you have a list of polygons that are all inside the frustrum (that is, are entirely within the viewing window within the minimum and maximum distance from the virtual camera). Each polygon is a set of vertices, with each vertex containing its 3D coordinates and a color or texture coordinate (usually a 2D texture vertex $[u, v]$ but sometimes a 3D texture vertex $[u, v, w]$ for materials).

3.6 Scan-Line Converting Polygons

So far, your data has been a set of noninteger values (floating or fixed point) representing points in space. Your final result is discrete pixels with integer locations on the screen. What occurs next is scan-line conversion where each polygon is scan-converted into a set of pixel rows.

First the vertices are projected into image coordinates, and then they are sorted into those on top and those on the left or right side. The minimum and maximum row number is determined, and a start and end column is found for every row using a line-drawing algorithm between vertices on the left and right side. In other words, you start with vertices and then fill in intermediate points so that you know where that edge starts and ends on every row.

Every start point on the row (let's assume you start on the left edge) has an (x, y, z) component as well as $(\delta x, \delta y, \delta z)$ deltas that tell us how much to increase or decrease (x, y, z) for every pixel (as you step to the right). Likewise, for the color or texture coordinates, you have an initial value and a delta for each as you step from that first pixel along to the right (see Figure 3.8).

The z-buffer comes into play as you scan-convert the polygons. The z-buffer is an array as large as the image—it stores a depth for each pixel.

Therefore, the storage requirement of the z-buffer is of comparable size to the image. When you start rendering, you first clear all elements by setting them to the maximum distance from the camera (usually equal to the distance of the far clipping plane). As you scan along each pixel, you first calculate the pixel's Z value and see whether it's less than the depth in the z-buffer at this pixel location. If so, you update both the image and the z-buffer. Thus, you can automatically handle cases of polygons intersecting each other in complex ways.

At this point, it's important to mention something you should understand about texture mapping. Each 3D vertex in your list of polygons must have 3D coordinates (initially in an object coordinate system) and also a color or texture coordinate. Actually, the color could be specified per polygon rather than per vertex, but OpenGL allows you to give each vertex a different color that produces a polygon that blends colors through the interior. Frequently, you have texture-mapped vertices—a texture vertex (u, v) for each 3D vertex. (u, v) are coordinate points in a texture image that will be stretched across the object. The triangle (or quad) section of the texture image will be stretched like a rubber sheet across these 3D vertices. Consistency in spacing is not required, so a small part of a texture image could be stretched across a large 3D space, and a large part of the texture could be stretched over a small 3D space.

3.7 Summary of Rendering Procedure

To summarize what you've learned so far, here are the basic principles we covered in this chapter:

- Pinhole projection (aka perspective projection) is used to simulate an ideal camera for computer graphics. 3D models are usually given in a local *object* coordinate system. Exceptions can include terrain or other parts of the environment; these would likely be in the *world* coordinate system.
- You will use matrices, either a 3 by 3 rotation matrix and a three-element translation vector or a single 4 by 4 matrix, to convert 3D points from one coordinate system to another.
- 4 by 4 matrices can be easily combined to provide a single matrix that contains all translation, rotation, and scaling operations. A 3 by 3 or 4 by 4 matrix can also be used to perform the pinhole projection to convert to screen coordinates. All object 3D points are

converted to camera coordinates, and the polygons using these 3D points are discarded or clipped by the viewing frustum. The frustum is a set of six planes that define a pyramidal region in the direction of the camera view. The polygon vertices are converted to image coordinates, and scan-line conversion is performed to produce the individual pixel values. A z-buffer is also used; it contains a depth value for each pixel in the image. The z-buffer is checked before updating a screen pixel.

Here are the steps to render an object model at any given position. Steps 1 and 2 are usually performed at start-up or when the user resizes the viewing window. Steps 3 and 4 are performed for every camera frame.

1. Create the pinhole (perspective) projection matrix.
2. Create the frustum—the set of cutting planes defining the visible space.
3. Clear the image and the z-buffer.
4. Create the camera pose transfer matrix, which can be performed by calculating a projection matrix directly (from a set of correspondences between the image and the real object, as ARTag does) or by creating a matrix to represent the camera pose and premultiplying this matrix by the pinhole matrix of step 1.
5. Create the "transfer from object to world coordinates" composite matrix (known in OpenGL as the modelview matrix). In OpenGL, you must start with the world coordinate system and move toward the object coordinate system.
6. The rendering engine now has all the required information. Next, it turns each 3D point into a 4D vector (adds a 1 in the fourth element) and passes each through the combination 4 by 4 matrices (possibly including the pinhole matrix as well). It also performs clipping and scan-line conversion and produces both a visible image and a z-buffer (which you usually don't use or view). Step 6 is performed for you by OpenGL.

Congratulations again if you made it all the way through this chapter. Complete knowledge of this material is not necessary to program computer graphics and AR applications, but the more you know, the better off you are.

Next, you're going to revisit these steps in OpenGL and learn how to get all this rendering work done for you with some simple code.

Chapter 4

Using OpenGL with Augmented Reality

Now that you've been introduced to AR, exposed to several examples, and learned a bit about how computer graphics work, it's high time to get down to some programming.

All of the AR examples in this book were written using OpenGL. If you're going to program 3D graphics, you should consider learning OpenGL. Like DirectX, it's freely available, but OpenGL has the benefit of being cross-platform. This chapter will help you create OpenGL applications. If you're already a seasoned OpenGL programmer, you may want to skip ahead to the AR-specific examples in the next chapter.

After enjoying this chapter, you will be able to do the following:

- Copy a standard template for an OpenGL program.
- Compile an OpenGL program for your platform (Windows, Linux or Mac OS X).
- Use the gluPerspective() or glFrustum() function to set your virtual camera's field of view (FOV) and zoom.
- Use the translate-rotate-scale (TRS) methodology for calling the glTranslate(), glRotate(), and glScale() functions and the matrix push/ pop functions to convert between coordinate systems. This will allow you to draw objects at arbitrary positions and orientations.
- Draw basic lines, triangles, and quad *primitive*s that are textured or untextured.
- Use more complex primitives and list-rendering functions.

The first part of this chapter will give you the tools you need to create OpenGL graphics programs. The second part will show you more ways to render 3D data.

4.1 About OpenGL

The *GL* in OpenGL stands for "graphics library." OpenGL is one of the most popular graphics standards partly because it can be used on Windows, Linux, or Mac OS X machines. Also, since OpenGL is so widely used, it works with the hardware-accelerated features of most video cards. In fact, the 3D graphics in most of today's computers, and many non-PC video games, are generated with accelerated graphics cards that run an OpenGL interface. Also, in many systems where the accelerated graphics hardware is not present, or more likely not configured, a software version of OpenGL is running.

This chapter is not meant to replace any of the standard OpenGL reference materials. If you're new to OpenGL and you want more information, you should refer to online resources such as the *OpenGL Programming Guide* (aka the Red Book) and the *OpenGL Reference Manual* (aka the Blue Book). This chapter will get you up and running with your own 3D applications, but as you expand in your programming glory, you will need to refer to resources such as the Web and other books dedicated to OpenGL. We recommend you go to http://www.opengl.org or do some web searches when you have questions.

The Red Book and Blue Book are considered to be the bibles of OpenGL programming. Once you know what the books look like, you'll notice them in the cubicles and bookshelves of a lot of computer graphics people. The Red Book is a programming guide, whereas the Blue Book is a reference manual. Some think purchasing the actual paper books is a wise investment; others believe that once you get started, you can find everything you want for free from the Web, including the text of the books themselves.

What is commonly referred to as OpenGL actually involves a few levels. The *top* level is GLUT, which is the Graphics Library Utility Toolkit written by Mark Kilgard. GLUT isn't officially part of OpenGL but is very useful for beginner and intermediate OpenGL programmers because it takes care of many complex operating system issues. You'll see files such as glut.h, glut.lib, and glut.dll mentioned as you read through this

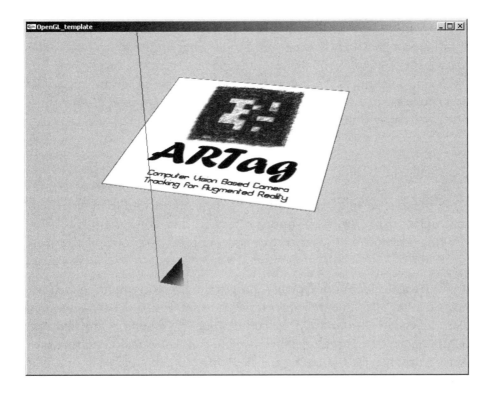

Figure 4.1: THE OPENGL TEMPLATE PROGRAM

book. When you see these, you'll know that they are part of GLUT. For more information about GLUT, refer to the website at http://www.opengl.org/documentation/specs/glut/spec3/spec3.html. Download the GLUT files from http://www.opengl.org/resources/libraries/glut/.

All right, enough introducing...more programming, you say? We could not agree more; we've stalled long enough, so let's get down to it.

4.2 Basic OpenGL Demo

To start, you will play with the OpenGL template program OPENGL_TEMPLATE_PROGRAM.CPP. Download this file from this book's website at http://www.pragprog.com/titles/cfar/source_code.

When you compile and run the template program, you will see the output shown in Figure 3.6, on page 49.

Before you go any further, ensure that you are able to compile and run this sample OpenGL program. To see what it should look like, refer to code\GetARRunning\opengl_only_test_compiled\ or the version for your platform. Sometimes getting a "Hello, world" type program to compile and run is a more difficult hurdle than expected. It should go smoothly, but you may as well check to make sure.

4.3 Compiling for Windows

First, make sure you have GLUT on your machine, and then find these three files: glut.h, glut32.lib, and glut32.dll. Either copy them into your working directory with your source code, or point your compiler to their locations.

If you plan to do lots of OpenGL programming, you might as well set up your compiler's search directories so that you don't have to copy files. In Visual Studio 2005, selecting Tools > Options > Projects and Solutions > VC++ Directories brings you to a list of include directories (see Figure 4.2, on the facing page). Find your copy of glut.h, and add its directory to the list of paths. To add a directory, click the New Line button, click the ellipses button, and then navigate to the directory containing glut.h. If glut32.dll is in a different directory, you will need to do the same for that folder.

Keep in mind that the version of GLUT must be right for your machine. If you have a version that isn't working, download a different one from the Web. You'll want to find the precompiled .h, .lib, and .dll files for GLUT. Get these for free from http://www.opengl.org (under "Coding Resources"). Remember that you want the precompiled versions, not the source code.

4.4 Compiling for Linux

Refreshingly, there are no changes required to get the programs in this chapter to compile for Linux, but as with Windows, you'll first have to find your GL and GLUT files. This may mean you'll have to download the correct version of GLUT for your machine.

You need to link in the GL, GLU, and GLUT libraries and provide a path to the GLUT header file and the files it includes. See whether there is a glut.h file in the /usr/include/GL directory; otherwise, look elsewhere for

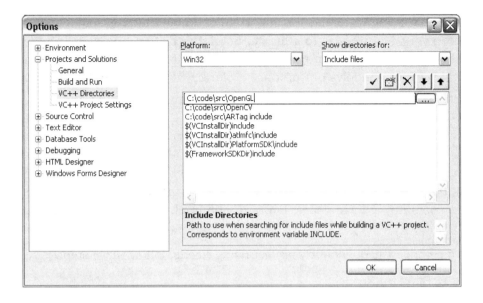

Figure 4.2: SETTING UP FOR OPENGL ON WINDOWS

it—you could use the command find / -name "glut.h" to search your entire machine, or you could use the locate command (locate glut.h).

You may need to customize the paths, but here is an example of the compile command:

```
gcc -o opengl_template opengl_template.cpp -I /usr/include/GL
    -I /usr/include -lGL -lGLU -lglut
```

gcc is a C/C++ compiler that should be present on your Linux or Unix machine. The -I /usr/include/GL command-line argument tells gcc to look in /usr/include/GL for the include files. In this case, you'll find glut.h and what it includes. When linking in libraries with gcc, you use the -lX switch—where X is the name of your library and there is a corresponding libX.a file somewhere in your path. For this example, you want to link in the library files libGL.a, libGLU.a, and libglut.a, so you will use the gcc arguments -lGL -lGLU -lglut. These three files are found in the default directory /usr/lib/, so you don't need to specify their location as you did with glut.h. If you did need to specify the library path, you would add -L to the path.

To run your compiled program, type ./opengl_template or, if the current directory is in your shell's paths, just opengl_template.

When working in Linux, it's important to know that you may need to keep your texture files to a maximum of 256 by 256 pixels or find the settings in your system to raise this limit. Often an OpenGL program will work in Windows but produce a blank white texture in Linux until the texture size is reduced.

4.5 Compiling for Mac OS X

When working with your OpenGL programs, Mac OS X gives you the option of using either Xcode or gcc. Note that there are two processor types associated with Macs: PowerPC and Intel. Make sure you're using the right version.

To compile the opengl_only project using Xcode, follow these steps:

1. Start up Xcode.

2. Create a new project.

3. Choose Carbon Application under Application.

4. Name your project opengl (the name doesn't matter).

5. Open the main.c file.

6. Delete all the contents of main.c, and replace it with the contents of opengl_only_test.cpp. Save the file.

7. From the Project window, navigate to External Frameworks and Libraries.

8. From the Action drop-down list, choose Add > Existing Frameworks.

9. Select Frameworks > GLUT.framework, and then click Add.

10. Click Add on the next screen to add it to the opengl target.

11. Go to Projects > Project Settings.

12. For the property Header Search Paths, set the value to /System/Library/Frameworks/GLUT.framework/Headers/.

13. Build the project, but do not run it yet. When you build, there should be no errors and only two warnings.

14. In the Finder, copy test_texture.ppm from the compiled_demos folder to the build/Debug/opengl1.app/Contents/Resources folder (for the current project).

Details: In the Finder (in the Debug directory), right-click the OpenGL icon, and select Show Package Contents from the context menu. In the new Finder window that appears, open the Contents directory, and then open the Resources directory. Copy test_texture.ppm to the directory.

15. Run the program from Build and Go on the Project window.

If you want to use gcc to compile your projects, use a command similar to this (you'll need to change the paths to match your system):

```
gcc -framework GLUT -framework OpenGL -Wall
    -o compiled_demos/opengl_only_test src/opengl_only_test.cpp
    -I include/ -I /System/Library/Frameworks/OpenGL.framework/Headers
    -I /System/Library/Frameworks/GLUT.framework/Headers
    -Llib -L/System/Library/Frameworks/OpenGL.framework/Libraries
    -lGL -lGLU -lm -lobjc -lstdc++
```

4.6 The OpenGL Template Program

Let's go over what's in the OpenGL Template demo. Better yet, let's review what you need to know for now and then use future examples to fill in the holes.

First, what does this program do? This OpenGL program draws a line, a triangle, a quad, and a textured quad on a gray background from an oblique angle. The texture used on the textured quad is loaded from a file called test_texture.ppm. This is not an AR example, because this is not an AR chapter. Everything you see when you run this application is created with OpenGL—no camera is used. This program is meant to provide you with some familiarity with OpenGL. Don't worry, you will get back to AR examples in the next chapter.

Next, let's look at the program structure. It is an event-driven structure, so code gets called when events happen. However, this doesn't occur in a constant linear flow as in conventional procedural programming. This is a software *framework*—it provides the structure and the callback functions (the *hooks*) for a user to fill in as required. After initialization, almost all the functionality is performed in the callback functions. This is true for everything except the keyboard reading, which allows the user to exit by pressing the Esc key.

The opengl_draw() function is the workhorse of the program. This function is called by the system when it's time to draw an image frame. In later AR examples, the opengl_tick() function grabs a camera image, but in this program a file is used for the texture image. The Main() function initializes things and sets callbacks for events with the glut*Func() functions (where * is Display, Idle, Reshape, Keyboard, PassiveMotion, or Mouse). Once you call glutMainLoop(), you lose procedural control, and your code gets to run only inside these callbacks. This is not necessarily bad since it allows you to avoid polling for things such as keyboard or mouse events in a main loop, and it also allows the rendering system to render as fast as it can.

Between glBegin() and glEnd(), you feed OpenGL 3D points using glVertex3f(x, y, z). You can input these points in several formats. The *f* in glVertex3f stands for *float*; the 3D values are each represented with single-precision floating-point numbers. Alternatively, you could have called glVertex3d() for double-precision floats (doubles), or you could have used short or full length integers with glVertex3s() or glVertex3i(), respectively. If *back-face culling* is turned on, you call the points in a clockwise order (when viewed from the front side) when you're drawing a triangle or quad. You can also pass a pointer to a list of three values with glVertex3fv(), glVertex3dv(), glVertex3sv(), or glVertex3iv(). For the sake of readability, the sample code is indented—with one space between glBegin() and glEnd().

If your entire primitive is a simple color, you can call it at the beginning —as with the green quad. You could also draw each vertex with a different color per vertex. This produces a blending effect, but you need to give the color or texture coordinates before giving the 3D coordinate. Calling glColor3f() just enters values into a buffer, which is then entered with glVertex*(). glVertex*() is the *active* command that actually performs the rendering. In this example, the color and 3D coordinate setting calls are on one line. This saves space and makes it easier for anyone reading the code to associate them. Here is the triangle rendering code:

`OpenGL/opengl_template_program/OPENGL_TEMPLATE_PROGRAM.CPP`

```
//draw multi-colored triangle
glDisable(GL_TEXTURE_2D);
glBegin(GL_TRIANGLES);
    glColor3f(1, 0, 0);
    glVertex3f(0,0,0);
    glColor3f(0, 1, 0);
    glVertex3f(10,0,0);
    glColor3f(0, 0, 1);
    glVertex3f(10,0,10);
glEnd();
```

You're not going to create a lot of plain-colored triangles for video games —almost everything in games is textured. To add the texture, you first need to enable texture mapping with the glEnable(GL_TEXTURE_2D) function call. Note that you called glDisable(GL_TEXTURE_2D) before drawing your line, triangle, and untextured quad. The textured quad drawing function is shown here:

OpenGL/opengl_template_program/OPENGL_TEMPLATE_PROGRAM.CPP

```
glEnable(GL_TEXTURE_2D);
glBindTexture(GL_TEXTURE_2D, pgm_texID);
glBegin(GL_QUADS);
    glColor3f(1.0f, 1.0f, 1.0f);
    glTexCoord2f(0.0f, 1.0f);  glVertex3f(-50,50,0);
    glTexCoord2f(0.0f, 0.0f);  glVertex3f(-50,150,0);
    glTexCoord2f(1.0f, 0.0f);  glVertex3f( 50,150,0);
    glTexCoord2f(1.0f, 1.0f);  glVertex3f( 50,50,0);
glEnd();
```

In both the color and texture coordinate cases, you need to set the non-3D coordinate data before you call glColor3f().

Before you call glBegin(GL_QUADS), you call glBindTexture() and give it the handle pgm_texID, which is a handle to a bitmap texture that's of data type GLuint. Let's hop to the end of the Main() function and look at the initialization of the texture. First, you get the handle with a call to glGenTextures(). Then, you call glBindTexture() to tell OpenGL that subsequent calls about textures will be about this texture. You can think of glBindTexture(GL_TEXTURE_2D, pgm_texID) as saying, "From now on, until I say otherwise, when I talk about a texture I mean the 2D texture with the handle pgm_texID." glBindTexture is called both during initialization and rendering.

GlTexParameteri() tells OpenGL how to handle textures when the texture is far away or close and when there are many texture pixels to one image pixel, or vice versa. When the bitmap texture resolution is higher than the screen resolution (that is, the virtual camera image resolution), then *aliasing* effects can occur. This usually happens when the virtual camera is viewing the object from a distance. This results in the appearance of *Moire effects*, which are false lines and patterns. With this texture parameter, one can set how OpenGL should mitigate these effects.

Once you get your bitmap into an unsigned char (byte) array, you call glTexImage2D() to load the full image. This function is notorious for being slow, so it should be done only in the initialization stage. If at all possible, don't use this function at other stages in your application. OpenGL textures will be used both to cover the polygons of the 3D models and to display the image from the camera.

Now, how do you get an image into an unsigned char array? In later chapters, you'll get one of your textures from a video camera, but in many cases, you will need to load one from a file. As mentioned earlier, the texture used on the textured quad is loaded from a file called test_texture.ppm.

This happens in the examples via the texture_read_ppm() function; this code reads a PPM file into memory. PPM files are RGB uncompressed image files. PPM and the grayscale version, PGM, are not very popular image formats—perhaps because of their large size. But they are easy to read and write, as is evidenced by the small texture_read_ppm() function provided with this example.

Now let's explore the initialization step that happens in Main() before glutMainLoop(). In the initialization, the first few lines in Main(), you see GLUT being initialized with glutInit(). You will also see the display mode being set with glutInitDisplayMode() to have double-buffering, to have an RGB screen, and to use the z-buffer. The z-buffer allows depth testing. Double-buffering is important to have a flicker-free display. You have two image buffers; you draw to one while the video card is outputting the other, and then you switch by calling glutSwapBuffers().

The size of your display window and the position of the upper-left corner, measured in screen pixels from the upper left of the desktop, is set with glutInitWindowSize() and glutInitWindowPosition(), respectively. Finally, the window title and background color, called ClearColor, is set with glutSetWindowTitle() and glClearColor(). Normally, one would use a black background, as per the commented out glClearColor() line, but you'll set it to gray for this demo. To create the gray color, the red, green, and blue values are set to 0.8.

During initialization, you will also turn on depth testing via the glEnable(GL_DEPTH_TEST) call and turn on back-face culling with glCullFace(GL_BACK). With back-face culling turned on, OpenGL will not render polygons with their backs to the user.

glFrontFace(GL_CW) defines a polygon as facing the user if the vertices go around in a clockwise direction. When it is facing the other way, it will appear counterclockwise to the user, and OpenGL will know the user is looking at the back of it. There may be some cases where you want to see the back faces of objects, but if they're closed, solid objects, then the polygons facing the other way will be hidden anyway. You can save rendering time since about one half of the polygons in closed, solid objects are facing the other way and the rendering engine doesn't need to consider them at all (for example, OpenGL doesn't need to scan-convert them, as discussed in the previous chapter).

Note that this implies that you have to make sure you give the polygon vertices to OpenGL so that the polygon vertices are ordered clockwise from an outside viewpoint. Finally, glShadeModel(GL_SMOOTH) sets the shading so that a *polyhedral* object will appear less tessellated; you'll see the effect of this later.

4.7 Setting the Frustum

In the previous chapter, the viewing frustum was introduced (see Figure 3.6, on page 49). You need this pyramidal frustum for two reasons: to provide parameters for the pinhole projection where 3D is mapped to the 2D image and for polygon clipping where points and parts of polygons outside the visible area are removed from consideration when rendering. You'll remember that points and parts of polygons inside the frustum's area are bounded by six planes. Anything outside of this area is discarded since it is out of the field of view (FOV) or is too close or too far to be visible to the gamer.

We'll explore two ways of setting the frustum to get the desired perspective view. First you'll use the glFrustum() function, because it fits in with the previous frustum discussions, and then you'll use gluPerspective()—which may be simpler to use when you're not doing AR and the virtual FOV doesn't have to match a real camera.

Here is the code from our template example again; it consists first of the glMatrixMode(GL_PROJECTION) call, which tells OpenGL that future matrix calls are modifying the projection matrix (to be distinguished from the modelview matrix). glFrustum() call post-multiplies the current matrix sitting in OpenGL's projection matrix variable; thus, you need to ensure that you have the identity matrix there first—hence the call to glLoadIdentity().

```
OpenGL/opengl_template_program/OPENGL_TEMPLATE_PROGRAM.CPP
//set viewing frustum to match camera FOV
glMatrixMode (GL_PROJECTION);
glLoadIdentity ();
camera_opengl_dRight = cam_width / (2.0 * DEFAULT_FX);
camera_opengl_dLeft = -camera_opengl_dRight;
camera_opengl_dTop = cam_height / (2.0 * DEFAULT_FY);
camera_opengl_dBottom = -camera_opengl_dTop;
glFrustum(camera_opengl_dLeft, camera_opengl_dRight, camera_opengl_dBottom,
        camera_opengl_dTop, 1.0, 1100.0);
```

The six elements in the glFrustum() call define the six planes that form the frustum. The format for calling glFrustum() is glFrustum(left, right, down, up, near, far). The near and far numbers are the distances along the camera's main axis of the top and bottom planes of the pyramid with the top chopped off. Left, right, down, and up are distances perpendicular to the camera main axis and define the width and height of the rectangular top of the pyramid. Together, five of the six numbers—left, right, down, up, and near—define the FOV. Usually, the frustum is symmetrical, so left is the opposite of (negative of) right, and up is the opposite of (negative of) down. Each pair has the same magnitude but opposite signs. As you'll see shortly, you need to give a little thought to the near and far settings. From these settings, you use your FOV to calculate the left, right, down, and up settings. In this example, you set the values near to 1.0 in your program. Figure 4.3, on the facing page, shows how the frustum settings in the previous code sample are determined.

Equivalent triangles are used to find *left* (and the magnitude of *right*) given *near* to match the desired FOV. The larger the focal lengths (DEFAULT_FX,Y in this program) are relative to the image dimensions (here, CAMERA_WIDTH, CAMERA_HEIGHT), the more zoomed in you are. This results in smaller left, right, down, and up values.

The second way of setting up the frustum is to use the gluPerspective() function. This function allows you to just specify the vertical FOV, the aspect ratio, and the position of the near and far cutting planes. The syntax is gluPerspective(vert_FOV, aspect_ratio, near, far).

With cameras, HMDs, and projectors, it can be tricky to understand which FOV the manufacturers are referring to in their specifications. Vendors often describe the diagonal FOV. This happens partly for historical reasons (that is, old vacuum tube video cameras) and partly because the vendors want to make the viewing angle sound larger. Here, the vertical FOV is used, which is just vert_fov=2 atan(up/near).

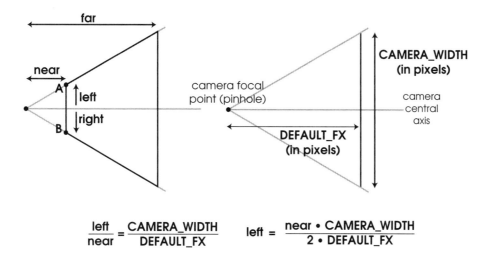

$$\frac{left}{near} = \frac{CAMERA\_WIDTH}{DEFAULT\_FX} \qquad left = \frac{near \cdot CAMERA\_WIDTH}{2 \cdot DEFAULT\_FX}$$

Figure 4.3: TOP VIEW OF VIEWING FRUSTUM

The aspect ratio is the horizontal resolution divided by the vertical. This is usually 1.333 with standard resolutions—such as 320 by 240 or 640 by 480.

The frustum is best understood with examples of different settings, so let's look at three examples with varying zoom (FOV) settings (see Figure 4.4, on the next page; Figure 4.5, on the following page; and Figure 4.6, on page 69). In each example, you'll see an outside view of the frustum on the left and what the camera sees on the right. The frustum edges are drawn as black lines. The camera's X-, Y-, and Z-axes are drawn as red, green, and blue lines, respectively. The blue Z-axis is the camera's main axis. All examples have near=1.0 and a virtual camera width and height of 320 by 240 pixels. The focal length changes to achieve different zoom factors. Note that these values just set the FOV and not the image resolution. The resolution is as large as the window that is created (or larger if you click Maximize to fill the full screen). As you can see in these examples, when you zoom in with a constant image size, the vertical FOV decreases, the focal length increases, the frustum tightens, and the magnitude of left, right, down, and up all decrease.

To get the zoomed-out view of Figure 4.4, on the following page, you could call gluPerspective(70.7, 1.3333, 1.0, 1025) or glFrustum(-0.94, 0.94, -0.71, 0.71, 1.0, 1025.0).

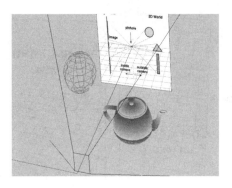
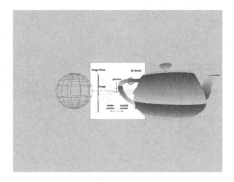

Figure 4.4: VERTICAL FOV=70.7 DEGREES. FX=FY=170. RIGHT=320/(2*170)=0.94. TOP=240/(2*170)=0.71.

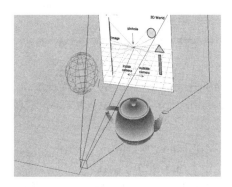
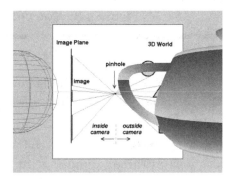

Figure 4.5: VERTICAL FOV=33.4 DEGREES. FX=FY=400. RIGHT=320/(2*400)=0.40. TOP=240/(2*400)= 0.30.

To get the view of Figure 4.5, you could call gluPerspective(33.4, 1.3333, 1.0, 1025) or glFrustum(-0.40, 0.40, -0.30, 0.30, 1.0, 1025.0).

To get the zoomed-in view of Figure 4.6, on the facing page, you could call gluPerspective(11.4, 1.3333, 1.0, 1025) or glFrustum(-0.13, 0.13, -0.10, 0.10, 1.0, 1025.0).

To nail down your depth resolution, you must consider one more issue. If possible, try to reduce the frustum's depth range. When the z-buffer-based depth testing is performed, it can resolve distance only with a finite accuracy (depth represents the distance from the camera). The z-buffer stores a depth for every pixel in the image; if the far/near ratio is too large, two points with similar depths may fall into the same quan-

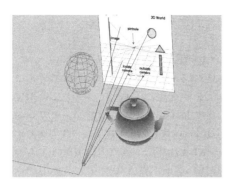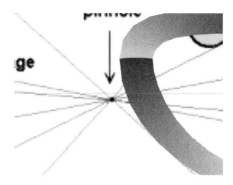

Figure 4.6: VERTICAL FOV=11.4 DEGREES. FX=FY=400. RIGHT=320/(2*1200)=0.13. TOP=240/(2*1200)=0.10.

tized number stored in the depth buffer, and the code might incorrectly identify which point is in front of the other. This effect of two points of different depths being quantized to the same depth value in the z-buffer becomes worse for points that are far away. Overall, the effect is worse the higher the far/near ratio is. Bad depth resolution is not a function of a large far minus near value, but of a large far divided by near value.

In the previous chapter, you learned that you shouldn't render points with a zero depth because you'll create a divide-by-zero problem. This may cause you to think any very small finite but positive near setting will work. However, this depth resolution consideration means you'll be better off with the largest near setting that you can tolerate. Think of it as compressing the depth of the frustum pyramid and moving the chopped-off top plane further down to meet the closest objects.

The take-away from these last two paragraphs is this: don't make the near plane too close to the camera, and don't make the far plane excessively far away. If you remember these points, you can avoid some unpleasant effects. You may also find that such issues are difficult to diagnose. For example, if you have an AR scenario where your camera is a camcorder and your scene takes place indoors, don't set your far plane 100 miles away and the near plane closer than an inch. You may as well use some reasonable distances. After all, if you used values too close, an object would end up hitting the lens of a real camera anyway. In many ways, it's easier to pick good values for near and far in AR settings than conventional graphics because your virtual objects and your scene are going to be in real-world units.

4.8 Translate Rotate Scale

So far you've compiled and run a basic OpenGL program that took care of setting things up and rendering. But in these examples, all objects were drawn in one coordinate system. Now let's learn how to use the glTranslate(), glRotate(), and glScale() functions to help you move between coordinate systems. This saves you the trouble of having to do the math for where to draw your polygons—which can get quite involved in 3D. Applications such as games, or animations, typically involve drawing polygon models that were created in a 3D design program, such as Autodesk 3D Studio Max, Autodesk Maya, Softimage, or Autodesk AutoCAD. As discussed in the previous chapter, it's convenient to use the concept of different coordinate systems so you can just render the polygons in their original coordinate system. You'll transform them for viewing by setting up matrix operations to handle the coordinate system transformations.

Translate-rotate-scale (TRS) is the mantra OpenGL programmers use when changing coordinate systems. It is a memory aid to apply whenever moving from world-to-object coordinates or from object-to-subobject coordinates. For each conversion of coordinate system, you first call glTranslate() to shift the origin of the coordinate system, then you call glRotate() to account for the rotation difference, and then you call glScale() to adjust the scale. If you were to convert between three coordinate systems, you would do a TRS for the world-to-object transformation, followed by a second TRS for the object-to-subobject transformation, followed by a third TRS for the final subobject-to-subsubobject transformation. You don't have to use all three operations each time; sometimes the relative pose between systems can be expressed simply as a rotation or translation. Often, you do only one scale operation right at the end to account for the scale of the 3D model as it came from the 3D software design program. This set of equations shows TRS coordinate system transformations represented as 4 by 4 matrices:

$$
\begin{pmatrix} x' \\ y' \\ z' \\ a' \end{pmatrix} = \begin{pmatrix} 1 & 0 & 0 & d_x \\ 0 & 1 & 0 & d_y \\ 0 & 0 & 1 & d_z \\ 0 & 0 & 0 & 1 \end{pmatrix} \begin{pmatrix} x \\ y \\ z \\ 1 \end{pmatrix} \tag{4.1}
$$

TRANSLATION BY DX, DY, DZ

$$
\begin{pmatrix} x' \\ y' \\ z' \\ a' \end{pmatrix} = \begin{pmatrix} \cos(\theta) & -sin(\theta) & 0 & 0 \\ \sin(\theta) & \cos(\theta) & 0 & 0 \\ 0 & 0 & 1 & 0 \\ 0 & 0 & 0 & 1 \end{pmatrix} \begin{pmatrix} x \\ y \\ z \\ 1 \end{pmatrix} \qquad (4.2)
$$

ROTATING COUNTERCLOCKWISE AROUND Z-AXIS BY θ DEGREES

$$
\begin{pmatrix} x' \\ y' \\ z' \\ a' \end{pmatrix} = \begin{pmatrix} s & 0 & 0 & 0 \\ 0 & s & 0 & 0 \\ 0 & 0 & s & 0 \\ 0 & 0 & 0 & 1 \end{pmatrix} \begin{pmatrix} x \\ y \\ z \\ 1 \end{pmatrix} \qquad (4.3)
$$

SCALING (ENLARGING) BY S

How do you call these functions? Let's go through some simple examples. In this book, we have been using the function names glTranslate(),
glRotate(), and glScale(), but these exact spellings won't compile. To use
these functions, you need to specify a data type; you need an *f* for
floating-point numbers or a *d* for double-precision floats. Don't get
confused with C's formatted print, printf(), or scanf() functions—where
an *f* represents a float, but a *d* represents an integer. There is also
an *x* type in embedded GL-ES for PDAs, where *x* means fixed point,
but herein we'll stick to what you'll usually find in Windows, Mac OS
X, and Linux. You must call glTranslatef(), glRotatef(), and glScalef(), or
glTranslated(), glRotated(), and glScaled(). In this book, *f* or *d* are simply
omitted to keep things more general.

The arguments for translation—using floats, for example—are glTrans-
late(Tx, Ty, Tz), where (Tx, Ty, Tz) is the offset of the object coordinate system
in the world system. For example, calling glTranslate(2, 3, 0) when in world
coordinates would put the origin of the new object coordinate system
at (2, 3, 0) in world coordinates. This means that (1, 1, 1) in object
coordinates maps to (3, 4, 1) in the real world.

glRotate() (either glRotatef() or glRotated()) allows you to rotate around
an arbitrary axis. The format (for floats) is glRotatef(theta, x, y, z). Theta
is in degrees, (x, y, z) is the axis of rotation, and the rotation is counterclockwise. glRotated(30, 0, 0, 1) would rotate the object coordinate system
30 degrees counterclockwise around the Z-axis. Rotating around the Z-
axis is probably the most common rotation, since in real life, objects
such as cars, or people, typically translate on a mostly horizontal surface and can rotate only around the vertical axis.

$$
\begin{pmatrix} x_{\text{world}} \\ y_{\text{world}} \\ z_{\text{world}} \\ 1 \end{pmatrix} = \begin{pmatrix} 1 & 0 & 0 & d_x \\ 0 & 1 & 0 & d_y \\ 0 & 0 & 1 & d_z \\ 0 & 0 & 0 & 1 \end{pmatrix} \begin{pmatrix} \cos(\theta) & -\sin(\theta) & 0 & 0 \\ \sin(\theta) & \cos(\theta) & 0 & 0 \\ 0 & 0 & 1 & 0 \\ 0 & 0 & 0 & 1 \end{pmatrix} \begin{pmatrix} s & 0 & 0 & 0 \\ 0 & s & 0 & 0 \\ 0 & 0 & s & 0 \\ 0 & 0 & 0 & 1 \end{pmatrix} \begin{pmatrix} x_{\text{object}} \\ y_{\text{object}} \\ z_{\text{object}} \\ 1 \end{pmatrix}
$$

$$
| \longleftarrow \quad \textit{Transfer from object} \quad \longrightarrow \quad |
$$
$$
\textit{to world coordinates}
$$

$$
\begin{pmatrix} x_{\text{world}} \\ y_{\text{world}} \\ z_{\text{world}} \\ 1 \end{pmatrix} = \begin{pmatrix} M_{11} & M_{12} & M_{13} & M_{14} \\ M_{21} & M_{22} & M_{23} & M_{24} \\ M_{31} & M_{32} & M_{33} & M_{34} \\ M_{41} & M_{42} & M_{43} & M_{44} \end{pmatrix} \begin{pmatrix} x_{\text{object}} \\ y_{\text{object}} \\ z_{\text{object}} \\ 1 \end{pmatrix}
$$

Figure 4.7: CONVERTING 3D POINTS BETWEEN COORDINATE SYSTEMS

To adjust scale, you call glScalef(sx, sy, sz) or glScaled(sx, sy, sz), where sx, sy, and sz are how much you scale along the object X-, Y-, and Z-axes. This allows you to stretch an object. Typically, you would have sx=sy=sz and scale in all directions equally. In the upcoming example, you will be doubling the size of an object (a teapot) with the command glScaled(2, 2, 2). Just for variety, you will use the double version of glScale() instead of the float version.

Each operation is performed with an appropriate 4 by 4 matrix. Having each TRS operation as a 4 by 4 matrix allows them to all be combined into one matrix (see equation 4.1, on page 70). From this point, every 3D object point can be converted to a world point with 16 multiply/accumulate (MAC) operations (see Figure 4.7). The order of matrix multiplication is shown again for the kettle example in Figure 4.8, on the next page. The kettle rotates with angle theta and moves with position (K_x, K_y, K_z) on a platform that itself is moving and has a position (P_x, P_y, P_z). This is how OpenGL handles things.

To reconcile this TRS and the world-to-object order of operations with the math from our previous chapter, you need to know that the glTranslate(), glRotate(), and glScale() functions post-multiply the existing modelview matrix by a new matrix created from the translation, rotation, or scale parameter. On paper, as in Figure 4.7, you write the object point on the right and the world point on the left, such that you are first doing the scale, then rotate, and then translate for the last coordinate system transformation.

$$\begin{pmatrix} x_{\text{world}} \\ y_{\text{world}} \\ z_{\text{world}} \\ 1 \end{pmatrix} = \begin{pmatrix} 1 & 0 & 0 & P_x \\ 0 & 1 & 0 & P_y \\ 0 & 0 & 1 & P_z \\ 0 & 0 & 0 & 1 \end{pmatrix} \begin{pmatrix} 1 & 0 & 0 & K_x \\ 0 & 1 & 0 & K_y \\ 0 & 0 & 1 & K_z \\ 0 & 0 & 0 & 1 \end{pmatrix} \begin{pmatrix} \cos(\theta) & -\sin(\theta) & 0 & 0 \\ \sin(\theta) & \cos(\theta) & 0 & 0 \\ 0 & 0 & 1 & 0 \\ 0 & 0 & 0 & 1 \end{pmatrix} \begin{pmatrix} x_{\text{object}} \\ y_{\text{object}} \\ z_{\text{object}} \\ 1 \end{pmatrix}$$

$\longleftarrow$ *Transfer from object* $\longrightarrow$
to world coordinates

Figure 4.8: ORDER OF MATRIX MULTIPLICATION FOR KETTLE EXAMPLE

Note that Figure 4.7, on the preceding page, has no scaling but has two transformations. The first is a rotation and translation (translating by A_x, A_y, A_z), and the second transformation is only a translation (translating by P_x, P_y, P_z). Next, move to the left on paper toward the world space, ultimately producing the 3D world coordinates. Therefore, on paper, you derive the operations from right to left, but in OpenGL you construct this matrix backward going left to right.

The left-to-right order is more practical because as you're higher in an object hierarchy, there will be many 3D points sharing the first few coordinate system transformations. Consider the example of a humanoid robot on a moving platform. You need to translate, rotate, and possibly scale to get from world to platform coordinates and a second translate and rotate for the position on the platform for all parts of the robot. When you TRS to the robot torso, this level will be useful for both the torso and the arms, because the modelview matrix can be used to calculate the modelview matrix at child elements—such as the arms (the children objects) compared to the torso (the parent object).

4.9 The Matrix Stack

Calculating the modelview matrix for child elements brings us to the other common commands: glPushMatrix() and glPopMatrix(). As you move down the object hierarchy, you can avoid repeating work by storing intermediate matrices. After you've moved your robot from world to platform, platform to robot, and robot to torso, you have a matrix that's useful for both the torso and the two arms. Imagine that you render the torso; then you move onto one of the arms. You will need the torso matrix when you come to the other arm. Before you move onto an arm,

Figure 4.9: SCREENSHOTS OF MOTION_EXAMPLE.CPP

you can do a glPushMatrix() operation on the torso. This saves the matrix in a *stack*, so you're able to reuse it later.

A stack is a list that is accessed only at the top. The last item put on is the first one retrieved. You can think of a stack as being like a track of cafeteria trays on a spring-loaded holder; the last one you *push* on the stack is the first one you'll *pop* off. This is called a *last in first out* (LIFO) system. As you add one item, the whole stack moves down under the weight, and as you take one off, the whole stack moves up such that you can always reach the same spot.

In the robot example, you probably want to push the matrix once you TRS onto the platform from world coordinates. You do this in case you have other objects that are sitting on the platform that need rendering. Then once you move to the robot pose, you might want to also push this matrix so that you can move down different branches of the subobject hierarchy of the robot parts and start again from the robot position. When you're done with the robot, you can pop the matrix stack so that you're back to the platform coordinate system.

It's vital to remember that there should be a pop instruction for every push instruction! If you don't plan to discard the matrix and start again, you need to pop to get back to where you started. This is necessary in the Motion_Example.CPP program since you are setting only the camera view (in the modelview matrix) once in the program initialization, and you rely on the glPopMatrix() command to bring you back to this camera view after every iteration loop. Program cleanly by popping every push. This avoids creating a growing memory stack. Matrix stack overflows crash OpenGL programs because OpenGL stacks have limited space; typically they have 32 stacks.

In addition, ensure that OpenGL knows which matrix you're using. There are a few matrices OpenGL uses, but all the operations that you repeat every frame in your demo programs are performed on the modelview matrix. The command glMatrixMode(GL_MODELVIEW) tells OpenGL that the next matrix operations are dealing with this matrix, and not, for example, the projection matrix.

4.10 Motion Example Program

The following example program uses the translate, rotate, scale, and matrix push/pop operations to create a moving animation. You can see screenshots of the motion program in action in Figure 4.9, on the facing page. The green platform translates up and down, while the teapot rotates and bounces around relative to the platform. This demonstrates two levels of coordinate system transfers. In this program, the wireframe sphere moves around under keyboard control using the I, J, K, and M keys. Here is a snippet from opengl_draw() in motion_example.cpp:

```
void opengl_draw(void)
{
...
    //save modelview matrix containing only camera pose
    glMatrixMode(GL_MODELVIEW);
    glPushMatrix();

    //convert from world to platform coordinates
    glTranslatef(0,platform_y,5);
    //---- Draw objects in platform coordinates ----
    glBegin(GL_QUADS);
        //draw platform top quad
        glColor3f(0, 1, 0);
        glVertex3f(0,0,0);
        glVertex3f(100,0,0);
        glVertex3f(100,100,0);
        glVertex3f(0,100,0);
        //draw platform front quad
        glColor3f(0, 0.7, 0);
        glVertex3f(0,0,0);
        glVertex3f(100,0,0);
        glVertex3f(100,0,-5);
        glVertex3f(0,0,-5);
    glEnd();

    //convert from platform to kettle coordinates
    //translate-rotate-scale
    glTranslatef(kettle_x,kettle_y,10);
    glRotatef(kettle_theta,0,0,1);
```

```
glRotatef(90,1,0,0);
glScaled(2,2,2);
//---- Draw objects in kettle coordinates ----
glEnable(GL_TEXTURE_2D);
glBindTexture(GL_TEXTURE_2D, grey_texID);
glColor3f(0.6f, 0.85f, 1.0f);
glutSolidTeapot(10);

//back to original modelview matrix containing
//only camera pose
glPopMatrix();

//save original modelview matrix again
glPushMatrix();
//convert from world to sphere coordinates
glTranslatef(sphere_x,sphere_y,5);
//---- Draw objects back in sphere coordinates ----
glColor3f(1.0f, 0.6f, 0.6f);
glutWireSphere(20,10,10);
//back to original modelview matrix again
glPopMatrix();

glutSwapBuffers();
}
```

Study the Motion_Example.CPP program and investigate what is drawn in each coordinate system and how the program moves between systems. A good exercise for an OpenGL beginner is to write down a list of which primitives are drawn in each coordinate system and when you need to perform transformations.

1. The Motion_Example.CPP program starts by setting the modelview matrix. This gives us the oblique camera view for the coordinate system transformation from world to camera coordinates. This happens in the Main() function—where you perform initialization. The modelview matrix has this setting every time the program enters the opengl_draw() function—you're not overwriting it in this example as you will in the other demos (where ARTag overwrites it with the new camera pose). In other words, the modelview matrix is set as the program enters opengl_draw() so that you're drawing in world coordinates. The grid and RGB axis marker is drawn at this level.

   Levels are steps within the tree of transformations. Therefore, the level refers to the matrix after just going from camera to world—it is here that you draw the grid and RGB axis markers. You later concatenate more matrices to represent more coordinate system transformations (that is, different *levels*).

2. You then call glPushMatrix() to save your state so that you can get it back later.

3. You translate to the platform coordinate system where you draw the platform—by performing a translate operation only. You are currently in platform coordinates.

4. You perform a full TRS to get to the teapot coordinate system where you draw the teapot.

5. You call glPopMatrix(), which returns you to world coordinates. It pulls the modelview matrix off the stack as you saved it in step 2.

6. Call glPushMatrix() another time before you leave the world coordinate system.

7. You perform a translation into sphere coordinates. Any drawing you do here is relative to the sphere's center.

8. You perform a final glPopMatrix(), which returns you to world coordinates. This is important because it ensures that the next time you reenter opengl_draw(), you are back in world coordinates.

As an experiment, remove the last glPopMatrix() and see what happens. There's a quick flash for the first time through opengl_draw(), where you see your expected view for one frame, and then you have a blank screen because your virtual camera is not facing the correct direction anymore.

We will explore some more aspects of this program and then make some small changes to the program to help you visualize the coordinate systems. For this example, two new *primitives* are introduced: teapots, which are actually pseudo-primitives, and spheres. You probably would not use them in a professional game or animation, but they're useful for programming because they allow you to quickly set up something.

You'll set the teapot size to 10 units wide and then use glScale() to double its size to 20. You could have simply drawn the teapot 20 units wide and not needed the scale, but for this example, we want a full TRS sequence in the program.

Notice here that you're creating a texture instead of loading it. It's just a simple grayscale ramp to give you some solid surface so that you can see the geometry of the teapot. You create the texture by making an unsigned char array of size 256 by 256—one byte per pixel—and fill it with a vertically increasing gray level. glTexImage2D() is called to load this texture into OpenGL. The GL_LUMINANCE setting is used to indicate that your texture has only one byte per pixel and does not have color information. When the program renders the teapot, you call glColor3f(0.6f, 0.85f, 1.0f) to give it a bluish tint. Note this means you're combining a color multiplier for the whole object with a texture map.

Another new element added to this program is the decoding of keyboard commands. You can move the sphere around on the X-Y plane with key presses. GLUT makes this easy—you can get keyboard input functionality with a few simple lines.

Let's have a look at what the coordinate systems look like. By now, you should clearly understand what it means to have the different coordinate systems—at least at the conceptual level. In this example you'll show the X-, Y-, and Z-axes for each coordinate system by drawing a red, green, and blue line segment, respectively, for each. In the last program, you did this only for the world coordinate system with large 100-unit-long line segments.

You'll enter the following code, which will put ten-unit-long segments for each axis (X, Y, Z) at the origin of each coordinate system. With C/C++, of course, it's OK to do multiple statements on a single line; this can save a lot of space. Also, when drawing primitives, you do not need to have a glBegin(), glEnd() around each primitive, just around the whole set of the same primitive type.

OpenGL/motion_example_2/motion_example_2.cpp

```
//draw RGB axis
glBegin(GL_LINES);
    //draw red x-axis
    glColor3f(1, 0, 0); glVertex3f(0,0,0); glVertex3f(20,0,0);
    //draw green y-axis
    glColor3f(0, 1, 0); glVertex3f(0,0,0); glVertex3f(0,20,0);
    //draw blue z-axis
    glColor3f(0, 0, 1); glVertex3f(0,0,0); glVertex3f(0,0,20);
glEnd();
```

This new code is added after the platform-, teapot-, and sphere-drawing code. The full code including these changes is in Motion_Example_2.CPP, which you can download with the rest of the book examples. Only the Z-axis of the platform axes is visible, and note that the teapot axes are twice as long as the sphere or platform. This is because of the glScale() operation. You can see the X- and Y-axes spinning around with the teapot. A screenshot is shown in Figure 4.10, on the next page. The axes are drawn for each coordinate system: Red = X-axis, Green = Y-axis, Blue = Z-axis.

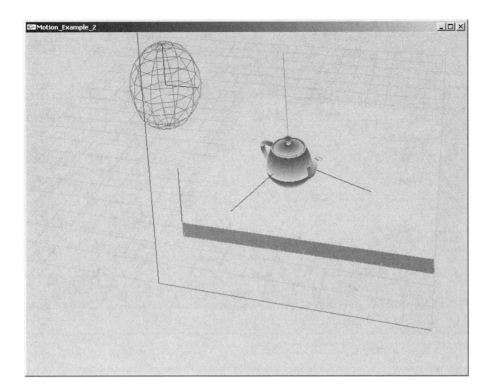

Figure 4.10: IMAGE MOTION AXIS

This would be a good point for OpenGL beginners, and those seeking to learn just what they need to get started, to skip ahead to the next chapter. At this point, you already have the tools to write some pretty good AR applications. The next few sections are for those who want to understand OpenGL in more detail.

4.11 Other Graphics Primitives: Polygons and Triangle Strips

Lines, triangles, and quads are the primitive types introduced so far (teapots and spheres don't really count, since they're composed of these primitives). When drawing triangles or quads, you don't need to draw them individually; you can draw more than one simultaneously.

When you draw a line, triangle, or quad, you need to supply the vertices to OpenGL. To provide a 3D point, you need to call glVertex3f(), glVertex3d(), glVertex3i(), or glVertex3s().

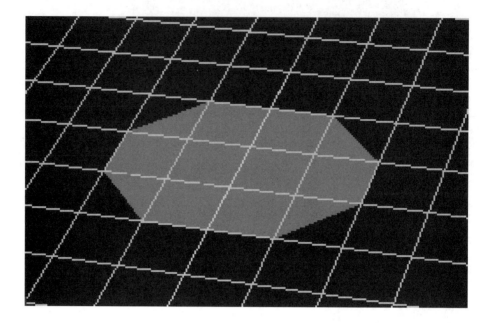

Figure 4.11: USING glBegin(GL_POLYGON)

Which one you use will depend on whether you have your vertex coordinates in floating-point, double-precision floating-point, or integer or short integer form, respectively. With the way we've been drawing triangles so far, with glBegin(GL_TRIANGLES), you need to provide three vertices for each triangle.

Most 3D models are polyhedral models composed of many triangles or quads. The model is solid or composed of solid sections of connected triangles or quads. Therefore, you are redundantly repeating 3D vertices.

For example, suppose you want to draw the octagon of Figure 4.11. You would need six triangles if you used one outside vertex for all triangles, or you would need eight triangles if you added a ninth point in the center. In this method, most vertices are repeated at least twice. You can provide each vertex only once by drawing a polygon. This saves ten vertices over the first method and sixteen over the second.

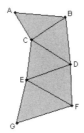

Figure 4.12: A TRIANGLE STRIP IS A CONNECTED SET OF TRIANGLES.

```
OpenGL/test_polygon_triangle_strips/test_polygon_triangle_strips.cpp
glBegin(GL_POLYGON);
  glColor3f(0.5,0.5,0.5);
  glVertex3f(-10,60,0);
  glVertex3f(-20,70,0);
  glVertex3f(-20,80,0);
  glVertex3f(-10,90,0);
  glVertex3f(10,90,0);
  glVertex3f(20,80,0);
  glVertex3f(20,70,0);
  glVertex3f(10,60,0);
glEnd();
```

A *triangle strip* is a connected list of triangles where subsequent triangles share an edge (see Figure 4.12). You can render triangle strips with glBegin(GL_TRIANGLE_STRIP). A triangle strip of five triangles would need only 3 + 4 = 7 vertices defined as opposed to 3 × 5 = 15 vertices with the GL_Begin/end method.

Look at Figure 4.12; how would you use the triangle strip method to create this polygon? Here is the code:

```
glBegin(GL_TRIANGLE_STRIP);
  glColor3f(0.7,0.8,0.7);
  glVertex3f(Ax,Ay,Az);
  glVertex3f(Bx,By,Bz);
  glVertex3f(Cx,Cy,Cz);
  glVertex3f(Dx,Dy,Dz);
  glVertex3f(Ex,Ey,Ez);
  glVertex3f(Fx,Fy,Fz);
  glVertex3f(Gx,Gy,Gz);
glEnd();
```

For contrast, here's how would you would render Figure 4.12 with individual triangles:

```
glBegin(GL_TRIANGLES);
  glColor3f(0.7,0.8,0.7);
  glVertex3f(Ax,Ay,Az);
  glVertex3f(Bx,By,Bz);
  glVertex3f(Cx,Cy,Cz);
glEnd();

glBegin(GL_TRIANGLES);
  glVertex3f(Cx,Cy,Cz);
  glVertex3f(Bx,By,Bz);
  glVertex3f(Dx,Dy,Dz);
glEnd();

glBegin(GL_TRIANGLES);
  glVertex3f(Cx,Cy,Cz);
  glVertex3f(Dx,Dy,Dz);
  glVertex3f(Ex,Ey,Ez);
glEnd();

glBegin(GL_TRIANGLES);
  glVertex3f(Ex,Ey,Ez);
  glVertex3f(Dx,Dy,Dz);
  glVertex3f(Fx,Fy,Fz);
glEnd();

glBegin(GL_TRIANGLES);
  glVertex3f(Ex,Ey,Ez);
  glVertex3f(Fx,Fy,Fz);
  glVertex3f(Gx,Gy,Gz);
glEnd();
```

This example doesn't just emphasize the code simplicity; it also demonstrates the subtle but important concept of vertex ordering.

If you have back-face culling on, you need to keep a consistent direction for your vertices. They are clockwise, since you specified that the vertices will look clockwise when you see the triangles from the front (this is set with glFrontFace(GL_CW)). OpenGL's triangle strip function takes care of this for you by flipping the order of every second triangle's vertices.

You get A, B, C - C, B, D - C, D, E - E, D, F - E, F, G, as opposed to A, B, C - B, C, D - C, D, E - D, E, F - E, F, G, as you might assume at first glance. The latter order would make every second triangle disappear when rendered from the front.

4.12 Rendering with Pointers

To provide a 3D point to OpenGL, you have used some variant of glVertex3f() and had to enter the x, y, and z elements separately and directly. Another way to provide 3D points is to give a pointer to a list of three consecutive numbers. Thus, your functions are called with only one argument. The whole set of glVertex functions has another version with v at the end of the function name. These versions allow you to provide pointers. For 3D points, you can call glVertex3fv(vert_f), glVertex3dv(vert_d), glVertex3iv(vert_i), or glVertex3sv(vert_s), where vert_f is a pointer that could be defined and used as follows:

```
float vert_f[3];
vert_f[0]=x;
vert_f[1]=y;
vert_f[2]=z;

glBegin(GL_TRIANGLES);
 glVertex3sv(vert_s);
glEnd();
```

Likewise, vert_d, vert_i, and vert_s are arrays of doubles, integers, and short integers, respectively.

4.13 Rendering with Indices

Instead of using pointers, you could refer to a piece of data by its position in a list. Imagine all the 3D vertices for a model or model section are in a linear list. You'd call glArrayElement(i) instead of glVertex3f(x, y, z). This way you reduce redundant data and therefore improve storage and execution efficiency.

Here is an example of a cube created with this technique. The vertices are given as a list of 3D coordinates, with an index number for each vertex:

```
Index number       3D coordinates
0:                  0.0,    0.0,    0.0
1:                 20.0,    0.0,    0.0
2:                  0.0,   20.0,    0.0
3:                 20.0,   20.0,    0.0
4:                  0.0,    0.0,   20.0
5:                 20.0,    0.0,   20.0
6                  20.0,   20.0,   20.0
7:                  0.0,   20.0,   20.0
```

The 3D coordinates don't really need the decimal and zero, but they are included here to highlight that this example is using floating-point data types. The next list shows your list of faces, and each face lists which 3D vertices constitute which face:

```
Face number      3D coordinate indices
0:                   0,1,2,3
1:                   4,5,1,0
2:                   5,6,2,1
3:                   6,7,3,2
4:                   7,4,0,3
5:                   7,6,5,4
```

The following code demonstrates rendering a wire frame and solid cube using this 3D vertex list and glDrawElements(). You have added the capability of rotating the cubes so that you can look at them with the < and > keys.

To create this program, you will add the global theta variable and replace the opengl_draw() and opengl_key_down() functions from one of the earlier example programs, such as OpenGL_Template_Program.CPP. This new program is named GLArrayElements_Vertex.CPP.

To add a global variable to store the rotation, add this line after the include statements at the top of the program:

OpenGL/glarrayelements_vertex/GLARRAYELEMENTS_VERTEX.CPP

```cpp
float theta=0;
```

Replace the opengl_draw() function with this version:

OpenGL/glarrayelements_vertex/GLARRAYELEMENTS_VERTEX.CPP

```cpp
void opengl_draw(void)
{
  //vertex list: 6 faces with 4 indices each
  float vertex[] = {
                    0.0,    0.0,    0.0,
                   20.0,    0.0,    0.0,
                   20.0,   20.0,    0.0,
                    0.0,   20.0,    0.0,
                    0.0,    0.0,   20.0,
                   20.0,    0.0,   20.0,
                   20.0,   20.0,   20.0,
                    0.0,   20.0,   20.0
                  };
```

```
glClear(GL_COLOR_BUFFER_BIT | GL_DEPTH_BUFFER_BIT | GL_STENCIL_BUFFER_BIT);
glDisable(GL_TEXTURE_2D);

//set up for drawing 3D vertex elements
glVertexPointer(3,GL_FLOAT,0,vertex);
glEnableClientState(GL_VERTEX_ARRAY);
//turn on back face culling to remove artifacts
glCullFace(GL_BACK);    glFrontFace(GL_CW);    glEnable(GL_CULL_FACE);

//set up coordinate system for left solid cube
glMatrixMode(GL_MODELVIEW);
glPushMatrix();
glRotatef(theta,0,0,1);

glBegin(GL_QUADS);
    glColor3f(0, 1, 0);
    glArrayElement(0); glArrayElement(1); glArrayElement(2); glArrayElement(3);
    glColor3f(1, 1, 0);
    glArrayElement(4); glArrayElement(5); glArrayElement(1); glArrayElement(0);
    glColor3f(0, 0, 1);
    glArrayElement(5); glArrayElement(6); glArrayElement(2); glArrayElement(1);
    glColor3f(0, 1, 1);
    glArrayElement(6); glArrayElement(7); glArrayElement(3); glArrayElement(2);
    glColor3f(1, 1, 1);
    glArrayElement(7); glArrayElement(4); glArrayElement(0); glArrayElement(3);
    glColor3f(1, 0, 0);
    glArrayElement(7); glArrayElement(6); glArrayElement(5); glArrayElement(4);
glEnd();

//set up coordinate system for right wire-frame cube
glPopMatrix();
glPushMatrix();
glTranslatef(60,0,0);
glRotatef(theta,0,0,1);

glBegin(GL_LINE_LOOP);
    glColor3f(0, 0, 0);
    glArrayElement(0); glArrayElement(1); glArrayElement(2); glArrayElement(3);
    glArrayElement(0); glArrayElement(4);
    glArrayElement(5); glArrayElement(1); glArrayElement(5);
    glArrayElement(6); glArrayElement(2); glArrayElement(6);
    glArrayElement(7); glArrayElement(3); glArrayElement(7);
    glArrayElement(4);
glEnd();

glPopMatrix();
glutSwapBuffers();
}
```

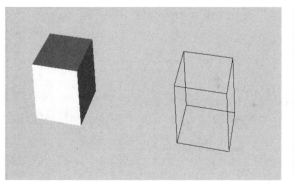

Figure 4.13: DRAWING A CUBE WITH GLARRAYELEMENT() AND A LINE LOOP
PRIMITIVE

Replace the opengl_key_down() function with this version:

OpenGL/glarrayelements_vertex/GLARRAYELEMENTS_VERTEX.CPP

```
void opengl_key_down(unsigned char k, int x, int y)
{
  if(k==27)  exit(0);        //escape key exits program
  else if(k==',') theta-=5;    //rotate cube left
  else if(k=='.') theta+=5;    //rotate cube right
}
```

Looking at this new code, you'll see that, as well as defining the vertices,
you needed to do the following two function calls to tell OpenGL where
your first vertex is in memory and to enable the vertex array pointer.

```
glVertexPointer(3,GL_FLOAT,0,vertex);
glEnableClientState(GL_VERTEX_ARRAY);
```

glVertexPointer() is supplied four arguments: three for the number of
dimensions per vertex, GL_FLOAT to tell it that the pointer is to floats,
0 to tell it not to skip vertices in between, and then the actual pointer.

In addition, in this code snippet, you put the 3D vertex definition into
the opengl_draw() function to increase readability. For the sake of execution speed, you should put this code in the initialization section of
Main(). In Figure 4.13, the right image shows how not using back-face
culling results in artifacts.

Note how you used a GL_LINE_LOOP primitive to draw the wire-frame
cube. It's a primitive type that was not described yet, but it's self-
explanatory. You also had to turn on the back-face culling to remove
rendering artifacts—something that may or may not appear on your

system. In this example, you saved on calling the 3D vertices but still had to set the color each time. The color is considered a primitive attribute, as are normal vectors and texture coordinates. Later you'll also use lists to render attributes.

This example also demonstrates storing the 3D vertices, and their color, texture, and normal attributes in lists and referring to them by indices. This may seem like unnecessary complexity at first, but for large models it will save on storage space because you can have a high resolution (and hence a high number of storage bits) for the 3D coordinates themselves but have a low resolution and number of storage bits for the indices. This is true because—in a closed solid model or model section—you'll be using each 3D vertex at least three to six times each. It's better to just repeat an index with fewer bits than the entire three-vertex component. With our cube example, if you represent the 3D vertices with floating-point numbers (floats) that are 32 bits each, you need six vertices times three elements (x, y, z) times four bytes, which equals 72 bytes, but only 32 more bytes for the indices if you only use 8-bit integers (unsigned chars). This gives you a total storage of 104 bytes for your cube. If you had stored the cube as quads—where you stored the 3D information for each—you'd need six faces times four vertices times three elements times 32 bits, which equals 288 bytes.

Remember that storage and execution speed are related, since for every byte you store, you will need to give that to OpenGL—perhaps even for every frame. So, it pays to make things a little more complex because you get rewards both in saved storage space and in how fast your program can run. This pays off most when you use *heavy* models, which is graphics parlance for models with lots of 3D geometry.

In the next section, you'll extend this technique to use indices for whole lists of 3D vertices, 2D textures, normal vectors, and colors.

4.14 The OpenGL glDrawElements Function

A good way to store a 3D model composed of lines, triangles, or quads is to have a list of the 3D coordinate, colors, texture coordinate, and normal vectors and separate lists that describe which of these go into which faces. This second set of lists contains integer list elements pointing to the members of the first lists. These second lists are called *lists of indices* because each element indexes, or *points to*, elements in another list.

This next sample shows the opengl_draw() function from gldrawelements_color.cpp:

```cpp
void opengl_draw(void)
{
  //vertex list: 8 vertices
  float vertex[] = {
    0.0,    0.0,  0.0,
    20.0,     0.0,   0.0,
    20.0,    20.0,    0.0,
    0.0,    20.0,   0.0,
    0.0,     0.0,  20.0,
    20.0,   0.0,  20.0,
    20.0,   20.0,  20.0,
    0.0,     20.0,   20.0
    };

  //color vertex list: 8 vertices
  float color[] = {
    0,1,0,
    1,1,0,
    0,0,1,
    0,1,1,
    0,1,0,
    1,1,1,
    1,0,0,
    0,1,0
    };

  //index list: 6 faces = 24 points
  unsigned int vertex_indices [] = {
    0,1,2,3,
    4,5,1,0,
    5,6,2,1,
    6,7,3,2,
    7,4,0,3,
    7,6,5,4
    };

glClear(GL_COLOR_BUFFER_BIT | GL_DEPTH_BUFFER_BIT | GL_STENCIL_BUFFER_BIT);
glDisable(GL_TEXTURE_2D);

//set up for drawing 3D vertex elements
glEnableClientState(GL_VERTEX_ARRAY);
glEnableClientState(GL_COLOR_ARRAY);
glVertexPointer(3,GL_FLOAT,0,vertex);
glColorPointer(3,GL_FLOAT,0,color);

//turn on back face culling to remove artifacts
glCullFace(GL_BACK);   glFrontFace(GL_CW);   glEnable(GL_CULL_FACE);
```

```
//set up coordinate system for rotating cube
glMatrixMode(GL_MODELVIEW);
glPushMatrix();
glRotatef(theta,0,0,1);

glDrawElements(GL_QUADS,24,GL_UNSIGNED_INT, vertex_indices);

glPopMatrix();
glutSwapBuffers();
}
```

As before, you nonoptimally put the data in the draw function (the *vertex, color, vertex_indices* arrays). In a real application this would be done elsewhere—such as in the initialization of the program.

In this example, you used the glDrawElements() function, which allows you to simply provide a pointer to a list of point indices and have it render them all as if you included them in a glBegin(GL_QUADS) instruction.

An attribute, in this case color, was drawn for each vertex. Note that, unlike your previous example program, the colors are per vertex, not per face (see Figure 4.14, on the following page).

In this example, you had to enable both vertex and color arrays and give them pointers like this:

OpenGL/gldrawelements_color/gldrawelements_color.cpp

```
//set up for drawing 3D vertex elements
glEnableClientState(GL_VERTEX_ARRAY);
glEnableClientState(GL_COLOR_ARRAY);
glVertexPointer(3,GL_FLOAT,0,vertex);
glColorPointer(3,GL_FLOAT,0,color);
```

Instead of calling glArrayElement(i) with a single index, *i*, you were able to give a pointer to a list of indices with glDrawElements(GL_QUADS,24,GL_UNSIGNED_INT, vertex_indices), where you have 24 to indicate how many vertices, GL_QUADS to tell it to group these vertices into quads, and the pointer to the index list and the pointer type.

Let's go through how to set up lists for the 3D vertices, color, texture coordinate, and normal vector attributes. For your 3D vertex data, you need to have an array of floats, doubles, integers, or short integers with $3 \times N$ elements—where N is the number of points. The array is filled in the order x0, y0, z0, x1, y1, z1, x2, y2, z2, . . . , x(N-1), y(N-1), z(N-1).

Figure 4.14: CUBE DRAWN WITH GLDRAWELEMENTS() WITH SEPARATE COLORS FOR EACH VERTEX

```
#define NUM_3D_VERTEX_ELEMENTS 10 //10 points
float vertex[NUM_3D_VERTEX_ELEMENTS];

glEnableClientState(GL_VERTEX_ARRAY);
glVertexPointer(3, GL_FLOAT, 0, vertex);
```

If you are applying a color to each vertex, turn on the GL_COLOR_ARRAY flag, and set the pointer to the first color value:

```
#define NUM_COLORS 20 //20 colors
float color_array[NUM_COLORS];

glEnableClientState(GL_COLOR_ARRAY);
glColorPointer(3, GL_FLOAT, 0, color_array);
```

If you're not applying a color to each vertex, make sure GL_COLOR_ARRAY is off so that glDrawElements() will not render anything:

```
glDisableClientState(GL_COLOR_ARRAY);
```

To wrap a texture around an object, turn on GL_TEXTURE_COORD_ARRAY, and set the pointer to the first texture coordinate:

```
//20 points, each with 2 elements (u,v)
#define NUM_TEXTURE_VERTEX_ELEMENTSS 20*2
float texvertices_array[NUM_TEXTURE_VERTEX_ELEMENTSS];

glEnableClientState(GL_TEXTURE_COORD_ARRAY);
glTexCoordPointer(2, GL_FLOAT, 0, texvertices_array);
```

If not, make sure GL_ TEXTURE_COORD is off:

```
glDisableClientState(GL_ TEXTURE_COORD _ARRAY);
```

Likewise, if you have normal vectors, turn on GL_NORMAL_ARRAY, and set the pointer to the first normal:

```
//20 points, each with 3 elements (x,y,z)
#define NUM_NORMALS 20*3
float normal_array[NUM_NORMALS];

glEnableClientState(GL_NORMAL_ARRAY);
glNormalPointer(3, GL_FLOAT, 0, normal_array);
```

If you have no normal vectors, you turn off GL_NORMAL_ARRAY so that glDrawElements() knows not to use normals.

```
glDisableClientState(GL_NORMAL_ARRAY);
```

In the example code, the texture and normal array drawing was not turned off explicitly, because it makes the code easier to read. However, in your programs it's good practice to do so. For example, if you weren't using color or normal attributes for vertices, you should turn them off with glDisableClientState()—especially if they are turned on elsewhere in your program. Rendering using unplanned attribute pointers can lead to strange rendering effects or a memory fault if one of the pointers is pointing to an invalid memory address. With a complex game or animation, where some objects are being rendered wrong or the program is crashing, it may be hard to recognize the source of the problem.

Chapter 5

Introduction to AR Programming

This chapter introduces how to develop augmented reality applications. Whether you want to compile the existing ARTag demos, make modifications, or create your own programs, this chapter will help you accomplish your goals. If you are an experienced C++ and OpenGL programmer, you may find that you can quickly skim through this chapter and move on to the more complicated examples. However, it is highly recommended that you try some of the demos in Chapter 2 before you try to compile an ARTag project.

Before you start to make modifications or even write your own applications from scratch, you might want to try compiling one of the existing ARTag sample projects. In the ARTag SDK, and the download for this book, you will find many sample applications and projects. There are samples for Linux, Windows, and Mac OS X, so when you create your ARTag applications, you have your choice of many development tools.

Regardless of which platform you're using, you should consider configuring paths to the ARTag library files. Depending on your platform, you may also want to provide paths to OpenGL, OpenCV, SharperCV, or the Tao OpenGL Framework. Read on for more details about what you may want to configure for your platform.

Before you start developing, you should refer to the instructions in Chapter 2. This will ensure that everything is ready for you to compile and run the sample projects. For example, the image_test project does not use any camera input—it loads a sample texture from a file. If this program works, then you will know that you have OpenGL and ARTag working. Similarly, if you want to use C# for your AR applications, you may want to try the same test with the Tao OpenGL Framework.

5.1 AR Development Setup

ARTag was developed in C++, and the original SDK contained C++ versions of the demos only. However, for this book, a basic C# wrapper was created, and a C# port of the 3D augmentations demo is provided. Together, the C++ and C# versions give you access to samples for Linux, Mac OS X, Windows with C++, and Windows with .NET.

Here are the steps for setting up and testing your ARTag development environment:

1. Download the ARTag library and header files.

   To get the ARTag library and header file, you will need to download the ARTag SDK (http://www.artag.net). These files are not included in the sample download for the book (http://www.pragprog.com/titles/cfar/source_code).

2. Download the source code and resources for the samples in the book.

   Although you could just use the ARTag SDK, you'll probably want to also download the source files for the book. These files are tailored more specifically for the examples in the text. In addition, the book download includes more C# content and the Tank Wars projects.

   When you have the files, try running some of the compiled demos (see Figure 5.1, on the next page).

3. Make some change to an ARTag project. For example, an easy change to make is swapping the test texture used by the basic demo. All you need to do to make this change is alter the name of the file that is loaded. Trying loading your own picture.

4. Compile the AR project.

5. Run your custom version of the AR project.

Now that you have compiled your own version of an ARTag demo, all you need to do is run the application and test that the new texture is displayed.

Figure 5.1: THE ORIGINAL 2D AR DEMO

5.2 A Note About Textures and OpenCV

Without the OpenCV highgui library, you can load only PGM and PPM image textures into your AR programs. With highgui you can load other image formats such as JPEG or BMP images. It's more convenient to work with formats such as JPEG because you don't have to convert the images you get when exporting a 3D model from a standard 3D package. In the ARTag download, the highgui library for Windows is included, and the other platforms use PPM images for the demo textures.

The image_test.cpp program, in the ARTag SDK download, has a line #define HIGHGUI. This line is commented out because when you aren't using highgui, you'll have to resort to the included PGM and PPM image-loading functions. If you have highgui, then uncomment this line and link in the highgui library.

5.3 Compiling AR Projects for Linux

Most of the ARTag projects were originally written on the Linux platform. Also, AR projects are most commonly being developed in research labs where Linux is popular. This all means you will probably find that most resources available for ARTag are geared toward Linux. However, this is beginning to change. For example, there is a project at Columbia University, by Ohan Oda and Steven K. Feiner, called Goblin XNA (http://www1.cs.columbia.edu/graphics/projects/goblin/goblinXNA.htm). Goblin XNA is an ARTag platform that uses Microsoft's new XNA game development platform.

In ARTag's Linux SDK, you will find a number of projects. Using the gcc compiler, you can compile your own versions of these projects. Here are some examples of Linux compiler commands for ARTag projects:

```
gcc -o opengl_template opengl_template.cpp
    -I /usr/include/GL -I /usr/include -lGL -lGLU -lglut
gcc -o opengl_only_test opengl_only_test.cpp
    -I /usr/include/GL -I /usr/include -lGL -lglut -lGLU
gcc -o artag_console_test artag_console_test.cpp -lm
    -I . -L . -lartag_rev2k -lGLU
gcc -o image_test image_test.cpp -lm -I . -L . -lartag_rev2k
    -I /usr/include/GL -I /usr/include -lGL -lglut -lGLU
gcc -o artag_create_marker artag_create_marker.cpp -lm
    -I . -L . -lartag_rev2k -lGLU
```

By using compiler commands such as these, you can get the ARTag projects working on your Linux box.

5.4 Compiling ARTag Projects

This section will help you deal with specific development setup requirements. The ARTag demos were written with platform portability as a primary goal.

Compiling ARTag Projects for Windows

If you are on the Windows platform, you can use your favorite Windows C++ compiler or C# compiler. For example, if you are a C++ developer, you can use Visual Studio 2005, Visual Studio 2003, Visual Studio 6, the free Visual C++ Express 2005 application, or any other Windows-compatible C++ compiler. If you are a C# developer, you can compile your AR projects with either Visual Studio 2005 or the free Visual C#

Express 2005 application. If you want to compile the ARTag wrapper, you will need Visual Studio 2005.

The ARTag SDK includes two versions of the ARTag library: artag_rev2_vs6.lib and artag_rev2_vs2005.lib. These two files allow you to choose between Visual Studio 6 (and Visual Studio 2003) or Visual Studio 2005. For convenience, we'll just refer to artag_rev2.lib in this book, but remember that the two versions are available as different files.

To set up Visual Studio or Visual C++ Express, it's a good idea to add the directories for the AR includes and other required libraries (for example, OpenGL). This will save you from having to copy some files into your project directories. To set up the folder, make sure you've downloaded the required files (for example, from the ARTag SDK), and then choose Tools > Options > Projects and Solutions > VC++ Directories. Then, under Show Directories For, choose Include Files. To add the include directories, click the New Line button, and then browse for your include directories. You should add the following: ARTag include, OpenCV, and OpenGL. Next, change Show Directories For to Library Files, and add entries for ARTag lib, OpenCV, and OpenGL.

Setting Up Your Windows Path Variable

Adding the include and lib folders under Visual C++ Express or Visual Studio 2005 will save you from having to make copies of a number of source files. Obviously, your programs will not run properly unless they can access the files they require at runtime. One option is to simply copy the files into the folder where you are running the executable—we have done this for you in the code\GetARRunning directory. But this is not necessarily the best way to organize your development environment. The other option is to have just one copy of the runtime files that your AR applications require and add the folders that contain these files to the Windows Path environment variable. Just bear in mind that if you have to deploy your solution to another machine, you must either reproduce these path changes, copy the file into a directory already in the Windows path (such as /Windows/system32), or copy the required files directly into the application's executable directory.

To add directories to your Path variable, right-click My Computer, and choose Properties. When the System Properties window opens, click the Advanced tab, and then choose Environment Variables. Next, from the Environment Variables window, find the Path variable under System Variables. Once you have the right entry, click Path, and then click

Edit. When the Edit System Variable window opens, simply add the paths that you require. For example, the \code\src\OpenCV directory contains the highgui.dll file, which is required to run image_test.exe. This technique will not work for every file (for example, it won't work for .cfg or .cf files), but it will save you from having to copy quite a few files. Note that the folders listed in the Path variable are separated with semicolons, and you'll probably have to restart before the changes take effect.

Once you have configured your machine, test your changes by compiling one of the ARTag sample projects.

If you have an older version of Visual Studio, you may be able to use the iartag_rev2_vs6.lib version of the ARTag library. This version was created for Visual Studio 6. You can find this file in the ARTag SDK along with the newer Visual Studio 2005 version.

Compiling C# ARTag Projects

If you are a .NET developer, you have the option of using the C# wrapper for the ARTag library. In the book's download, you will also find a C# port of the basic demo—the wrapper code can be found in code\ IntroARProg\CSharp Projects\ARTag Wrapper Project\. The compiled wrapper is in the ARTag SDK folder code\src\ARTag CSharp wrapper\ and in the book download at code\lib\CSharp ARTagWrapper.

To set up a C# development environment for ARTag, do the following:

1. Install the Rhodes University SharperCV implementation of Open-CV (http://www.cs.ru.ac.za/research/groups/SharperCV/). Unlike the Tao OpenGL Framework, you will have to browse when you want to add a reference to SharperCV in your C# projects. The Tao Framework install registers assemblies in the *global assembly cache* (GAC), but the SharperCV install does not.

   To add the SharperCV reference to your Visual Studio 2005 project, right-click References in the Solution Explorer, and choose Add Reference. Then select the Browse tab, and browse to the folder where you installed SharperCV. Once in the right folder, select openCVWrapper.dll.

2. Install the Tao OpenGL Framework (http://www.taoframework.com). Tao OpenGL requires version 2.0 of the .NET Framework. You may have a newer version of the framework installed, but Tao OpenGL will not install on a machine without the .NET Framework version

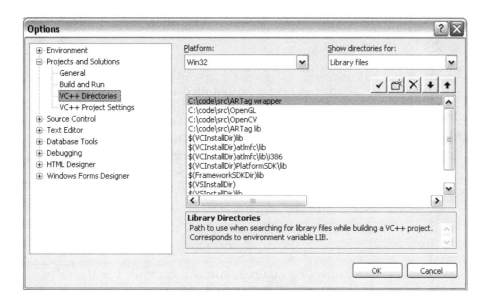

Figure 5.2: ADDING THE ARTAG WRAPPER FOLDER IN VISUAL STUDIO 2005

2.0. Even if you have a newer version, you can install the .NET Framework 1.1 through Microsoft Update or Windows Update—multiple versions of the framework will happily coexist on the same machine. If you choose the default option, installing the Tao assemblies in the GAC, you'll have an easier time adding Tao to your projects.

To check whether Tao OpenGL is installed correctly, open the TaoOpenGLTest solution and check whether you can get them properly referenced within the project. If they appear with caution signs, then the Tao OpenGL files are not correctly referenced.

The Tao OpenGL assemblies required for ARTag projects are Tao Framework FreeGLUT Binding for .NET (Tao.FreeGlut), Tao.OpenGL (Tao.OpenGL), and Tao Framework OpenGL GLU Binding for .NET (Tao.OpenGL.Glu). To add the Tao references, right-click References in the Solution Explorer, and choose Add Reference. Then scroll down the list of .NET assemblies, and find the Tao Framework. If there are broken references, you may need first to remove them and add them back again. If the Tao Framework assemblies are not in the .NET list, then they were not properly added to the GAC.

As was mentioned in Chapter 2, you can test whether the Tao OpenGL framework is properly installed by running the application in \code\GetARRunning\Tao OpenGL Test_compiled.

3. To use ARTag with .NET, use the C# wrapper provided in the sample project (see Figure 5.2, on the preceding page). To use the wrapper, copy ARTagWrapper.dll from code\src\ARTag wrapper into your executable's directory. Copy code\src\ARTag wrapper\ ARTagWrapper.dll into the same folder as your executable, or add code\src\ARTag wrapper to the list of library files under the VC++ directories.

Once you have the project configured, you can compile it in Visual Studio 2005 or Visual C# Express and try it.

Compiling the ARTag C# Wrapper

To use ARTag with .NET, you can use the ARTagWrapper DLL provided in the ARTag SDK (http://www.artag.net). For licensing reasons, the compiled version of the wrapper can also be found in the ARTag SDK. The code for this wrapper is provided in book download's sample projects (\code\src\ARTag wrapper). Although the code is provided, it is a basic .NET interop wrapper, and not all of ARTag's functionality has been exposed. You may want to add something, or you may want to improve the wrapper. To get information about the ARTag library, refer to the ARTag header file—currently artag_rev2.h. Add what you need, and recompile the project. Refer to MSDN (http://www.msdn.com) for more information about .NET interop.

The C# sample wrapper for ARTag is written in C++ and creates an interface between the ARTag library .lib file and your C# applications. The C++ wrapper project requires Visual Studio 2005 Standard Edition or newer. Visual C++ Express Edition does not support ATL, so it won't work with this project.

To configure the wrapper project, you will need to download the book download (which includes the wrapper code) and the ARTag SDK, and then you'll need to check two file references. First, you must properly reference the file ARTag header file (artag_rev2.h). The path used in the sample project is C:\ARTag Lib\. If you don't have the file at this location, you will need to remove the file from the project and add it back at its proper location. To change the path, go to the Solution Explorer, and open the Header Files folder. Then, click artag_rev2.h, and change the Relative Path shown in the Properties window.

To add the file from a different location, right-click Header Files, and then choose Add > Existing Item.

You may also need to configure the name or path for the ARTag .lib file. To do this, open .ARTagWrapper.h, and change line 14, #pragma comment(lib, "artag_rev2_vs2005.lib"). After making these two configuration changes and adding references to the supporting files, you should be able to compile the ARTagWrapper solution.

To use the ARTag C# wrapper, add it to the same directory as your application, or configure Visual Studio 2005 to find the DLL. When referencing the ARTag functions (and helper functions) in ARTagWrapper.dll, the input and output types must be properly marshaled. For example, void and int can be used as is, but unsigned char* must be changed to IntPtr in the C# version.

Here are some examples of importing the C++ wrapper functions into a C# application:

```csharp
// ARTag Wrapper: ARTag Init
[DllImport("ARTagWrapper.dll", EntryPoint = "init_artag_wrapped")]
public static extern char init_artag_wrapped
    (int width, int height, int bpp);

// ARTag Wrapper: load_array_file
[DllImport("ARTagWrapper.dll", EntryPoint = "load_array_file_wrapped")]
public static extern int load_array_file_wrapped(string filename);

// ARTag Wrapper: artag_find_objects
[DllImport("ARTagWrapper.dll", EntryPoint = "artag_find_objects_wrapped")]
public static extern int artag_find_objects_wrapped
    ([In,Out] IntPtr rgb_cam_image,char rgb_greybar);

// ARTag Wrapper: artag_create_marker
[DllImport("ARTagWrapper.dll", EntryPoint = "artag_create_marker_wrapped")]
public static extern int artag_create_marker_wrapped
    (int artag_id,int scale,[In][Out]ref IntPtr image);

// ARTag Utils
// ARTag Wrapper: read_ppm_wrapped
[DllImport("ARTagWrapper.dll", EntryPoint = "read_ppm_wrapped")]
public static extern IntPtr read_ppm_wrapped
    (string file_name,ref int width,ref int height);
```

Here is a sample that demonstrates how to use the wrapper functions in a C# application:

`IntroARProg/CSharp Projects/ARTagBasicDemo_CSharp/ARTagBasicDemo_CSharp/Form1.cs`

```csharp
// Reference for interop with the Win32 DLL
using System.Runtime.InteropServices;

// Reference for writing and reading files
//(e.g. writing a marker tag to a file)
using System.IO;

// Reference for the Tao OpenGL Library for C#
// http://www.taoframework.com/Home
using Tao.OpenGl;
using Tao.FreeGlut;

// Reference for the OpenCV 'SharperCV' Library for C#
// http://www.cs.ru.ac.za/research/groups/SharperCV
using SharperCV;
```

`IntroARProg/CSharp Projects/ARTagBasicDemo_CSharp/ARTagBasicDemo_CSharp/Form1.cs`

```csharp
artag_find_objects_wrapped(pPPM, (char)1);
char foundResult = artag_is_object_found_wrapped(artag_object_id);
MessageBox.Show("Found object result: " + (int)foundResult,
    "Find Objects Test", MessageBoxButtons.OK, MessageBoxIcon.Error);
```

Compiling ARTag Projects on Mac OS X

Mac OS X users can compile ARTag C++ projects. In Chapter 4, you were shown an example of compiling the opengl_only project using Xcode. Another option for Mac OS X users is to use the gcc compiler. If your paths to OpenGL and GLUT are the same as these examples, they may work as is. If they don't work, you need to locate your GLUT and gl libraries and headers (for example, find / -name "glut.h"):

```
ranlib lib/libartag_rev2k.a

gcc -framework GLUT -framework OpenGL -Wall
    -o compiled_demos/opengl_only_test src/opengl_only_test.cpp
    -I include/ -I /System/Library/Frameworks/OpenGL.framework/Headers
    -I /System/Library/Frameworks/GLUT.framework/Headers
    -Llib -L/System/Library/Frameworks/OpenGL.framework/Libraries
    -lGL -lGLU -lm -lobjc -lstdc++

gcc -framework GLUT -framework OpenGL -Wall
    -o compiled_demos/image_test src/image_test.cpp
    -I include/ -I /System/Library/Frameworks/OpenGL.framework/Headers
    -I /System/Library/Frameworks/GLUT.framework/Headers
    -Llib -L/System/Library/Frameworks/OpenGL.framework/Libraries
    -lGL -lGLU -lm -lobjc -lstdc++ -lartag_rev2k
```

```
gcc -framework GLUT -framework OpenGL -Wall
    -o compiled_demos/artag_console_test src/artag_console_test.cpp
    -I include/ -I /System/Library/Frameworks/OpenGL.framework/Headers
    -I /System/Library/Frameworks/GLUT.framework/Headers
    -Llib -L/System/Library/Frameworks/OpenGL.framework/Libraries
    -lGL -lGLU -lm -lobjc -lstdc++ -lartag_rev2k

gcc -framework GLUT -framework OpenGL -Wall
    -o compiled_demos/artag_create_marker src/artag_create_marker.cpp
    -I include/ -I /System/Library/Frameworks/OpenGL.framework/Headers
    -I /System/Library/Frameworks/GLUT.framework/Headers
    -Llib -L/System/Library/Frameworks/OpenGL.framework/Libraries
    -lGL -lGLU -lm -lobjc -lstdc++ -lartag_rev2k
```

OpenGL Development Help

If you have any questions about OpenGL, your first step should be to refer to http://www.opengl.org. This page from the FAQ is a good place to start: http://www.opengl.org/resources/faq/technical/gettingstarted.htm#0010.

Mac OS X users can also refer to these pages:

- OpenGL: http://developer.apple.com/graphicsimaging/opengl/ and developer.apple.com/graphicsimaging/opengl/opengl_serious.html

- GLUT: http://developer.apple.com/samplecode/glut/index.html

Here are some Linux resources:

- OpenGL: http://www.opengl.org

- GLUT: www.linux.com/howtos/Nvidia-OpenGL-Configuration/instglut.shtml

If you are on the Windows platform and you don't have the required OpenGL components, you can get the OpenGL files by downloading the Windows SDK (http://www.microsoft.com/downloads/details.aspx?FamilyID=c2b1e300-f358-4523-b479-f53d234cdccf). The Windows SDK works on Windows Vista beta 2 (or later), Windows Server 2003 Release 2, and Windows XP Service Pack 1. After installing the SDK, look in the folder C:\Program Files\Microsoft Platform SDK for Windows Server 2003 R2\Include\gl.

You can download GLUT from http://www.xmission.com/~nate/glut.html.

For additional information about using OpenGL with Visual Studio, please refer to the website at http://www.cecs.csulb.edu/~pnguyen/Using%20OpenGL%20in%20Visual%20Studio%202005.htm.

Files Required to Build ARTag Projects on Windows

This reference section is meant to help you understand which resources are needed for each ARTag sample project. Many of these files can be found in the book download (code\lib\ARTag include and ARTag lib). However, the ARTag library and header can be found only in the ARTag SDK (http://www.artag.net). Check the readme file in each project folder for more details about specific files that may be required.

Files Required to Build C++ ARTag Projects

These are the required files:

```
artag_rev2.lib

glut32.dll
glut32.lib
```

The cv* files and highgui* files are necessary only if you are using the CVcam USB camera interface and loading JPEG textures.

```
cv.dll
cv.h
cv.lib
cvcam.h
cvcam.lib
cvcompat.h
cverror.h
cvtypes.h
highgui.dll
highgui.h
highgui.lib
```

Different versions of OpenCV don't coexist well, so make sure you're not linking one library file from one version to a component from another. One way to make sure is to put them all into the directory you're compiling from the include/, lib/, opencv/, and opengl/ directories in the ARTag SDK download.

These files are required to build some ARTag projects (code\lib\ARTag include):

```
ase_parse.c
mesh_management.c
obj_parse.c
read_line.c
wrl_parse.c
```

The following files are required to build all OpenGL/GLUT projects (code\lib\OpenGL):

```
glut.h
glut32.dll
glut32.lib

highgui.dll
highgui.h
highgui.lib
```

These files are required to build CVcam projects (code\lib\OpenCV):

```
cv.dll
cv.h
cv.lib
cvcam.h
cvcam.lib
cvcompat.h
cverror.h
cvtypes.h
```

Files Required to Build C# ARTag Projects

To create ARTag projects in C#, you will need to gather a few elements. The C# wrapper and the ARTag library can be downloaded only from the National Research Council of Canada; you can find the link on http://www.artag.net.

```
ARTagWrapper.dll - the ARTag wrapper for .Net.
highguisharper.dll - part of the SharperCV wrapper from Rhodes University
```

To run ARTag C# applications, you will also need SharperCV and the Tao OpenGL Framework.

5.5   Revisiting Demo Customization

In the "3D Demo Configuration Changes" section in Chapter 2, you saw how you can easily swap the 3D objects that appear in the 3d_augmentations demo. The same can de done with other ARTag demos. image_test.exe is used to test ARTag and augmentations without using a camera—this can help you debug issues or simply try things if you don't have a camera. The grayscale image camera_image.pgm is loaded and presented to the program at every frame. Usually, the image presented would be a live video feed.

You can change setup_artag_test.cfg to make different objects appear. In this way, the file is similar to the setup_artag_3d.cfg file from the

3d_magic_mirror/ directory. You can also replace the camera_image.pgm file with others to see how they affect augmentations. The supplied camera_image.pgm was captured with a Point Grey Research Dragonfly camera that had a *focal length* of $f_x = f_x = 1110$ pixels, so values other than this in setup_artag_3d.cfg will result in a squashed or stretched 3D model.

You can modify the objects shown by editing the setup_artag_3d.cfg file. For example, you can replace the default objects with your own. You can do this with any 3D object that you can export to VRML, OBJ, or ASE format (remember to export a material library if you export an OBJ). Here are a few important lines of this configuration file:

```
//USB 2.0 camera
camera_fx 410
camera_fy 410
//- enter array files below
array_file panel_set.cf
//- enter objects below - export OBJ, WRL, or ASE formats from
//3DSMax, etc. Create a .mtl material library for .OBJ's.
object fish.obj              array base0 center resize
object peters_car.mesh       array toolbar0  center resize
object fish.obj              array toolbar1  center resize
object CanOfAspargus.mesh    single 1023 center resize
```

The camera parameters are entered here, as is the array file panel_set.cf. panel_set.cf contains information about the individual marker's IDs and positions so that they can be associated with what's shown in the image. This allows them to measure the camera pose for each image frame.

Next, each line begins with an object keyword followed by the name of the 3D model (which must be in the same directory) and then by either the array or single keywords. The name following an array must be a name of a *coordframe* inside the panel_set.cf file. If you want to associate a 3D model to an individual marker and not an array, specify the single keyword and follow it with the ARTag ID. There are 1,001 possible markers in the range 0–1023. To make ARTag more reliable, 23 values are illegal—these tags did not perform well enough to be included in the library (see Figure 6.5, on page 143).

The center, resize, or no_rotate keywords allow you to modify how the model is displayed. center centers the model, and resize scales it to fit within the extents of the array or individual marker. Otherwise, the model can be too large or small. The no_rotate keyword allows the rotation to stay fixed for billboarding effects such as "cardboard cutout" figures or flames, which are always facing the same direction.

5.6 Configuring Your Camera

For best results, you should take the time to properly calibrate your AR camera. This section will help you ensure that you have the optimal setup for your hardware.

Camera Resolution

When it comes to camera resolution, bigger images equal better AR marker performance. In other words, the larger the input camera image is, the smaller the markers can be and still be detected, and the less the JPEG artifacts will disturb the detection (should your camera have some form of internal compression). Unfortunately, the OpenCV CVcam interface that is used in these demos is not able to properly set the camera resolution. It usually defaults to a lower resolution such as 160 by 120 or 320 by 240. Some users have found that if they run another program that allows them to set the camera resolution first, then the demos will run with the set resolution. Programs downloaded from http://www.shrinkwrapvb.com/ezvidcap.htm do the trick on some computers.

The camera resolution should not be confused with the resolution of the graphics window. The demo program window can be 640 by 480, while the camera resolution is still only 160 by 120—the background will just appear grainier and more pixelated. Your AR system will work better if the camera can be set to a higher resolution.

Calibrating Your Camera

If you are creating an AR application and have a medium-sized budget, you should consider buying an IEEE 1394 (FireWire) camera such as the offerings from Point Grey Research (http://www.ptgrey.com). Using these cameras, you can capture a much better picture than any USB webcam we have tried. This may be because the camera uses a quality CCD sensor and not a low-cost CMOS imager that most webcams tend to use. With CMOS technology, it's possible to combine both the imager and processing onto one small silicon chip. However, the quality tends to suffer. Most of the USB and USB2.0 webcams we tried had some sort of JPEG compression that interfered with the marker detection. With a quality camera, such as Point Grey Research's Dragonfly, the markers could be seen down to about 17 pixels wide. With the poorer JPEG-compressed video from a webcam, this size frequently had to be at least 30 pixels. The downside of needing larger markers is not only that you have to move the camera closer (or make the markers larger) but that the augmentation can also jitter more if fewer markers are visible.

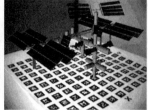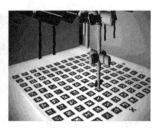

Figure 5.3: THREE DIFFERENT PERSPECTIVES

The Canadian National Research Council uses the 1.4r27 and 1.5003 release versions of the Dragonfly drivers, so the ARTag download has wrapper code for these two driver versions.

When using a camera for AR, it's important to get an approximation of your camera's internal parameters; for ARTag Rev2 the ideal pinhole model is used, which has four parameters: fx, fy, cx, and cy. fx and fy are the horizontal and vertical focal lengths, measured in pixels, whereas cx and cy are the image center (aka center of projection). The fx and fy variables have a greater impact on the augmentation appearance and so are more important to get correct. You can usually just set cx and cy to half the width and height of the resolution.

For example, for a 640 by 480 camera, cx and cy would be 320 and 240. However, fx and fy should be measured or more closely approximated. For most webcams, the pixels are square (that is, the aspect ratio is 1.0) and so fx=fy, meaning you can usually just measure the focal length in one direction. The focal length (fx=fy) is a larger number when zoomed in and a smaller number when zoomed out and seeing a wide angle.

When rendering in OpenGL, the program needs to know fx, fy to make the virtual object's perspective look right. Figure 5.3 shows some examples of how the 3D object will appear squashed or stretched with an incorrect fx, fy. The figure shows three renderings of a space station model; the left is fx=fy set to an incorrect value of 400 pixels, the middle shows the correct rendering with fx=fx=1100 pixels (the correct value for this camera, a 640 by 480 Dragonfly with an 8mm lens), and the rightmost image shows what happens with fx=fy=3000 pixels.

fx and fy are set either in the program you are writing or in the setup_artag_3d.cfg file in the 3d_magic_mirror demo where they are set with the lines:

```
camera_fx 1100
camera_fy 1100
```

In the sample project's basic_artag_opengl, fx and fy are hard-coded with the defines:

```
#define DEFAULT_FX      1100
#define DEFAULT_FY      1100
```

These numbers are used both in setting up the viewing frustum for OpenGL and for initializing ARTag. This is the function call in basic_artag_opengl.cpp that does the latter:

```
//set camera params
artag_set_camera_params(DEFAULT_FX,DEFAULT_FY,cam_width/2.0,cam_height/2.0);
```

A quick and dirty way to get going is to keep guessing numbers and changing them in a program—such as in the setup_artag_3d.cfg file for the 3d_magic_mirror demo—until a virtual object looks good. But, if you want to be more scientific, read on.

Here's how you properly calibrate your camera. As mentioned, in most cases, fx=fy, so you need to perform only one measurement; set up the camera facing some object of known width—such as a doorway or book (see Figure 5.4, on the next page). A planar object is best, and it should be perpendicular to the camera. In the figure, you can see the Logitech Quickcam Pro 3000 USB2 webcam being calibrated—it's aiming at the door.

Move the camera so that the object fills roughly the middle 50% of the screen. Don't make it too small because the expected error of the measurement will be higher. Don't make it so large that it fills the image because this will cause *radial distortion* (a barrel-like effect where lines curve near the image edges).

In this case, we're measuring fx. fx can be measured from the equation Fx=U*Z/X, where U is the width of the door (in pixels) in the captured image. Z is the distance of the door from the lens of the webcam (try to estimate where the center of the lens is), and X is the width of the door. A tape measure is used to measure Z and X. The units don't matter as long as you're consistent between Z and X. Figure 5.5, on the following page, shows an image from the webcam.

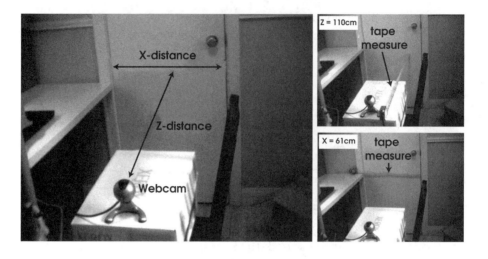

Figure 5.4: CALIBRATING A CAMERA

Figure 5.5: THE VIEW FROM THE CAMERA

From these figures, we see X = 61cm, Z = 110cm, and U = 220 pixels. From our equation, fx = U*Z/X = 220*110/61 = 397 pixels. In our case we're assuming square pixels, so we say that both fx and fy are 397 pixels.

Be careful that the image resolution (when you're capturing this test image) is the same as in the program you want to run. As already mentioned, CVcam's controls to set the resolution may not work—make sure to look at the return values of the init_camera() function. This information is printed in many of the demo program's console windows. If the program started with 160 by 120 pixels for the camera, then you would need to cut the fx estimate in half to 199 pixels.

When would you not assume fx=fy, and what should you do in this case? If you have a video frame grabber, then your aspect ratio will likely not be 1:0. In this scenario, you should repeat the experiment in the Y direction. You can either use a rectangular target or just repeat the experiment twice by rotating the camera 90 degrees between tests. fy=V*Z/Y, where V is the height of the target object in the image and Y is its height in the real world.

Why Add Markers?

Aligning the virtual camera with the real camera can be done with specialized sonar, magnetic, RF, or LED positioning systems or can be done less expensively (and often more accurately) using computer vision on the imagery from the camera itself. Passive computer vision systems such as conventional video cameras or webcams just use the light in the environment—as compared to laser-scanning systems. Computer vision algorithms for finding pose can be classified into marker-based and "markerless" vision systems. Markerless systems are starting to appear but are still in their infancy with respect to performance and speed. Also, with markerless systems, one often needs to add texture to objects. This is the case because objects such as tables and walls tend to have lots of smooth featureless regions. But if you're going to that much trouble, why not just use markers?

5.7 ARTag Marker Format

Inside the code\GetARRunning\artag_create_marker_compiled directory, you will find the artag_create_marker.exe program. This utility will create Portable Graymap (PGM) files for individual ARTag markers. PGM is one variant of the Portable Pixmap format.

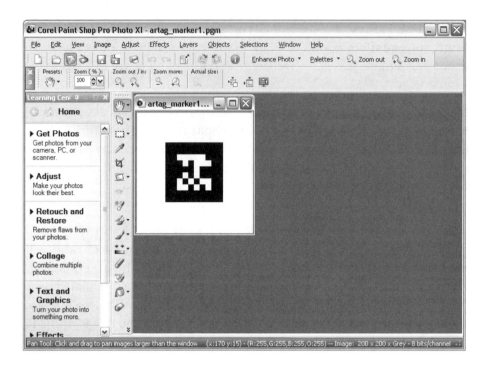

Figure 5.6: Opening an ARTag marker in Corel Paint Shop Pro

To open the marker files, you can use Corel Paint Shop Pro Photo (http://www.corel.com) or the GIMP (http://www.gimp.org), or if you have Adobe Photoshop, you can download a plug-in that supports the PGM format (for example, http://www.telegraphics.com.au/sw/#netpbmformats). (See Figure 5.6, above, and Figure 5.7, on the facing page.) The GIMP is a free option that can be used on any platform, but we didn't fully test it with the examples in this book. Whichever platform you use, remember that if you want to resize the markers, you must ensure that the application you are using does not extrapolate extra data into the larger versions. You can check this visually since the added pixels are usually gray. ARTag markers are pure black and white.

PGM is not the most commonly used format these days, so you may be wondering why ARTag uses it. The answer is simply that it's an easy format to manipulate in code. Read more about the Portable Graymap format at Wikipedia (http://en.wikipedia.org/wiki/Portable_pixmap). Opening an ARTag marker tag in a hex editor shows the transparency of the PGM format (see Figure 5.8, on page 114).

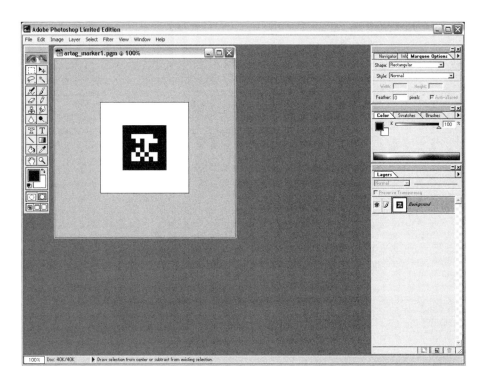

Figure 5.7: Opening an ARTag marker in Adobe Photoshop

These points define the Portable Pixmap file format:

- Line 1 contains a magic number. P1 = ASCII bitmap (black and white), P2 = ASCII grayscale, P3 = ASCII color, P5 = BINARY grayscale, and P6 = BINARY color.

- Line 2 starts any number of comment lines that are preceded by the character #.

- After the comment lines come the horizontal and vertical image resolution (for example, 640 480). These two values are separated by a space.

- The next line gives the maximum value of the color component. Usually it's 255 for 8-bit images and 65535 for 16-bit images.

- The rest of the file contains RGB, grayscale, or black-and-white data. This information is read in the order red, green, and then blue. If the data is RGB, there will be a red, green, and blue integer. If the image is grayscale, there will be a grayscale integer. If the file is a bitmap, there will be either a 0 (white) or a 1 (black).

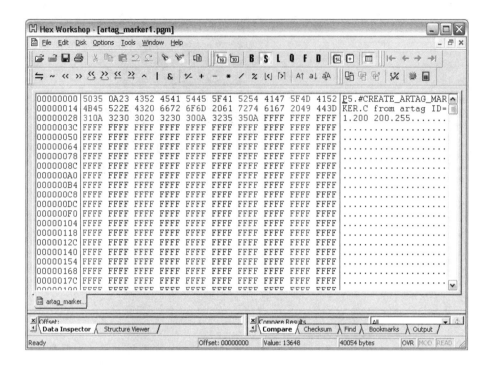

Figure 5.8: ARTAG MARKER 1 OPEN IN HEX WORKSHOP

This write_pgm function (from code/src/ARTag include/pgm_functions.c) shows how simple it is to work with the PGM format:

src/ARTag include/pgm_functions.c

```c
void write_pgm(char *file_name, char *comment, unsigned char *image,
    int width, int height)
{
FILE *out;
int i,j;

out=(FILE*)fopen(file_name,"wb");
if(out==NULL)
    {printf("PGM_FUNCTIONS.C error: Couldn't open %s for writing\n",
        file_name);exit(1);}
fprintf(out,"P5\n#%s\n",comment);
fprintf(out,"%d %d\n255\n",width,height);
for(i=0;i<width*height;i++)
    {
    j=(int)(*(image+i));
    fputc(j,out);
    }
fclose(out);
}
```

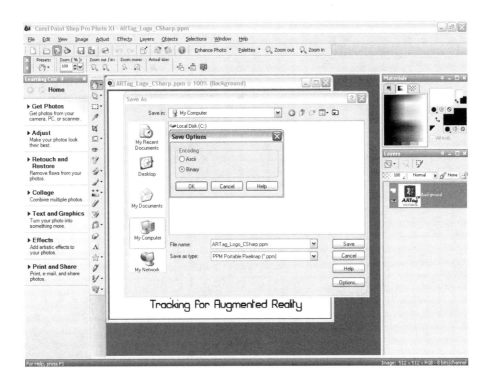

Figure 5.9: USING BINARY PPM OR PGM

When working with PPM or PGM files, make sure to save them in binary format. At this time, the ARTag functions don't support ASCII format. So, unless you want to use your own code, when saving a PPM or PGM, select binary, not ASCII, mode (see Figure 5.9).

If you have a PPM or PGM file that isn't working for you, it may be because the file is not in the format used by ARTag. A last-ditch option is to manually edit the file in hex. For example, the newline characters may not be in the right place. When editing a particular PPM file to match the proper format, 5036203531322035313220 32353520 became 50360A353132203531320A3235350A. This change inserted newline characters (0A) at the appropriate locations in the header. This change allowed the PGM-loading function to read the file.

That's it for this introduction to AR coding. The next chapter will build upon everything you've learned here.

Chapter 6

Writing Applications for ARTag

6.1 Introduction to ARTag Applications

This chapter shows you how to integrate ARTag into your OpenGL programming to create your own AR applications. Using AR, you will be able to take your 3D objects, animations, and games out of the computer and into the real world (see Figure 6.1, on the next page). By the end of this chapter, you will have created some simple programs that use the functions from the ARTag library. You will also learn about the initialization functions that start things up and the three functions that you will call every frame: artag_find_objects(), artag_is_object_found(), and artag_set_object_opengl_matrix().

As you know from previous chapters, ARTag is a computer vision software system that uses markers to align real and virtual cameras. ARTag recognizes special black-and-white square markers, finds the pose, and then sets the modelview matrix so that subsequent rendering operations appear relative to the array and, therefore, relative to the real 3D world. Because you learned about OpenGL in a previous chapter, creating a new AR OpenGL program or adding ARTag to an existing one will be quite simple. The hardest part might be getting your webcam installed and measuring its focal-length parameter.

6.2 ARTag Functions

To use ARTag in an existing OpenGL application, you need to add only a few functions:

- init_artag(width,height,bytes_per_pixel): When you start the program, you use this function to tell ARTag the dimensions of images you will be using.

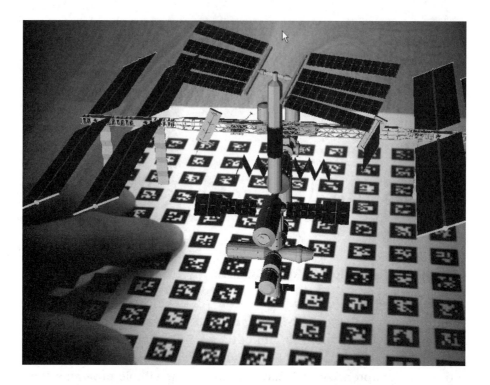

Figure 6.1: A 3D MODEL RENDERED IN AR

- close_artag(): This is the opposite of init_artag. This function frees memory when your application is finished.
- load_array_file(array_filename): This loads a .cf file with array data.
- artag_associate_array(array_name): Used to get a handle number for an array within the array file. You'll use the handle when referring to the array.
- artag_find_objects(cam_image, rgb_greybar): This is the function that does all the image-processing work. Give it a pointer to an unsigned char (byte) array containing the image and a flag telling it whether the image is color or grayscale (1 = color, 0 = grayscale).
- (artag_is_object_found(handle)): This function returns true (nonzero) if the ARTag array, or marker, was detected in the last call to artag_find_objects.
- artag_set_object_opengl_matrix(handle,mirror_on): Call this function if artag_is_object_found(handle) returns true. This sets the modelview camera-to-object matrix. Subsequent rendering will appear relative to the array or marker corresponding to the handle number.

6.3   Using ARTag Functions

Before going into too much detail, let's classify the ARTag functions into ones required for initialization (or cleanup) and those for use with every video frame. The ones done at initialization are setup functions—they're done just once. The others are done every frame.

These are the functions for initialization and cleanup:

1. First call init_artag().

2. Load an array (.cf) file with load_array_file() if you want to use arrays.

3. Associate arrays or single markers with handles (aka objects) by using artag_associate_array() or artag_associate_marker(), respectively. Use the returned artag_object_id for future calls.

These functions are called for every frame:

1. artag_find_objects(). This function searches an image for objects.

2. For all objects associated in step 3 of the initialization, call artag_is_object_found(obj#) if the result is true (1), and then perform the following steps:

3. Call artag_set_object_opengl_matrix(), which sets the modelview matrix for you to start rendering.

4. Other calls you could make instead of, or as well as, setting the matrix are artag_project_point() and artag_project_between_objects(). These functions transfer object coordinates to image coordinates or transfer object coordinates between arrays.

The three functions artag_find_objects(), artag_is_object_found(), and artag_set_object_opengl_matrix() are the most commonly used functions when ARTag is running with an OpenGL application.

6.4   Getting the ARTag SDK

Before you go any further, make sure you have the ARTag SDK. If you don't have it already, jump online, and download the ARTag SDK for Windows, Linux, or Mac OS X. At the time of writing, the latest version is Rev2k. To find the SDK, follow the links from http://www.artag.net.

Once you have the SDK, first try to run the demos in the directory compiled_demos\. You may need to wrestle with your webcam for a bit and set up the camera parameters as per the instructions in the previous chapter.

6.5 Camera Input to Your Program

To make a live AR system, you'll need to get video imagery—in the form of image frames—into your program. The ARTag library requires the image in an uncompressed sequential array of bytes in memory (that is, an unsigned char array).

The demos use the CVcam video capture program from the OpenCV library, which provides imagery from USB webcams and other video cameras that have the necessary drivers—such as a camcorder plugged into a frame grabber. Unfortunately, CVcam does not give you control over the input image resolution, so if you have a specialized camera, you may need to write a wrapper similar to ours. Otherwise, you may want to delve into DirectShow or Video for Windows (VFW) programming, both of which are beyond the scope of this book. If you work in a lab with a Dragonfly IEEE 1394 camera (from Point Grey Research at http://www.ptgrey.com), then you can use one of the wrappers provided in its SDK to get superior, faster, and higher-resolution video than your USB webcam will give you.

Before you try to compile this code, here's one thing to remember: if you get errors that appear in camera_cvcam_windows.c, you may have the wrong version of OpenCV installed on your machine.

6.6 Basic OpenGL Program Running with ARTag

The basic_artag_opengl program demonstrates the following:

- Initializing ARTag.

- Loading an array file.

- Associating an individual array from this file. An array file can contain many arrays, starting and ending with the coordframe and \coordframe keywords.

- Calling the main artag_find_objects() function.

- Calling artag_is_object_found() to see whether an object is loaded.

- Using the artag_get_object_opengl_matrix() function to set the OpenGL modelview matrix. This allows rendering relative to the array.

- Using either OpenCV's CVcam for camera capture with USB and USB 2 webcams or pgrflycapture for Point Grey Research's Dragonfly FireWire camera.

OpenGL lines, nontextured triangles, nontextured quads, and textured quads are used in this demo. The ismar_logo.ppm image is used to texture a quad. Also, in this demo application, the modelview matrix of OpenGL is set by an ARTag function call.

Since this demo works with both USB and Dragonfly cameras, you should uncomment the appropriate include line and link in the correct library for your setup. Refer to the license agreements for both Intel's OpenCV and Point Grey Research's Pgrflycapture software. Use one of these two camera inputs if you agree with their license terms:

```
//USING OpenCV's "cvcam"
#include wrapper "camera_dragonfly_640_480_windows.c"

//USING DRAGONFLY
#include wrapper "camera_cvcam_windows.c"
```

You will also need to link in artag_rev2_vs2005.lib (from the ARTag SDK) and cv.lib and highgui.lib (from Intel). For this first example, link in artag_rev2_vs2005.lib (from the ARTag SDK). To link files in Visual Studio 2005, go to Solution Explorer, and choose Properties from the right-click menu. Then under Configuration Properties, expand Linker, and select Input. Once you are able to see the Input links, add artag_rev2_vs2005.lib and highgui.lib as Additional Dependencies.

Note: in Visual Studio 6, you would select the Settings tab, choose Link, and add the files to the Object/Library modules list. The Visual Studio 6 version of the ARTag library is artag_rev2_vs6.lib. For more details about development setup, including Linux and Mac OS X, refer to Chapter 5.

The include files that you need to add for this demo are stdio.h, stdlib.h, string.h, and math.h. stdio.h is for input and output functions (for example, printf), stdlib.h is a general-purpose standard C library (for example, memory allocation), string.h includes functions for string handling, and math.h gives you access to mathematical functions. Defining M_PI sets the value for pi during the compilation of the program.

Figure 6.2: THE OPENGL TEMPLATE APPLICATION

Let's leap in, get some code working, and then get into how everything works. For your first program, you will convert the OPENGL_TEMPLATE_ PROGRAM.CPP program from the previous chapter so that it runs ARTag (see Figure 6.2). The graphics will be rendered relative to the *base0* array. This array will define the world coordinate system.

You can download the OpenGL_Template_Program_ARTag.CPP example or the OpenGL_Temp_ARTag project in the book download at http://www. pragprog.com/titles/cfar/source_code.

Obviously, for this example, it's necessary only for you to look at the lines that are different from the program in the OpenGL chapter. The first altered code block consists of the includes. The previous example used a flat file instead of video input and didn't use AR at all. To use a camera and ARTag, you must include the ARTag header file and one of the camera interfaces. The demos use the CVcam video capture program from the OpenCV library (that is, camera_cvcam_windows.c).

If you have a Dragonfly camera, then you can use the other interface (that is, camera_dragonfly_640_480_windows.c). You use camera 0 for all the demo projects for this book—the camera number is a provision for future expansion or ARTag.

WriteApps/opengl_template_program_artag/OPENGL_TEMPLATE_PROGRAM_ARTAG.CPP

```
#include "camera_cvcam_windows.c"
//#include "camera_dragonfly_640_480_windows.c"
#define CAM_NUM 0          //which camera input
#include "artag_rev2.h"
```

In this example, you'll be using the panel_set.cf file from the demo or SDK download. This configuration file contains the *base0* array that will be used to define the world coordinate system.

WriteApps/opengl_template_program_artag/OPENGL_TEMPLATE_PROGRAM_ARTAG.CPP

```
#define ARRAY_FILENAME "panel_set.cf"
```

The next sample line creates pointers to your "raw" camera image and a potentially larger one that is 2^n dimensions of your texture. Remember that OpenGL textures cannot be of arbitrary dimensions, so you'll have to stick with 2^n. In this case, it is 1024 by 1024.

WriteApps/opengl_template_program_artag/OPENGL_TEMPLATE_PROGRAM_ARTAG.CPP

```
//cam_image is cam_width*cam_height from camera,
//cam_tex_img is 1024*1024
unsigned char *cam_image,*cam_tex_img;
```

The next few lines provide information—other than the pointers—that ARTag needs about your image. For example, is it a color image or a black-and-white image, and what are its dimensions?

WriteApps/opengl_template_program_artag/OPENGL_TEMPLATE_PROGRAM_ARTAG.CPP

```
//1=RGB, 0=greyscale
char rgb_greybar;
int cam_width, cam_height;
//set to 1 to flip image horizontally for
//"magic mirror" effect
char mirror_on=0;
```

The global variable mirror_on lets you toggle the mirror effect with the spacebar. This allows you to flip the image as the program is running. Figure 6.3, on the next page, shows the effect of mirroring. The image on the left shows mirror_on=0, and the right one shows mirror_on=1. In other words, the spacebar was pressed to create the right image. The textured quad—in the background containing the camera image—is also drawn with reversed X coordinates so that the real and virtual line up.

Figure 6.3: THE EFFECT OF MIRROR_ON IN ARTAG_SET_OBJECT_ OPENGL_MATRIX()

WriteApps/opengl_template_program_artag/OPENGL_TEMPLATE_PROGRAM_ARTAG.CPP

```
//artag object # for array
int artag_object_id;
```

The handle artag_object_id is declared as a global variable so that it can be accessed by both main() and opengl_draw():

WriteApps/opengl_template_program_artag/OPENGL_TEMPLATE_PROGRAM_ARTAG.CPP

```
//space bar toggles "magic mirror" mode
else if(k==' ') mirror_on=mirror_on?0:1;    (hor. mirroring)
```

You need to add a texture for the camera image, which you'll be putting in the background behind your virtual objects. In addition, you need the previously calculated frustum dimensions in your drawing function. Therefore, the right, left, top, and bottom variables are created as global variables:

WriteApps/opengl_template_program_artag/OPENGL_TEMPLATE_PROGRAM_ARTAG.CPP

```
//texture variables
//handle to camera image texture
GLuint camera_texID;
double camera_opengl_dRight,camera_opengl_dLeft,
    camera_opengl_dTop,camera_opengl_dBottom;
```

In the opengl_tick() function, you've added the camera capture and the call to artag_find_objects(), and you've copied the camera image into a camera texture. The camera texture image is set to the next 2^n size above the camera image. In this example, you're attempting to set your camera to 640 by 480, so you use a texture size of 1024 by 1024. The reason for this is that OpenGL textures have to be 2^n, and they must be square. The first size that fits the height of 640 is 1024, and therefore you must use a 1024 by 1024 texture.

WriteApps/opengl_template_program_artag/OPENGL_TEMPLATE_PROGRAM_ARTAG.CPP

```
void opengl_tick(void)
{
    int j=0;
    int source_offset,dest_offset;
    //grab camera image
    camera_grab_bgr_blocking(CAM_NUM,cam_image,cam_width,cam_height);

    //main ARTag function - process image for markers and arrays
    artag_find_objects(cam_image,rgb_greybar);

    //copy camera image into 1024x1024 texture image
    source_offset=0; dest_offset=0;
    for(j=0;j<cam_height;j++)  {
    memcpy(cam_tex_img+dest_offset,cam_image+source_offset,cam_width*3);
        source_offset+=cam_width*3;   dest_offset+=1024*3;
}

//copy image into OpenGL buffer
glBindTexture(GL_TEXTURE_2D, camera_texID);
glTexImage2D(GL_TEXTURE_2D,0,GL_RGB,1024,1024,0,GL_BGR_EXT,
                        GL_UNSIGNED_BYTE,cam_tex_img);

glutPostRedisplay();
}
```

The following code, in the opengl_draw() callback function, sets up the camera texture for rendering:

WriteApps/opengl_template_program_artag/OPENGL_TEMPLATE_PROGRAM_ARTAG.CPP

```
// draw a quad for the background video
glLoadIdentity();
glDisable(GL_LIGHTING);
glEnable(GL_TEXTURE_2D);
glBindTexture(GL_TEXTURE_2D, camera_texID);
glBegin(GL_QUADS);
```

The quad is then drawn, either clockwise or counterclockwise, depending on whether you're using the mirror image. Since the camera image was copied into the upper-left corner of a larger 1024 by 1024 texture image, you apply the texture coordinates from (0,0) to (0.64,0.48). This way you're just using the useful area of the camera image. Afterward, you call artag_is_object_found() with the handle of the base object; if the *base0* array object is visible, you set the OpenGL matrix and do your rendering from there.

WriteApps/opengl_template_program_artag/OPENGL_TEMPLATE_PROGRAM_ARTAG.CPP

```
//draw simple augmentations
if(artag_is_object_found(artag_object_id))  {
  artag_set_object_opengl_matrix(artag_object_id,mirror_on);

//draw multi-colored triangle
glDisable(GL_TEXTURE_2D);
glBegin(GL_TRIANGLES);
glColor3f(1, 0, 0);
glVertex3f(0,0,0);
glColor3f(0, 1, 0);
glVertex3f(10,0,0);
glColor3f(0, 0, 1);
glVertex3f(10,0,10);
glEnd();

//draw green quad
glBegin(GL_QUADS);
glColor3f(0, 1, 0);
glVertex3f(-5,25,0);
glVertex3f(-5,35,0);
glVertex3f( 5,35,0);
glVertex3f( 5,25,0);
glEnd();

//draw vertical line
glBegin(GL_LINES);
glColor3f(1, 0, 0);
glVertex3f(0,0,0);
glColor3f(0, 0, 1);
glVertex3f(00,0,100);
glEnd();

//draw textured quad
if(texpgm!=NULL)  {
   glEnable(GL_TEXTURE_2D);
   glBindTexture(GL_TEXTURE_2D, pgm_texID);
   glBegin(GL_QUADS);
   glColor3f(1.0f, 1.0f, 1.0f);
   glTexCoord2f(0.0f, 1.0f);  glVertex3f(-50,50,0);
   glTexCoord2f(0.0f, 0.0f);  glVertex3f(-50,150,0);
   glTexCoord2f(1.0f, 0.0f);  glVertex3f( 50,150,0);
   glTexCoord2f(1.0f, 1.0f);  glVertex3f( 50,50,0);
   glEnd();
  }
 }
glutSwapBuffers();
}
```

In the main() function, you perform the initialization using the wrapper function init_camera(). This function gives back the image dimensions from the camera driver.

WriteApps/opengl_template_program_artag/OPENGL_TEMPLATE_PROGRAM_ARTAG.CPP

```
//initialize camera
rgb_greybar=1;
if(init_camera(CAM_NUM,640,480,rgb_greybar,&cam_width,&cam_height))
    {printf("Can't start camera\n");exit(1);}
printf("Camera started with resolution=%dx%d\n",cam_width,cam_height);
```

Next, the sample displays the ARTag library version—this is clearly an optional step.

WriteApps/opengl_template_program_artag/OPENGL_TEMPLATE_PROGRAM_ARTAG.CPP

```
//display version (optional)
char version_string[256];
artag_get_version(version_string);
printf("version: <%s>\n",version_string);
```

At this point, you actually initialize ARTag by telling it to set up its internal memory buffers for your desired image size. It is vital that the image size and color depth are correct. If you attempt to process a larger image than what was initialized, you can have memory faults because your pointers will reach out of the allocated memory range.

WriteApps/opengl_template_program_artag/OPENGL_TEMPLATE_PROGRAM_ARTAG.CPP

```
// ARTag initialization
if(init_artag(cam_width,cam_height,3)) {printf("ERROR:
    Can't start ARTag\n");exit(1);}
```

The next step, setting the camera parameters, is not optional. The program will still function without it, but the 3D augmentations will not look correct. You need to tell ARTag what your camera parameters are (see equation 3.8, on page 42). The real and virtual camera's parameters need to match for the 3D object to look correct.

WriteApps/opengl_template_program_artag/OPENGL_TEMPLATE_PROGRAM_ARTAG.CPP

```
//set camera params
artag_set_camera_params(DEFAULT_FX,DEFAULT_FY,
    cam_width/2.0,cam_height/2.0);
```

When you set the viewing frustum, you use the cam_width variable returned by your init_camera() function, rather than the global CAM_WIDTH that you used in the original program (before you had real camera input).

```
//set viewing frustum to match camera FOV
glMatrixMode (GL_PROJECTION);
glLoadIdentity ();
camera_opengl_dRight = cam_width / (2.0 * DEFAULT_FX);
camera_opengl_dLeft = -camera_opengl_dRight;
camera_opengl_dTop = cam_height / (2.0 * DEFAULT_FY);
camera_opengl_dBottom = -camera_opengl_dTop;
glFrustum(camera_opengl_dLeft, camera_opengl_dRight,
    camera_opengl_dBottom, camera_opengl_dTop, 1.0, 1100.0);
```

Next, you load the array file panel_set.cf and associate the handle artag_object_id with the array *base0* from your file.

```
//load array file
if(load_array_file(ARRAY_FILENAME))
    printf("ERROR loading <%s>\n",ARRAY_FILENAME);
else
    printf("Loaded array file <%s>\n",ARRAY_FILENAME);

//associate object with array named "base0"
artag_object_id=artag_associate_array("base0");
```

By the way, in this example, you are associating an array; this is the recommended technique for ARTag. It is possible to use single markers, but arrays work better. Sometimes you may want to use the function artag_associate_marker(). This function assigns a handle to an individual marker rather than an array of markers.

Next, you allocate memory for the camera image, both the raw image coming from the camera and a texture image that will be displayed. The code is the same as in the previous example where you had only a static texture loaded from disk. Remember that you must allocate sufficient memory.

```
//camera rgb image
cam_image=(unsigned char*)malloc(cam_width*cam_height*4+100);
if(cam_image==NULL) {printf("failed malloc\n");exit(1);}

//camera texture
cam_tex_img=(unsigned char*)malloc(1024*1024*4+100);
if(cam_tex_img==NULL) {printf("failed malloc\n");exit(1);}

// make a texture for the video
glGenTextures(1, &camera_texID);
glBindTexture(GL_TEXTURE_2D, camera_texID);
glTexParameteri(GL_TEXTURE_2D,GL_TEXTURE_MAG_FILTER,GL_LINEAR);
glTexParameteri(GL_TEXTURE_2D,GL_TEXTURE_MIN_FILTER,GL_LINEAR);
```

Finally, when you exit, you should free the memory being used by ARTag and the camera.

```
void terminate(void)
{
    close_artag();
    close_camera(CAM_NUM);
}
```

6.7 Motion and Multiple Array Objects

The previous example used only one array, so let's look at an example with two. Using more than one array will allow you to add multiple virtual objects. To do this, morph your code from the OpenGL chapter's moving platform example program (Motion_Example.CPP) to attach the moving platform with the bouncing kettle on the *base0* array and the sphere to the *toolbar4* array.

This is another example of modifying a regular OpenGL program to work with ARTag. Here are the additions to Motion_Example.CPP that are used in Motion_Example_ARTag.CPP. As with the previous example, you must add these includes at the top of the file:

```
#include "camera_cvcam_windows.c"
//#include "camera_dragonfly_640_480_windows.c"
#define CAM_NUM 0        //which camera input
#include "artag_rev2.h"
```

In the global variables, you add the following:

```
#define ARRAY_FILENAME "panel_set.cf"

//cam_image is cam_width*cam_height from camera,
//cam_tex_img is 1024*1024
unsigned char *cam_image,*cam_tex_img;
//1=RGB, 0=greyscale
char rgb_greybar;
int cam_width, cam_height;
//set to 1 to flip image horizontally for
//"magic mirror" effect
char mirror_on=0;

int base_array_id,toolbar4_array_id;
double camera_opengl_dRight,camera_opengl_dLeft,
//camera_opengl_dTop,camera_opengl_dBottom;
```

```
//texture variables
//handle to camera image texture
GLuint camera_texID;
```

Here is the new opengl_tick() function combining both the platform moving and the camera texture processing:

WriteApps/motion_example_artag/motion_example_artag.cpp

```cpp
void opengl_tick(void)
{
    int j=0;
    int source_offset,dest_offset;

    //grab camera image
    camera_grab_bgr_blocking(CAM_NUM,cam_image,cam_width,cam_height);

    //main ARTag function - process image for markers and arrays
    artag_find_objects(cam_image,rgb_greybar);

    //copy camera image into 1024x1024 texture image
    source_offset=0; dest_offset=0;
    for(j=0;j<cam_height;j++)  {
        memcpy(cam_tex_img+dest_offset,cam_image+source_offset,cam_width*3);
        source_offset+=cam_width*3;  dest_offset+=1024*3;
    }
    //copy image into OpenGL buffer
    glBindTexture(GL_TEXTURE_2D, camera_texID);
    glTexImage2D(GL_TEXTURE_2D, 0, GL_RGB, 1024, 1024, 0, GL_BGR_EXT,
        GL_UNSIGNED_BYTE,cam_tex_img);

    //--update position of platform--
    platform_y+=platform_dy;
    //if platform hits either end, reverse direction of motion
    if(( platform_y >= 100.0 )&&( platform_dy > 0 )) platform_dy*=-1.0;
    if(( platform_y <= 0.0 )&&( platform_dy < 0 )) platform_dy*=-1.0;

    //--update position of kettle--
    kettle_x+=kettle_dx;
    kettle_y+=kettle_dy;
    //if platform hits platform edges, 'bounce' reverse direction
    //of motion along that axis
    if(( kettle_x >= 90.0 )&&( kettle_x > 0.0 ))  kettle_dx*=-1.0;
    if(( kettle_x <= 10.0 )&&( kettle_x < 0.0 ))  kettle_dx*=-1.0;
    if(( kettle_y >= 90.0 )&&( kettle_y > 0.0 ))  kettle_dy*=-1.0;
    if(( kettle_y <= 10.0 )&&( kettle_y < 0.0 ))  kettle_dy*=-1.0;

    //--update kettle angle--
    kettle_theta+=kettle_dtheta;
    //keep in 0-360 degree bounds
    if( kettle_theta >= 360.0 ) kettle_theta-=360.0;

    glutPostRedisplay();
}
```

The important changes come in the next block of code. You will add the new drawing functions in the section where you use ARTag to set the modelview matrix for each object.

WriteApps/motion_example_artag/motion_example_artag.cpp

```cpp
void opengl_draw(void)
{
glClear(GL_COLOR_BUFFER_BIT | GL_DEPTH_BUFFER_BIT | GL_STENCIL_BUFFER_BIT);

// draw a quad for the background video
glLoadIdentity();
glDisable(GL_LIGHTING);
glEnable(GL_TEXTURE_2D);
glBindTexture(GL_TEXTURE_2D, camera_texID);
glBegin(GL_QUADS);
glColor3f(1.0f, 1.0f, 1.0f);
//draw camera texture, set with offset to aim only at cam_width x
//cam_height upper left bit
//normal operation (magic mirror off)
if(mirror_on==0)  {
   glTexCoord2f(0.0f, (float)cam_height/1024.0);
   glVertex3f(camera_opengl_dLeft*1024, camera_opengl_dBottom*1024, -1024);
   glTexCoord2f(0.0f, 0.0f);
   glVertex3f(camera_opengl_dLeft*1024, camera_opengl_dTop*1024, -1024);
   glTexCoord2f((float)cam_width/1024.0, 0.0f);
   glVertex3f(camera_opengl_dRight*1024, camera_opengl_dTop*1024, -1024);
   glTexCoord2f((float)cam_width/1024.0, (float)cam_height/1024.0);
   glVertex3f(camera_opengl_dRight*1024, camera_opengl_dBottom*1024, -1024);
   glEnd();
}
//flip background image for "magic mirror" effect
else  {
   glTexCoord2f(0.0f, (float)cam_height/1024.0);
   glVertex3f(camera_opengl_dRight*1024, camera_opengl_dBottom*1024, -1024);
   glTexCoord2f(0.0f, 0.0f);
   glVertex3f(camera_opengl_dRight*1024, camera_opengl_dTop*1024, -1024);
   glTexCoord2f((float)cam_width/1024.0, 0.0f);
   glVertex3f(camera_opengl_dLeft*1024, camera_opengl_dTop*1024, -1024);
   glTexCoord2f((float)cam_width/1024.0, (float)cam_height/1024.0);
   glVertex3f(camera_opengl_dLeft*1024, camera_opengl_dBottom*1024, -1024);
   glEnd();
}


//draw grid, platform, and kettle relative to base0 array
if(artag_is_object_found(base_array_id))  {
    artag_set_object_opengl_matrix(base_array_id,mirror_on);

   //------------ Draw objects in base0 coordinates ---------
   glTranslatef(0,-80,0);  //move back to start of array
```

```
//draw grid and axis
glDisable(GL_TEXTURE_2D);

//draw red x-axis
glBegin(GL_LINES);
  glColor3f(1, 0, 0);
  glVertex3f(0,0,0);
  glVertex3f(100,0,0);
glEnd();

//draw green y-axis
glBegin(GL_LINES);
  glColor3f(0, 1, 0);
  glVertex3f(0,0,0);
  glVertex3f(0,100,0);
glEnd();

//draw blue z-axis
glBegin(GL_LINES);
  glColor3f(0, 0, 1);
  glVertex3f(0,0,0);
  glVertex3f(0,0,100);
glEnd();

//draw grey grid
for(float x=100 ; x<=100 ; x+=10 )  {
    glBegin(GL_LINES);
      glColor3f(0.75, 0.75, 0.75);
      glVertex3f(x,0,0);
      glVertex3f(x,200,0);
    glEnd();
    }
for(float y=0 ; y <= 200; y+=10 )  {
    glBegin(GL_LINES);
      glColor3f(0.75, 0.75, 0.75);
      glVertex3f(-100,y,0);
      glVertex3f(100,y,0);
    glEnd();
    }

//save modelview matrix containing only camera pose
glMatrixMode(GL_MODELVIEW);
glPushMatrix();


//convert from world to platform coordinates
glTranslatef(0,platform_y,5);
//---- Draw objects in platform coordinates -----
glBegin(GL_QUADS);

  //draw platform top quad
```

```
        glColor3f(0, 1, 0);
        glVertex3f(0,0,0);
        glVertex3f(100,0,0);
        glVertex3f(100,100,0);
        glVertex3f(0,100,0);

            //draw platform front quad
        glColor3f(0, 0.7, 0);
        glVertex3f(0,0,0);
        glVertex3f(100,0,0);
        glVertex3f(100,0,-5);
        glVertex3f(0,0,-5);
    glEnd();


    //convert from platform to kettle coordinates
    //-translate-rotate-scale
    glTranslatef(kettle_x,kettle_y,10);
    glRotatef(kettle_theta,0,0,1);
    glRotatef(90,1,0,0);
    glScaled(2,2,2);
    //---- Draw objects in kettle coordinates ----
    glEnable(GL_TEXTURE_2D);
    glBindTexture(GL_TEXTURE_2D, grey_texID);
    glColor3f(0.6f, 0.85f, 1.0f);
    glutSolidTeapot(5);



    //back to original modelview matrix containing
    //only camera pose
    glPopMatrix();
}



//draw grid, platform, and kettle relative to base0 array
if(artag_is_object_found(toolbar4_array_id))  {
    artag_set_object_opengl_matrix(toolbar4_array_id,mirror_on);

    //----- Draw sphere in toolbar4 coordinates -----

    glColor3f(1.0f, 0.6f, 0.6f);

    glutWireSphere(20,10,10);
}

glutSwapBuffers();
}
```

As before, you should add the camera and ARTag closing functions to terminate():

WriteApps/motion_example_artag/motion_example_artag.cpp

```
void terminate(void)
{
    close_artag();
    close_camera(CAM_NUM);
}
```

The program will now run at a slower frame rate because it must wait for the camera image to be acquired and the ARTag processing to be complete. To compensate, you will increase the platform and kettle movement speeds (platform_dx, dy and kettle_dx, dy, respectively).

WriteApps/motion_example_artag/motion_example_artag.cpp

```
//initialize object variables
platform_y=0; platform_dy=1;
kettle_x=50; kettle_dx=2;
kettle_y=50; kettle_dy=3;
kettle_theta=0; kettle_dtheta=4;
sphere_x=-50; sphere_y=130;
```

The same initialization code (that was added to main() in OpenGL_ Template_Program_ARTag.CPP) is repeated for this example. The difference here is the addition of the second association for the *toolbar4* array (see Figure 6.4, on page 137).

WriteApps/motion_example_artag/motion_example_artag.cpp

```
//initialize camera
rgb_greybar=1;
if(init_camera(CAM_NUM,640,480,rgb_greybar,&cam_width,&cam_height))
    {printf("Can't start camera\n");exit(1);}
printf("Camera started with resolution=%dx%d\n",cam_width,cam_height);

//display version (optional)
char version_string[256];
artag_get_version(version_string);
printf("version: <%s>\n",version_string);

// ARTag initialization
if(init_artag(cam_width,cam_height,3))
{printf("ERROR: Can't start ARTag\n");exit(1);}

//set camera params
artag_set_camera_params(DEFAULT_FX,DEFAULT_FY,cam_width/2.0,cam_height/2.0);
```

```
//load array file
if(load_array_file(ARRAY_FILENAME))
    printf("ERROR loading <%s>\n",ARRAY_FILENAME);
else
    printf("Loaded array file <%s>\n",ARRAY_FILENAME);

//associate object with
//arrays in <panel_set.cf>
base_array_id=artag_associate_array("base0");
toolbar4_array_id=artag_associate_array("toolbar4");

//set viewing frustum
//to match camera FOV
glMatrixMode (GL_PROJECTION);
glLoadIdentity ();
camera_opengl_dRight = CAM_WIDTH / (2.0 * DEFAULT_FX);
camera_opengl_dLeft = -camera_opengl_dRight;
camera_opengl_dTop = CAM_HEIGHT / (2.0 * DEFAULT_FY);
camera_opengl_dBottom = -camera_opengl_dTop;
glFrustum(camera_opengl_dLeft, camera_opengl_dRight,
    camera_opengl_dBottom, camera_opengl_dTop, 1.0, 1100.0);

//set Modelview matrix
glMatrixMode(GL_MODELVIEW);
float opengl_matrix[16]={0.844278,-0.109951,0.524505,0.000000,

0.244976,0.554910,-1.689997,0.000000,
    0.064337,0.950853,0.302886,0.000000,
    -29.162102,-25.714951,-504.337860,1.000000};
glLoadMatrixf(opengl_matrix);

//make greyscale texture
//for teapot
glGenTextures(1, &grey_texID);
glBindTexture(GL_TEXTURE_2D, grey_texID);
glTexParameteri(GL_TEXTURE_2D,GL_TEXTURE_MAG_FILTER,GL_LINEAR);
glTexParameteri(GL_TEXTURE_2D,GL_TEXTURE_MIN_FILTER,GL_LINEAR);

grey=(unsigned char*)malloc(256*256);
for(int i=0;i<256*256;i++) grey[i]=(unsigned char)(i/512)+128;
glTexImage2D(GL_TEXTURE_2D, 0, GL_LUMINANCE, 256, 256, 0,
    GL_LUMINANCE, GL_UNSIGNED_BYTE,grey);

//initialize object variables
platform_y=0; platform_dy=1;
kettle_x=50; kettle_dx=2;
kettle_y=50; kettle_dy=3;
kettle_theta=0; kettle_dtheta=4;
sphere_x=-50; sphere_y=130;
```

```
//set viewing frustum to match camera FOV
glMatrixMode (GL_PROJECTION);
glLoadIdentity ();
camera_opengl_dRight = cam_width / (2.0 * DEFAULT_FX);
camera_opengl_dLeft = -camera_opengl_dRight;
camera_opengl_dTop = cam_height / (2.0 * DEFAULT_FY);
camera_opengl_dBottom = -camera_opengl_dTop;
glFrustum(camera_opengl_dLeft, camera_opengl_dRight,

     camera_opengl_dBottom, camera_opengl_dTop, 1.0, 1100.0);
//set Modelview matrix
glMatrixMode(GL_MODELVIEW);

//camera rgb image
cam_image=(unsigned char*)malloc(cam_width*cam_height*4+100);
if(cam_image==NULL) {printf("failed malloc\n");exit(1);}

//camera texture
cam_tex_img=(unsigned char*)malloc(1024*1024*4+100);
if(cam_tex_img==NULL) {printf("failed malloc\n");exit(1);}

// make a texture for the video
glGenTextures(1, &camera_texID);
glBindTexture(GL_TEXTURE_2D, camera_texID);
glTexParameteri(GL_TEXTURE_2D,GL_TEXTURE_MAG_FILTER,GL_LINEAR);
glTexParameteri(GL_TEXTURE_2D,GL_TEXTURE_MIN_FILTER,GL_LINEAR);
```

After you make these changes, the platform and kettle will move back and forth along the *base0* array while the sphere holds its position relative to *toolbar4*.

Now let's examine the ARTag library in more detail.

6.8   Initializing and Terminating AR Applications

From the ARTag header file, the prototypes for these functions are as follows:

```
char  init_artag(int width, int height, int bpp);   //bpp=bytes/pixel
void  close_artag(void);
```

Each function should be called only once inside your program—once to allocate the necessary memory and the other to free the memory.

The ARTag image processing happens in several stages. Obviously, some of these stages require memory storage allocation. The init_artag() function sets up this memory, and it tells ARTag how big the image will be when you later call artag_find_objects(). When you're done with ARTag processing and are not going to be calling artag_find_objects() anymore,

Figure 6.4: THE MOTION EXAMPLE DEMO MODIFIED TO WORK WITH ARTAG

call close_artag() to free up ARTag's storage memory. You have to allocate the memory for the image itself. For example:

```
unsigned char *image_pointer;
//for grayscale image, color is * 3
image_pointer=(unsigned char*)malloc(width*height);
```

Remember that you must give ARTag the correct parameters; otherwise, you may get a memory fault. You also need the number of bytes per pixel set correctly. If you call init_artag(width,height,1), meaning one byte per pixel, and then later call artag_find_objects(image_pointer,1)—where the last argument means an RGB image—then you'll have problems since the function will read three times the memory. This will create a memory overrun error.

Here are two combinations that work. The first is for a grayscale image (only one byte per pixel) in your image_pointer array:

```
//GRAYSCALE IMAGE
unsigned char *image_pointer;
int width=640,height=480;
//1 byte per pixel for grayscale image
image_pointer=(unsigned char*)malloc(width*height);
if(image_pointer==NULL)
{
 printf("Error: can't malloc image_pointer\n");
 exit(1);
}
init_artag(width,height,1);
...
//acquire camera
//rgb_greybar=0 for grayscale
image artag_find_objects(image_pointer,0);
```

Alternatively, for color images, the code is as follows:

```
//RGB COLOR IMAGE
unsigned char *image_pointer;
int width=640,height=480;
//3 bytes per pixel for color RGB image
image_pointer=(unsigned char*)malloc(width*height*3);
if(image_pointer==NULL)
  {
   printf("Error: can't malloc image_pointer\n");
   exit(1);
  }
init_artag(width,height,3);
...
//acquire camera image
//rgb_greybar=1 for RGB
artag_find_objects(image_pointer,1);
```

You may ask, why are there two settings for the pixel depth? You have to set it both in the initialization and every frame when you call artag_find_objects(). This is done for historical reasons. An earlier version of ARTag had "drop-in functions" for users of an older marker system called ARToolkit.

6.9 Detecting Markers

The ARTag_Find_Objects function is the workhorse of ARTag. It processes the image, finds markers, and groups them into arrays. To find the markers, this function uses many stages, including finding outlines, hypothesizing marker locations, and reading the embedded digital code.

From the ARTag header file, the prototype for ARTag_Find_Objects is as follows:

```
void artag_find_objects(unsigned char *rgb_cam_image, char rgb_greybar);
```

You will call this function every time you get an image frame. Because it is a CPU-intensive operation, this function consumes the most time. The larger the image and the more four-sided objects there are, the more time it will take to process.

All ARTag image processing is done on grayscale images, so when you give it an RGB image, the first thing it does is convert it to grayscale. If you have a special camera or camera interface and you have the option of getting a grayscale image straight from your camera or camera driver, you could save processing time by using that option. However, you'll probably want to have a color image to display to the user, so you may be stuck with processing color images.

6.10 Setting Virtual Camera Viewpoint

After you have called artag_find_objects(), you can later query ARTag for the locations of arrays (and/or individual markers) and set the ARTag modelview matrix so that rendering can happen relative to the array. An *object* in this context is a single ARTag marker, or array, that has been initialized with artag_associate_array() or artag_associate_marker(). In the prototypes, the handle artag_object_num is used. This variable is returned from the artag_associate_array() or artag_associate_marker() function that was called during initialization.

You call the artag_is_object_found() function to see whether the array or marker was found, and you can call artag_set_object_opengl_matrix() to set the OpenGL modelview matrix. You should call the second function only if the first function returned true (that is, nonzero).

```
char artag_is_object_found(int artag_object_num);
void artag_set_object_opengl_matrix(int object_num, char mirror_on);
```

Earlier, you learned that ARTag sets the OpenGL modelview matrix with camera-to-world transformation so that you can render in world coordinates. More precisely, each marker or array of markers that you initialize as an *ARTag object* is treated the same so that the ARTag software sets the modelview matrix for each camera-to-object coordinate system. In many applications, such as tabletop AR programs, you have only one array (the tabletop) that you are using as the world coordinate system; in this case, artag_set_object_opengl_matrix is setting the camera-to-world coordinate system transfer for you. Together, the artag_find_objects(), artag_is_object_found(), and artag_set_object_opengl_matrix() functions are called every frame. Other than the initialization, these three functions perform the essential operations of ARTag and allow you to use OpenGL applications with ARTag.

The mirror_on option for the last function is usually 0. You will set it to 1 for cases where you want to have a horizontally mirrored display, for example, in *magic mirror* scenarios where you stand in front of a large screen that acts as a mirror. Since the camera will be looking back at you, both the camera image and augmentations must be flipped horizontally when they are drawn. In most cases, such as a webcam and computer screen combination, you will use 0 for this setting.

6.11 Finding Marker Array Size

Objects rendered, after artag_set_object_opengl_matrix() is called, will be drawn to scale with the units in the array definition that is in the array file. The scale of objects rendered will depend on the relative size between the virtual object and the array definition—the augmentation will be drawn in the same units. If one marker is 100 units wide in the .cf file, then a virtual 3D object will need to be 100 units wide so that it appears as wide as the marker. This is true regardless of how large the marker array is printed.

One way to adapt to the scale, other than carefully sizing your 3D models or rewriting the .cf array file, is to read the size of an array and call glScale accordingly:

```
void artag_get_object_coordframe_range(int object_num,
        float *min_x, float *max_x,
        float *min_y, float *max_y,
        float *min_z, float *max_z);
```

For example, the following code queries and prints the range spanned by the array:

```
base_array_id=artag_associate_array("base0");
float min_x,max_x,min_y,max_y,min_z,max_z;
atag_get_object_coordframe_range(base_array_id,&min_x,
&max_x,&min_y,
&max_y,&min_z,
&max_z);
printf("MIN,MAX X=%4.1f,%4.1f Y=%4.1f,%4.1f Z=%4.1f,%4.1f\n",
    _x,max_x,min_y,max_y,min_z,max_z);
```

The output is as follows:

```
MIN,MAX   X=-80.0,80.0    Y=-80.0,80.0    Z= 0,0, 0,0
```

The next chapter contains a section that delves a bit deeper into the issue of getting the scale right. It includes an example that uses ARTag_ Get_Object_Coordframe_Range.

6.12 Mapping Between Objects

The artag_project_between_objects() function is provided for interactions between virtual objects attached to different array patterns. This function maps from a location (x, y, z) in the coordinate system (attached to one array) to a location (x, y, z) in a second array. The real-world relative size of the units must be considered before using this function. For example, in the next chapter's sections on scaling, the *base0* array is 1.19 mm/unit when printed out as letter size, whereas *toolbar0* is 0.81 mm/unit. Therefore, you must call artag_project_between_objects() with a scale of 1.19/0.81=1.47 to get the correct results.

Note that because of amplification in extrapolated 3D data from the image data, the projected coordinates will be subject to greater inaccuracy and noise than the augmentations themselves. This error is a numerical instability problem. Errors because of noise in the detected marker positions produce some jittering in the projection matrix that ARTag calculates. The jittering does not affect a 3D object rendered using the projection matrix but does affect the 3D point that is calculated when the inverse operation is performed. The root of the instability is that a small error in the image location converts into a potentially large error in the depth direction (that is, along the direction from the camera to the 3D point). This noisy 3D point is then mapped over to the other coordinate system where it is more noticeable. This issue can be mitigated by having a good camera, focusing the camera, properly calculating the scale factor between units in the two array coordinate systems, and calibrating the camera (that is, calculating the zoom and setting the image center properly).

The prototype for artag_project_between_objects() is as follows:

```
void artag_project_between_objects(int object_num1,
    double source2dest_scale, int object_num2, double x1,
    double y1, double z1, double *x2, double *y2, double *z2);
```

This function is demonstrated by the artag_cad program. With artag_ project_between_objects(), you can convert a 3D point from one object's coordinate system to another. For example, you can convert (20, 10, 5) from the coordinate system of *toolbar0* to where it would lie in *toolbar1*. In the artag_cad example, a virtual pointer from the *pointer1* array is mapped to the *base0* array's space to create polygons. To make the application easier to use, we removed the ball from a wireless mouse and taped the mouse to a card with *pointer1* mounted on it. With this setup, we could more easily click and draw polygons. The power of this interaction technique, as well as the limitations with the propagating error of the math involved, is apparent when trying this demo—you'll see how the transferred point is noisy (that is, it flickers).

6.13 Mapping from Objects to the Image

You are not likely to use these next few functions, but they are briefly explained for your reference.

If you are doing *billboard*-type sprite animations, where you have flat polygons textured with an alpha channel texture—such as in id Software's legendary Doom game—you may want to know the mapping between a point in object space and the screen. An indirect way to accomplish this is with artag_project_point() where an (x, y, z) location in object space is mapped to a pixel position (u, v) in the original camera image. Note that you must correctly map this to the screen image by scaling the (u, v) coordinates because the camera image and screen image are different sizes.

The function prototype for artag_project_point() is as follows:

```
void artag_project_point(int object_num, float x, float y,
    float z, float *u, float *v);
```

6.14 Creating Marker Patterns

Most of the time, you'll be able to use the supplied images of marker arrays and their corresponding .cf files. But in the event you want to make your own, you need to generate the ARTag marker for a given ID number. The function prototype for artag_create_marker() is as follows:

```
int artag_create_marker(int artag_id, int scale, unsigned char *image);
```

To create a marker, you tell this function which marker ID you want and what scale it should be, and you provide a pointer for the function to fill in the pattern. If you provide a scale of 1, the pattern created will be 100 bytes (that is, 10 by 10). Likewise, as in the demo download

ARTag Marker Not Recommended		Reason	ARTag Marker Not Recommended		Reason
ARTag ID	sub-ID		ARTag ID	sub-ID	
75,1099	75	HD=4 to sub-ID 692 at 90° ccw	655,1679	655	HD=4 to sub-ID 898 at 180°
192,1216	192	HD=4 to sub-ID 686 at 90° ccw	686,1710	686	HD=4 to sub-ID 192 at 90° cw
182,1206	182	HD=4 to itself mirrored at 90° cw	692,1716	692	HD=4 to sub-ID 75 at 90° cw
270,1294	270	HD=2 to itself mirrored at 90° cw	736,1760	736	HD=4 to sub-ID 574 at 180°
377,1401	377	HD=4 to sub-ID 933 at 90° ccw	791,1815	791	HD=4 to itself mirrored at 90° ccw
384,1408	384	HD=4 to itself mirrored at 90° ccw	828,1852	828	HD=4 to sub-ID 609 mirrored at 0°
507,1531	507	HD=4 to sub-ID 966 mirrored at 0°	898,1922	898	HD=4 to sub-ID 655 at 180°
574,1598	574	HD=4 to sub-ID 736 at 180°	927,1951	927	HD=4 to sub-ID 938 at 90° ccw
609,1633	609	HD=4 to sub-ID 828 mirrored at 0°	933,1957	933	HD=4 to sub-ID 377 at 90° cw
643,1667	643	HD=4 to itself mirrored at 180°	938,1962	938	HD=4 to sub-ID 927 at 90° cw
648,1672	648	HD=4 to itself mirrored at 90° ccw	966,1990	966	HD=4 to sub-ID 507 mirrored at 0°

Figure 6.5: TABLE OF ILLEGAL ARTAG MARKER IDS

program artag_create_marker.cpp, if you set the scale to 10, then the pattern created is 100 by 100, and thus you need to allocate 10,000 bytes for the pattern before calling the function. Each pixel gets fill with a value of 255 for white or 0 for black.

When using this function, you set the ARTag ID variable (artag_id in the prototype) to the ARTag ID for the marker you want to create. ARTag has a range 0–1023, of which 1,001 are valid. Twenty-three markers were removed from the possible space for reasons of uniqueness (see Figure 6.5). Removing these markers made the remaining set of markers as different from each other as possible and therefore reduced the intermarker confusion rate. Since some IDs are invalid (such as 682), you should check the return value—1 means that marker ID is invalid.

Figure 6.6: ARTAG MARKER PATTERN CREATED WITH ARTAG_
CREATE_MARKER.CPP

Here is some sample code that creates an AR marker pattern:

```
unsigned char *pattern_image;
int scale,pattern_width;
int artag_id;

scale=10;
pattern_width=10*scale;
pattern_image=(unsigned char*)malloc(pattern_width*pattern_width);
if(pattern_image==NULL) {printf("Can't malloc pattern_image\n");exit(1);}
//call artag_create_marker() to get pattern
if(artag_create_marker(artag_id,scale,pattern_image))
    {printf("Error calling artag_create_marker()\n");exit(1);}
```

For an example that uses the artag_create_marker() function, look at the sample project in the code\IntroARProg\artag_create_marker\ directory of the book's download. artag_create_marker.exe is a command-line program that calls this function, adds a label on top, and writes it out as a PGM file. Figure 6.6 shows the example of creating marker artag_id=99. The command-line statement and the output for this command are as follows:

```
C:\>artag_create_marker.exe 99
CREATE_ARTAG_MARKER.C Wrote <artag_create_marker.pgm>
```

Note: this program requires a GLUT DLL because the ARTag library currently requires glut32.dll. The create marker pattern program doesn't actually use GLUT.

6.15 Miscellaneous Functions

This section covers the rest of the functions that are available in the ARTag Rev2 SDK. You are not likely to use these, but we'll mention them briefly here for sake of completeness. The functions are artag_ get_setting_repair_broken_border(), artag_set_setting_repair_broken_border(), artag_get_version(version_string), artag_get_object_type(), and artag_ remove_object_rotation(). The first two functions affect whether ARTag will detect markers with partial occlusion (that is, they are partially blocked or have a side or corner missing from the edge of the image). artag_get_version() gives you a string with the version and expiry date of the ARTag library. The function artag_get_object_type() is for future expansion. Research is being conducted with flexible and connected objects, as well as objects that can be constrained in some dimensions, such as a flame animation object like a medieval torch that always points up regardless of the rotation of the array.

The prototypes for these functions are as follows:

```
//broken border heuristics can repair broken marker border
// 1=enable/0=disable repairing incomplete marker borders (default=1)
char artag_get_setting_repair_broken_border(void);
void artag_set_setting_repair_broken_border(char setting);

//Read version information
void artag_get_version(char *str);

//-remove rotation of selected object, so X,Y,Z axis are
//aligned with virtual camera, useful
//for effects where you want a virtual object to move but
//not rotate, such as fire effects,
void artag_remove_object_rotation(int object_num);

//-find out whether object is a single marker, array,
//(or future expansion types)
//type=artag_get_object_type(object_num);
//0=single marker
//1=normal coordframe
int artag_get_object_type(int object_num);
```

The following function removes the rotation of an array's coordinate system so that it remains perpendicular to the camera's main axis.

This is useful for sprite "cardboard cutout" effects.

```
void artag_remove_object_rotation(int object_num);
```

6.16 Performance Issues

Depending on your image size and computer speed, the execution time taken by ARTag (in the artag_find_objects() function) may or may not pose a problem. As previously mentioned, if you use a grayscale image, then you'll shave off a few milliseconds. Also, if you can avoid having gridlike structures or a background with lots of polygonal objects, it will also save time since ARTag won't search them all to see whether they are valid markers.

However, the action with the largest effect is to use the artag_set_setting_use_full_res() function. ARTag does its image processing at three scale levels. It *de-rezs* (which is slang for reducing resolution) the image twice so it has a full-size, a half-size, and a quarter-size image to work with. You can save processing time by turning off the processing for the full-resolution image. If your image is blurry, then there may not be much image information at the full resolution anyway. You can test with the artag_viewer_*.exe programs and see the trade-off between how far away you are able to see the marker and the processing time in milliseconds per frame.

Here is the format, from artag_rev2.h, for these functions:

```
//1=use full resolution as well as half,
//quarter resolution  (default state)
//0=only process half, quarter resolution
//(faster but smaller markers will be missed)
char artag_get_setting_use_full_res(void);
void artag_set_setting_use_full_res(char setting);
```

Call artag_set_setting_use_full_res(0) to turn off full image processing. This should speed things up by a factor of 2 to 4. This improvement will be at the cost of possibly missing smaller markers.

6.17 Scale Issues with Array Dimensions

The physical size of one unit, in each array definition, must be the same so that the correct distance and scale allows the correct *occlusion* relationship. For example, if two arrays are printed so that they both have one centimeter for one array unit, then the virtual objects will correctly block one another. If this interaction is not important, then you can simply just scale the 3D models to the desirable size.

Correctly setting the scale of the arrays and 3D objects is important for three reasons:

- So that the 3D object is not too large or too small.
- It allows the relative depth of objects to be correct so that they pass in front of, behind, and through each other correctly.
- The X, Y, Z values projected between array objects using the artag_project_point() function will not be correct. But you don't need the same relative sizing if you know the scale factor between arrays.

If there won't be any interaction between objects rendered with different arrays, then the second point does not matter, like if you're using only one large array such as a tabletop scenario. Thus, if you have several arrays, you simply scale 3D objects to be the size you want to use. However, if you want correct depth performance, you need to consider the relative scale of units inside the arrays. Otherwise, when you pass one array in front of another, the wrong 3D object may be rendered in front. More complex interactions that require correct relative scale are, for example, a space shuttle docking at a space station and a handheld array with a virtual sword stabbing a virtual dragon (rendered relative to another array). In these cases, if the units in the array file are not the same between the physically printed out arrays, then the depth and the object intersection will not be correct. The space shuttle may appear behind the space station when it should be in front, or the sword may not correctly pierce the dragon.

Rendering the scale of an object correctly is a function of both the scale of the 3D model you're rendering and the scale of the array points in the array file. Each array in an array file is a set of the 3D coordinates storing the marker corners. The camera-array pose is calculated by the ARTag library, but the pose is in the units that the array is using. For example, the *base0* array spans plus/minus 80 units in the X and Y directions, meaning that it is 160 units wide. When this array is printed at full size on a letter-size 8.5" by 11" page, the pattern comes out 19.1 cm wide, giving us 1.19 mm/unit. The toolbars are 100 units long on the Y-axis, which was printed out 8.1 cm long, giving us 0.81 mm/unit—which is not the same.

The measurements must be to the outside corners of the markers themselves. The array ranges can be found either by manually inspecting

Figure 6.7: DEPTH ERROR WITH IMPROPERLY SCALED OBJECTS

the panel.cf file or by running the code in the next section. Rendering objects relative to these marker arrays will create errors in rendering depth (see Figure 6.7). Note how the fish and the can models should be intersecting the space station—instead they are behind. The toolbar with the fish has to be brought about 1/3 of the way closer toward the camera before the models start to intersect. This is because of the difference in the units in the coordinate systems.

To get the models to intersect or appear as you would expect, you need to print the patterns so that they have the same scale (see Figure 6.8, on the next page).

In the previous chapter, the artag_get_object_coordframe_range() function was introduced. This function provides the range of 3D coordinates within an array.

Figure 6.8: PROPERLY SCALED OBJECTS

Here is some example code that prints the extents of the arrays in the array file panel_set.cf to a file:

```
#define ARRAY_FILENAME "panel_set.cf"
int base_array_id,toolbar_array_id[16],pointer0_array_id,pointer1_array_id;

//load array file
if(load_array_file(ARRAY_FILENAME))
  printf("ERROR loading <%s>\n",ARRAY_FILENAME);
else
  printf("Loaded array file <%s>\n",ARRAY_FILENAME);

//associate objects with arrays in panel_set.cf
base_array_id=artag_associate_array("base0");
for(int i=0;i<16;i++)
{
  char toolbar_name[32];
  sprintf(toolbar_name,"toolbar%d",i);
  toolbar_array_id[i]=artag_associate_array(toolbar_name);
}
pointer0_array_id=artag_associate_array("pointer0");
pointer1_array_id=artag_associate_array("pointer1");
```

```
//print out range of array markers
float min_x,max_x,min_y,max_y,min_z,max_z;

FILE *rangefile=fopen("array_ranges.txt","wb");
artag_get_object_coordframe_range
    (base_array_id,&min_x,&max_x,&min_y,&max_y,
    &min_z,&max_z);
fprintf(rangefile,"base0 array: MIN,MAX X=%4.1f,%4.1f Y=%4.1f,
    %4.1f Z=%4.1f,%4.1f\n",min_x,max_x,min_y,max_y,min_z,max_z);

for(i=0;i<16;i++)
{
  artag_get_object_coordframe_range(toolbar_array_id
  [i],&min_x,&max_x,&min_y,&max_y,&min_z,&max_z);
  fprintf(rangefile,"toolbar%d array: MIN,MAX X=%4.1f,%4.1f Y=%4.1f,%4.1f
    Z=%4.1f,% 4.1f\n",i,min_x,max_x,min_y,max_y,min_z,max_z);
}

artag_get_object_coordframe_range(pointer0_array_id,&min_x,&max_x,
    &min_y,&max_y,&min_z,&max_z);
fprintf(rangefile,"pointer0 array: MIN,MAX X=%4.1f,%4.1f Y=%4.1f,%4.1f
    Z=%4.1f,% 4.1f\n",min_x,max_x,min_y,max_y,min_z,max_z);
artag_get_object_coordframe_range(pointer1_array_id,&min_x,&max_x,
    &min_y,&max_y,&min_z,&max_z);
fprintf(rangefile,"pointer1 array: MIN,MAX X=%4.1f,%4.1f Y=%4.1f,%4.1f
    Z=%4.1f,% 4.1f\n",min_x,max_x,min_y,max_y,min_z,max_z);
fclose(rangefile);
```

The output of this program is as follows:

```
base0 array: MIN,MAX    X=-80.0,80.0    Y=-80.0,80.0   Z= 0.0, 0.0
toolbar0 array: MIN,MAX    X= 0.0,40.0   Y= 0.0,100.0   Z= 0.0, 0.0
toolbar1 array: MIN,MAX    X= 0.0,40.0   Y= 0.0,100.0   Z= 0.0, 0.0
...
toolbar15 array: MIN,MAX   X= 0.0,40.0   Y= 0.0,100.0   Z= 0.0, 0.0
pointer0 array: MIN,MAX    X=-40.0,40.0  Y= 0.0,110.0   Z= 0.0, 0.0
pointer1 array: MIN,MAX    X=-35.0,35.0  Y= 0.0,110.0   Z= 0.0, 0.0
```

6.18 Automatically Sizing Augmentations to Array Size

When you load a model from a file, you may need to adjust the scale of how large it is rendered. If incorrect scaling issues don't affect your application, then you can just scale your 3D model to fit the extent of the array (that is, you are not going to have interactions between augmentations or have one appear in front of the other). This way you do not need to consider the scale of the model and the scale of the coordinates in the array definition. The artag_get_object_coordframe_range() function is used to scale the 3D models loaded in the 3d_magic_mirror\ project in the ARTag SDK. The following code demonstrates the use of the artag_get_object_coordframe_range() function—not with any 3D models but simply by drawing a wire-frame cube above all visible toolbars. You can see how you could scale your 3D objects with the glScale() function using the shorter of the two dimensions in the array.

In these code snippets, only the significant changes to ARTag_Get_Object_Coordframe_Range_Test.CPP from the OpenGL template program are shown (see Figure 6.9, on page 154).

Here is the beginning of the opengl_draw() function where you just draw the camera texture.

`OpenGL/artag_get_object_coordframe_range_test/artag_get_object_coordframe_range_test.cpp`

```
void opengl_draw(void)
{
glClear(GL_COLOR_BUFFER_BIT | GL_DEPTH_BUFFER_BIT | GL_STENCIL_BUFFER_BIT);

// draw a quad for the background video
glLoadIdentity();
glDisable(GL_LIGHTING);
glEnable(GL_TEXTURE_2D);
glBindTexture(GL_TEXTURE_2D, camera_texID);
glBegin(GL_QUADS);
glColor3f(1.0f, 1.0f, 1.0f);
//draw camera texture, set with offset to aim only at cam_width x cam_height
// upper left bit
//normal operation (magic mirror off)
if( mirror_on == 0 )  {
   glTexCoord2f(0.0f, (float)cam_height/1024.0);
   glVertex3f(camera_opengl_dLeft*1024, camera_opengl_dBottom*1024, -1024);
   glTexCoord2f(0.0f, 0.0f);
   glVertex3f(camera_opengl_dLeft*1024, camera_opengl_dTop*1024, -1024);
   glTexCoord2f((float)cam_width/1024.0, 0.0f);
   glVertex3f(camera_opengl_dRight*1024, camera_opengl_dTop*1024, -1024);
   glTexCoord2f((float)cam_width/1024.0, (float)cam_height/1024.0);
   glVertex3f(camera_opengl_dRight*1024, camera_opengl_dBottom*1024, -1024);
   glEnd();
}
//flip background image for "magic mirror" effect
else  {
   glTexCoord2f(0.0f, (float)cam_height/1024.0);
   glVertex3f(camera_opengl_dRight*1024, camera_opengl_dBottom*1024, -1024);
   glTexCoord2f(0.0f, 0.0f);
   glVertex3f(camera_opengl_dRight*1024, camera_opengl_dTop*1024, -1024);
   glTexCoord2f((float)cam_width/1024.0, 0.0f);
   glVertex3f(camera_opengl_dLeft*1024, camera_opengl_dTop*1024, -1024);
   glTexCoord2f((float)cam_width/1024.0, (float)cam_height/1024.0);
   glVertex3f(camera_opengl_dLeft*1024, camera_opengl_dBottom*1024, -1024);
   glEnd();
}
```

Now when you draw the base array, you first call the artag_get_object_
coordframe_range() function to give us the extents X, Y, and Z extents of
the array. You then use those extents to draw a wire-frame cube with
the OpenGL line-drawing commands.

OpenGL/artag_get_object_coordframe_range_test/artag_get_object_coordframe_range_test.cpp

```
//draw simple augmentations
if(artag_is_object_found(base_array_id)) {
  artag_set_object_opengl_matrix(base_array_id,mirror_on);

  float min_x,max_x,min_y,max_y,min_z,max_z;
  float delta_x,delta_y,height;
  atag_get_object_coordframe_range(base_array_id,&min_x,
    &max_x,&min_y,&max_y,&min_z,&max_z);
  delta_x=max_x-min_x;
  delta_y=max_y-min_y;
  //pick shorter length for box height
  height = (delta_y>delta_x) ? delta_x : delta_y;

  //draw lines along cube sides
  glColor3f(1, 0, 0);
  glBegin(GL_LINES);
    //vertical lines
    glVertex3f(min_x,min_y,0); glVertex3f(min_x,min_y,height);
    glVertex3f(min_x,max_y,0); glVertex3f(min_x,max_y,height);
    glVertex3f(max_x,min_y,0); glVertex3f(max_x,min_y,height);
    glVertex3f(max_x,max_y,0); glVertex3f(max_x,max_y,height);
    //bottom
    glVertex3f(min_x,min_y,0); glVertex3f(max_x,min_y,0);
    glVertex3f(min_x,max_y,0); glVertex3f(max_x,max_y,0);
    glVertex3f(min_x,min_y,0); glVertex3f(min_x,max_y,0);
    glVertex3f(max_x,min_y,0); glVertex3f(max_x,max_y,0);
    //top
    glVertex3f(min_x,min_y,height); glVertex3f(max_x,min_y,height);
    glVertex3f(min_x,max_y,height); glVertex3f(max_x,max_y,height);
    glVertex3f(min_x,min_y,height); glVertex3f(min_x,max_y,height);
    glVertex3f(max_x,min_y,height); glVertex3f(max_x,max_y,height);
  glEnd();
}
```

Next, the same is done for the toolbar arrays:

OpenGL/artag_get_object_coordframe_range_test/artag_get_object_coordframe_range_test.cpp

```
//draw quads on toolbars
for(int i=0 ; i<16 ; i++)
  if(artag_is_object_found(toolbar_array_id[i])) {
    artag_set_object_opengl_matrix(toolbar_array_id[i],mirror_on);

    float min_x,max_x,min_y,max_y,min_z,max_z;
    float delta_x,delta_y,height;
```

```
   atag_get_object_coordframe_range(toolbar_array_id[i],&min_x,
      &max_x,&min_y,&max_y,&min_z,&max_z);
   delta_x=max_x-min_x;
   delta_y=max_y-min_y;
   //pick shorter length for box height
   height = (delta_y>delta_x) ? delta_x : delta_y;

   //draw lines along cube sides
   glColor3f(0, 0, 1);
   glBegin(GL_LINES);
      //vertical lines
      glVertex3f(min_x,min_y,0); glVertex3f(min_x,min_y,height);
      glVertex3f(min_x,max_y,0); glVertex3f(min_x,max_y,height);
      glVertex3f(max_x,min_y,0); glVertex3f(max_x,min_y,height);
      glVertex3f(max_x,max_y,0); glVertex3f(max_x,max_y,height);
      //bottom
      glVertex3f(min_x,min_y,0); glVertex3f(max_x,min_y,0);
      glVertex3f(min_x,max_y,0); glVertex3f(max_x,max_y,0);
      glVertex3f(min_x,min_y,0); glVertex3f(min_x,max_y,0);
      glVertex3f(max_x,min_y,0); glVertex3f(max_x,max_y,0);
      //top
      glVertex3f(min_x,min_y,height); glVertex3f(max_x,min_y,height);
      glVertex3f(min_x,max_y,height); glVertex3f(max_x,max_y,height);
      glVertex3f(min_x,min_y,height); glVertex3f(min_x,max_y,height);
      glVertex3f(max_x,min_y,height); glVertex3f(max_x,max_y,height);
   glEnd();
   }

   glutSwapBuffers();
}
```

Similar code can be found in \Sample_projects\3d_magic_mirror\ 3d_augmentations.cpp in the ARTag SDK. A 3D model is scaled and translated to fit in a rectangular prism given by the limits of the array and a height created from the minimum length.

```
artag_get_object_coordframe_range(objec[object_num].artag_object_id,
      &min_x,&max_x,&min_y,&max_y,&min_z,&max_z);
//choose a good height - can't use z-range since coordframes are planar
float max_height=2.0*(max_x-min_x);
if(2.0*(max_y-min_y)<max_height)  max_height=2.0*(max_y-min_y);
meshman_fit_to_limits(object[object_num].meshman_model_num,
      min_x,max_x,min_y,max_y,0.0,max_height);
```

6.19 Using artag_project_between_objects

The artag_project_between_objects() function is useful for interactions between objects attached to different arrays. The following program demonstrates the mapping of a 3D point from the coordinate system

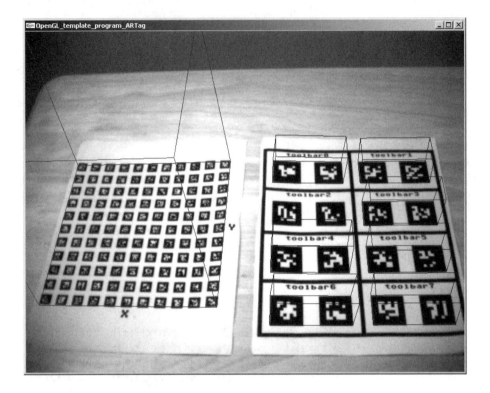

Figure 6.9: USING THE ARTAG_GET_OBJECT_COORDFRAME_RANGE() FUNCTION TO DRAW OUTLINES OF ARRAY BOUNDARIES

of one array into that of another. In this example, you extend a *pointer* line from the center of a toolbar out into space. You have a pie-shaped object with different sectors attached to *base0*. If the endpoint of the pointer line ends in the sector, it is colored red. As you saw earlier in this chapter, the relative scale of 1.47 mapping from the *base0* array to the *toolbar* arrays is 1.47. Since you are mapping in the other direction, you use the inverse: 0.68.

A screenshot of this example is shown in Figure 6.10, on the next page. The code is included at the end of this chapter. As usual, only the code that is added to the ARTag_Get_Object_Coordframe_Range_Test.CPP program is shown for Project_Points_Between_Arrays_Demo.CPP. Only the opengl_draw() function has new code.

Figure 6.10: THE PROJECT POINTS BETWEEN ARRAYS DEMO

Figure 6.10 demonstrates using the artag_project_between_objects()
function to project the endpoint of the red pointer emanating from the
toolbar array into the coordinate system of the *base0* array. The sector
where the pointer maps to is indicated in red.

This is the beginning of the opengl_draw() function:

OpenGL/project_points_between_arrays_demo/PROJECT_POINTS_BETWEEN_ARRAYS_DEMO.CPP

```
void opengl_draw(void)
{
glClear(GL_COLOR_BUFFER_BIT | GL_DEPTH_BUFFER_BIT | GL_STENCIL_BUFFER_BIT);

// draw a quad for the background video
glLoadIdentity();
glDisable(GL_LIGHTING);
glEnable(GL_TEXTURE_2D);
glBindTexture(GL_TEXTURE_2D, camera_texID);
glBegin(GL_QUADS);
glColor3f(1.0f, 1.0f, 1.0f);
```

```
//draw camera texture, set with offset to aim only at cam_width x cam_height
//upper left bit
//normal operation (magic mirror off)
if(mirror_on==0)  {
    glTexCoord2f(0.0f, (float)cam_height/1024.0);
    glVertex3f(camera_opengl_dLeft*1024, camera_opengl_dBottom*1024, -1024);
    glTexCoord2f(0.0f, 0.0f);
    glVertex3f(camera_opengl_dLeft*1024, camera_opengl_dTop*1024, -1024);
    glTexCoord2f((float)cam_width/1024.0, 0.0f);
    glVertex3f(camera_opengl_dRight*1024, camera_opengl_dTop*1024, -1024);
    glTexCoord2f((float)cam_width/1024.0, (float)cam_height/1024.0);
    glVertex3f(camera_opengl_dRight*1024, camera_opengl_dBottom*1024, -1024);
    glEnd();
}
//flip background image for "magic mirror" effect
else  {
    glTexCoord2f(0.0f, (float)cam_height/1024.0);
    glVertex3f(camera_opengl_dRight*1024, camera_opengl_dBottom*1024, -1024);
    glTexCoord2f(0.0f, 0.0f);
    glVertex3f(camera_opengl_dRight*1024, camera_opengl_dTop*1024, -1024);
    glTexCoord2f((float)cam_width/1024.0, 0.0f);
    glVertex3f(camera_opengl_dLeft*1024, camera_opengl_dTop*1024, -1024);
    glTexCoord2f((float)cam_width/1024.0, (float)cam_height/1024.0);
    glVertex3f(camera_opengl_dLeft*1024, camera_opengl_dBottom*1024, -1024);
    glEnd();
}
```

Next, the artag_project_between_objects() function is used to find where points in toolbar space correspond to points in *base0*. This is used to draw the lines emanating from the toolbar. The values of the endpoint of the pointer line are stored.

OpenGL/project_points_between_arrays_demo/PROJECT_POINTS_BETWEEN_ARRAYS_DEMO.CPP

```
//variables for endpoint of toolbar pointers in base0 space
double toolbar_px[12],toolbar_py[12],toolbar_pz[12];
bool toolbar_seen[12];

//clear flags for toolbar end
for(int i=0; i<12; i++ ) toolbar_seen[i]=false;

//draw pointer lines coming out of toolbars
for(i=0; i<16; i++ )
    if(artag_is_object_found(toolbar_array_id[i]))  {
        artag_set_object_opengl_matrix(toolbar_array_id[i],mirror_on);
        glColor3f(1, 0, 0);
        glBegin(GL_LINES);
            glVertex3f(20,100,0); glVertex3f(20,-50,0);
        glEnd();
```

```
    //map endpoint to pie -both toolbar and base0 must be seen
    if(artag_is_object_found(base_array_id))  {
      double px,py,pz;
      artag_project_between_objects(toolbar_array_id[i],0.68,
          base_array_id,20,-50,0,&px,&py,&pz);
      toolbar_px[i]=px; toolbar_py[i]=py; toolbar_pz[i]=pz;
      toolbar_seen[i]=true;
    }
  }
```

Finally, the stored endpoints are used to determine whether an end-point of any array lies within a pie slice. This controls whether it is red (to indicate that it is selected) or whether it is blue (meaning that it is unselected).

OpenGL/project_points_between_arrays_demo/PROJECT_POINTS_BETWEEN_ARRAYS_DEMO.CPP

```
//draw 12 pie slices
//draw either light blue or red if toolbar endpoints are near
 if(artag_is_object_found(base_array_id))  {
    artag_set_object_opengl_matrix(base_array_id,mirror_on);

    bool not_first_time=false;
    double radius=50.0;
    double last_x,last_y,last_angle;
    for(int slice_num=0;slice_num<=12;slice_num++)  {
      double angle=-2.0*M_PI/24.0+(double)slice_num*2.0*M_PI/12.0;
      double last_angle=-2.0*M_PI/24.0+(double)(slice_num-1)*2.0*M_PI/12.0;
      double x=radius*cos(angle),y=radius*sin(angle);
      bool pointer_in_slice=false;

    //see if any pointer endpoints end in pie slice, if so color=red
    for(int i=0;i<16;i++)
      if((toolbar_seen[i])&&(toolbar_pz[i]>=0)&&(toolbar_pz[i]<=30)) {
        double px=toolbar_px[i],py=toolbar_py[i];
        double rad=sqrt(px*px+py*py);
        double pointer_angle=atan2(py,px);
        if(pointer_angle<0) pointer_angle+=2.0*M_PI;
        if( (pointer_angle<=angle)&&(pointer_angle>=last_angle)
          &&(rad<=radius) ) pointer_in_slice=true;
      }
    if(pointer_in_slice) glColor3f(1,0,0);
    else  {
      //pie slice not selected, set color = a shade of blue
      float blue=1.0-0.2*(float)(slice_num%3);
      glColor3f(0.5,0.5,blue);
        }
```

```
        if(not_first_time)  {
          //draw pie wedge
          glBegin(GL_QUADS);
          glVertex3f(x,y,0);
          glVertex3f(last_x,last_y,0);
          glVertex3f(last_x,last_y,30);
          glVertex3f(x,y,30);
          glEnd();
          glBegin(GL_TRIANGLES);
          glVertex3f(x,y,30);
          glVertex3f(last_x,last_y,30);
          glVertex3f(0,0,30);
          glEnd();
        }
        last_x=x; last_y=y; last_angle=angle;
        not_first_time=true;
    }
  }

  glutSwapBuffers();
}
```

In this chapter, you learned how to use the ARTag library to create AR with OpenGL programs. You learned the minimal set of functions that are needed to get a program running: the initialization functions and the functions called for every camera and rendering frame. The initialization functions are init_artag(), load_array_file(), and artag_associate_array(). The artag_find_objects() function is called every camera frame. The artag_is_object_found() and artag_set_object_opengl_matrix() functions are called every time you render to the screen.

You also saw how the knowledge you acquired about OpenGL programming is easily applied to ARTag applications (that is, you are getting the ARTag library to set the virtual camera pose [the modelview matrix] for each array). You also learned that you can modify an existing OpenGL application to use ARTag simply by putting these two functions at the beginning of your rendering code (that is, in place of your initial camera pose–setting code). At the end of the chapter, you learned how to calibrate your camera so that your augmentations don't appear too stretched or squashed, and you also learned how to create ARTag markers. Have fun with your AR applications!

## Chapter 7

Model Loading and Rendering

In the previous chapters, you learned how to render 3D graphics using OpenGL, how to use the ARTag system to align the virtual camera to a real camera, and how to compile or run AR software on your computer. Based on this, you can now have a textured quad or two, some rectangular boxes, some spheres, and maybe a teapot appearing in your AR software creation. But you're probably wondering whether there is more to life. We're here to reassure you that there is.

The goal of this chapter is to get you to use typical video game design flow to create 3D models in a specialized 3D program and then import them into the AR program you're writing. In a game design studio, this work is typically divided into 3D artwork, 2D texture and background work, and game engine programming. This chapter may well be voted by readers as the least exciting, but if you want to learn how to load your own 3D models, it will be valuable to you.

As you read on, you will learn how to read in 3D textured models from files that you export from a 3D design package—such as 3D Studio Max, Softimage, Maya, or Cinema4D. You will also learn the type of data that a 3D model file must convey and how to parse it. Specifically, you will learn about Wavefront OBJ files and VRML 1.0 and 2.0.

If you use the source code provided in the ARTag downloads, you won't need to write any code to use the examples in this chapter. Specifically, you can use mesh_management.c and one of the 3D model parsing files (obj_parse.c, wrl_parse.c, or ase_parse.c). However, this code is not as developed as you may require, so you may need to write more for your application.

For example, the sample code does not use the OpenGL glDrawElements() function. glDrawElements() runs faster and saves memory but is harder to program.

7.1 A Textured Polyhedral Model

This book discusses the simple but prevalent form of 3D graphics composed of many polygons—usually triangles and quads—that have a 2D image texture stretched over them. These polygons may also use colors and normal vectors to add shading. This chapter will not cover *nonuniform rational basis spline* (NURBS) or other nonplanar graphics primitives. However, most modern 3D games out there use textured planar polygons—you're not missing a lot by sticking to a textured *polyhedral* model.

3D models are usually broken into meshes, especially if the model is large. Typically, there is only one texture image per mesh. A 3D model can be defined as a composition of one or more meshes, and each mesh can have only one texture associated with it. Therefore, a model using different bitmap textures must be broken into at least as many meshes.

So, what goes into a 3D model? Specifically, a model composed of planar polygons with 2D texture images stretched across them? More specifically, what goes into a mesh? If you don't have much experience with 3D file formats or haven't used the glDrawElements() function, you might provide a list such as this:

- A list of faces; each face contains the following:
  - A list of vertices; each vertex contains the following:
    * (x, y, z): The 3D coordinates of the vertex
    * (u, v): The 2D texture coordinates of this vertex
    * (n_x, n_y, n_z): The normal vector of this vertex, used for shading
  - The name of the texture image used for this face.
  - The color of this face, if the face is not textured. A polygon may also be shaded with a different color at every vertex.

This would not be an entirely unreasonable way to represent a 3D model, but you can more efficiently use memory and processing if you remove redundant information. Most models are a set of joined faces (that is, connected faces that share some of the same 3D vertices and 2D texture coordinates). For example, picture a terrain model of the ground composed of a stretched grid of quads.

In this scenario, you would repeat most of the 3D (x, y, z) and 2D (u, v) information four times.

As discussed in the glDrawElements section of Chapter 4, it's less wasteful to have parallel lists that repeat index numbers instead of all the vertex information. This method breaks down as follows:

- A list of faces; each face contains the following:
    - A list of indices to list 2 = 3D (x, y, z) coordinates—this is mandatory.
    - A list of indices to list 3 = 2D (u, v) coordinates—this is optional.
    - A list of indices to list 4 = 3D normal vectors (n_x, n_y, n_z)—this is optional.
    - A list of indices to list 5 = color values—this is optional.
- A list of 3D (x, y, z) vertex coordinates.
- A list of 2D (u, v) texture coordinates.
- A list of 3D (n_x, n_y, n_z) normal coordinates (a vector).
- A list of color components.

This new representation is far more efficient in cases where connected polygons share vertices. Instead of repeating data, you describe the 3D vertex information once and then repeat the index number that points to it. This provides a significant savings since you repeat one number (on most platforms, a short int is 2 bytes) rather than the entire vertex information, which is usually going to be on the order of 20 or 32 bytes. 3D coordinates are typically floating-point numbers of 4 bytes each (that is, 12 bytes). 2D texture coordinates also use 32-bit floats (4 bytes each) consuming 8 more bytes, and sometimes there is also a normal vector (which is 12 more bytes).

This more compact representation is used for storing models on a hard drive, but it is also used much of the time for storage within your program. This is true since you'll likely be using glDrawElements() most—if not all of the time—with large models.

To illustrate this point, take a look at this simple textured cube described in both of the methods that have been discussed. Figure 7.1, on the next page, shows a view of the 3D cube with the 3D vertex numbers labeled. This example has no color or normal vectors, but it has a texture bitmap applied to it (see Figure 7.2, on page 163). In Figure 7.2, on page 163, the faces are numbered in white, and the texture vertices are numbered in black.

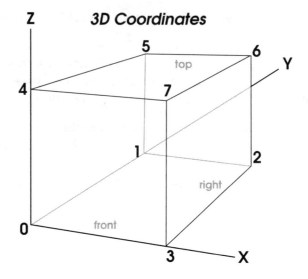

Figure 7.1: 3D CUBE WITH THE 3D VERTEX NUMBERS LABELED

Here is a 3D model, listed in the nonoptimal method:

```
Face #0:  vertex (0,0,0)   texture vertex (0.25,0.67) bottom face
          vertex (0,1,0)   texture vertex (0.25,1.0)
          vertex (1,1,0)   texture vertex (0.5,1.0)
          vertex (1,0,0)   texture vertex (0.5,0.67)
Face #1:  vertex (0,0,1)   texture vertex (0.25,0.33) top face
          vertex (0,1,1)   texture vertex (0.5,0.33)
          vertex (1,1,1)   texture vertex (0.5,0.0)
          vertex (1,0,1)   texture vertex (0.25,0.0)
Face #2:  vertex (0,0,0)   texture vertex (0.25,0.67) front face
          vertex (1,0,0)   texture vertex (0.5,0.67)
          vertex (1,0,1)   texture vertex (0.5,0.33)
          vertex (0,0,1)   texture vertex (0.25,0.33)
Face #3:  vertex (1,0,0)   texture vertex (0.5,0.67)  right face
          vertex (1,1,0)   texture vertex (0.75,0.67)
          vertex (1,1,1)   texture vertex (0.75,0.33)
          vertex (1,0,1)   texture vertex (0.5,0.33)
Face #4:  vertex (1,1,0)   texture vertex (0.75,0.67) back face
          vertex (0,1,0)   texture vertex (1.0,0.67)
          vertex (0,1,1)   texture vertex (1.0,0.33)
          vertex (1,1,1)   texture vertex (0.75,0.33)
Face #5:  vertex (0,1,0)   texture vertex (0.0,0.67)  left face
          vertex (0,0,0)   texture vertex (0.25,0.67)
          vertex (0,0,1)   texture vertex (0.25,0.33)
          vertex (0,1,1)   texture vertex (0.0,0.33)
```

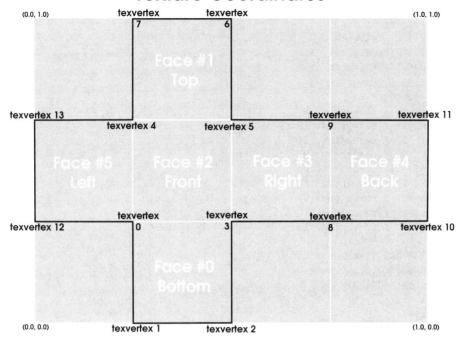

Figure 7.2: 3D TEXTURED CUBE

If you count the floating-point numbers in this example, you will see that you need the following: 6 faces × 4 vertices per face × 5 floats per face—with no normal vectors, this is 120 floats, or 480 bytes.

Here is the same model described using the indexed lists method:

```
List 1) - faces
Face #0:  bottom face
vertex 0  / texvertex    0
vertex 1  / texvertex 1
vertex 2  / texvertex 2
vertex 3  / texvertex 3
Face #1: top face
vertex 4  / texvertex    4
vertex 5  / texvertex    5
vertex 6  / texvertex    6
vertex 7  / texvertex    7
Face #2:  front face
vertex 0  / texvertex    0
vertex 3  / texvertex    3
```

```
vertex 7  / texvertex  5
vertex 4  / texvertex  4
Face #3:  right face
vertex 3  / texvertex  3
vertex 2  / texvertex  8
vertex 6  / texvertex  9
vertex 7  / texvertex  5
Face #4:  back face
vertex  2  / texvertex  8
vertex  1  / texvertex  10
vertex  5  / texvertex  11
vertex  6  / texvertex  9
Face #5:  left face
vertex  1  / texvertex  12
vertex  0  / texvertex  0
vertex  4  / texvertex  4
vertex  5  / texvertex  13

List 2) - 3D vertices
Vertex #0: (0,0,0)
Vertex #1: (0,1,0)
Vertex #2: (1,1,0)
Vertex #3: (1,0,0)
Vertex #4: (0,0,1)
Vertex #5: (0,1,1)
Vertex #6: (1,1,1)
Vertex #7: (1,0,1)

List 3) - 2D texture vertices
Texvertex #0: (0.25,0.67)
Texvertex #1: (0.25,1.0)
Texvertex #2: (0.5,1.0)
Texvertex #3: (0.5,0.67)
Texvertex #4: (0.25,0.33)
Texvertex #5: (0.5,0.33)
Texvertex #6: (0.5,0.0)
Texvertex #7: (0.25,0.0)
Texvertex #8: (0.75,0.67)
Texvertex #9: (0.75,0.33)
Texvertex #10: (1.0,0.67)
Texvertex #11: (1.0,0.33)
Texvertex #12: (0.0,0.67)
Texvertex #13: (0.0,0.33)
```

Note how list 1 has several different index types for each corner. Counting integers, which are only in list 1, you require the following: 6 faces $\times$ 4 vertices $\times$ 2 ints per face = 48 indices = 96 bytes. (Note that this is using 16-bit short integers, as is commonly done for these indices.) Counting floating-point numbers, we count lists 2 and 3. In this case, we need 6 vertices $\times$ 3 floats/vertex = 18 floats for list 2. We have 14 texture vertices (called *texvertexs*) in list 3, and each has 2 floats = 28 floats. So overall, we use 96 bytes + 42 floats, giving us a grand total of 264 bytes.

The previous example illustrated the concept of using indexed lists to represent 3D geometry and showed the resulting decrease in memory consumption. This particular example had only a modest size decrease: from 240/480 bytes down to 180/264. However, the savings are greater when you use larger meshes.

7.2 OBJ File Format: Sneak Peek

Now let's have a brief look at a Wavefront Object (OBJ) file format version for the cube. The OBJ format is a good example of indexed list storage—except that the data is switched around in a few ways.

Here is the cube in OBJ format:

```
mtllib cube.mtl
g default
v 0 0 -1
v 1 0 -1
v 1 0 0
v 0 1 0
v 0 1 -1
v 1 1 -1
v 1 1 0
v 0 0 0
vt  0.25 1.0
vt  0.5 1.0
vt  0.5 0.67
vt  0.25 0.33
vt  0.5 0.33
vt  0.5 0.0
vt  0.25 0.0
vt  0.75 0.67
vt  0.75 0.33
vt  1.0 0.67
vt  1.0 0.33
vt  0.0 0.67
vt  0.0 0.33
vt  0.25 0.67
s off
g Box01
usemtl initialShadingGroup
f 8/14 1/1 2/2 3/3
f 4/4 5/5 6/6 7/7
f 8/14 3/3 7/5 4/4
f 3/3 2/8 6/9 7/5
f 2/8 1/10 5/11 6/9
f 1/12 8/14 4/4 5/13
```

Take a look at the lines that begin with *v*, *vt*, or *f*—for now, ignore the other lines. The lines that begin with *v* are the 3D vertex coordinates, *vt* lines are texture coordinates, and *f* are the faces. Note that this is three sets of lists, with the *f* list indexing entries in the *v* and *vt* lists.

The *f* line type lists sets of index values. You'll see that we have six lines for six faces. Looking at the second *f* row, you see four groups of index pairs. The number before the forward slash is the 3D vertex index number, and the number after is the texvertex index number.

The data is a bit rearranged because OBJ files number the first element in a list 1; this is different from our example and VRML, which are zero-based. 3D vertex 0 is now put to the end of the list and called 8 so that we don't have to reorder the others; likewise, texvertex 0 is moved to the end and is called 14. This explains our first *f* row where 0/0 from our original list is replaced with 8/14. The nonzero elements line up with our example.

The second way our data is switched around a bit is that the Y and Z elements are switched, and the Z data is inverted. OBJ files use a different convention for what is up, and you need to rotate points around the X-axis to convert to your definition (where Z is up). For example, take this line:

```
v xfile yfile zfile
```

If you read off this line, then your xreal is xfile, your yreal is -zfile, and your zfile is yfile. When exporting a 3D model as an OBJ file, there is the option in programs such as Autodesk 3D Studio Max (3DSMax) to use rotated or *inverted* coordinates. For example, there is a checkbox for this setting in 3DSMax's export screen for OBJ files. The parsing code obj_parse.c provided in the ARTag download, and described later in this chapter, expects the data in the rotated/inverted convention; thus, we follow it for this example.

Figure 7.3, on the facing page, shows the cube rendered (left) and the bitmap image (right). Note that the bitmap is flipped vertically since OBJ files have the origin at the bottom left instead of the conventional upper right—this is the third data switcheroo.

7.3 Reorganizing a Model for Single Indices

There are a few things to note from our previous example. For example, the number of 3D and texture vertices is not the same. This may sound

 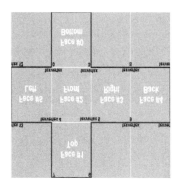

Figure 7.3: Cube rendered (left) and the bitmap image (right)

counterintuitive, but it is true for meshes that wrap around—such as a mesh that creates the surface of a solid object. Our example cube has eight 3D vertices, but the way the texture image is arranged, it has 14 texture vertices (see Figure 7.2, on page 163). If the faces were not partially joined in the texture image—if they were all freely floating and not connected—then there would be 6 faces × 4 vertex/face = 24 texture vertices. In general, a large sheet (that doesn't wrap around or have holes) can have the same number of 3D vertices as texture vertices, in the worst case.

The next section deals with the specifics of using OpenGL and how you ought to represent things in memory. When you read it, it's important to remember the mismatch between the number of 3D and texture vertices.

Note that you have two types of 3D points in your cube: those that are always associated with the same texvertex in all faces and those that are at points where the texture wraps around and are associated with different texvertices in different faces. We will call the first type *interior mesh points* and the latter type *boundary mesh points*. The 3D points 0, 3, 4, 7, 8, and 9 have a one-to-one mapping with texvertices 0, 3, 4, 5, 2, and 6, respectively—they are interior mesh points. Others do not follow this rule, such as 3D vertex 2, which is associated with texvertices 1, 11, and 12.

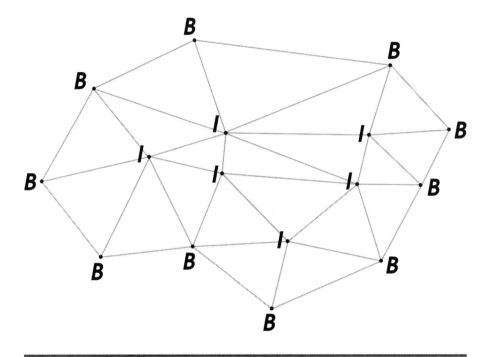

Figure 7.4: MESH WITH INTERIOR

Figure 7.4 shows an example mesh with interior (labeled with *I*) and boundary (labeled with *B*) mesh points. This diagram assumes that this mesh connects with other meshes on all sides so that the points labeled *B* will touch points from other meshes.

So far, we have only covered 3D vertices and 2D *texvertices*, but we will extend our definition of interior points to include cases with normal vectors and colors. We'll also label any points as interior points when all data is the same. In other words, an interior mesh point is one where all faces using a 3D vertex also use the same texture, normal vectors, and color.

This distinction is not important for the 3D model files that you'll read about here but needs to be considered when you arrange the data for rendering with OpenGL's glDrawElements() function.

7.4 More About OpenGL's glDrawElements

In the glDrawElements() section of Chapter 4, you learned about the OpenGL glDrawElements() function that enables efficient storage and rendering speed. Sometimes, it is the only function available in embedded systems (such as for portable platforms). In this chapter, you're going to stick to using glDrawElements() instead of the more introductory glBegin() and glEnd() functions.

In coming sections, you're going to load in the face index, 3D vertex, and store them as arrays in memory. Optionally, you can also load a texture vertex, a normal vector, and color lists. However, one drawback of using glDrawElements() is that there is only one index number per face corner, so you cannot point separately to the 3D vertex, texture vertex, normal vector, or color. This means the memory usage is not optimal since vertex information has to be repeated.

In the indexed mesh model from the previous section, list 1 has several different index types for each face corner. Therefore, you can't use this directly when using glDrawElements(). The only way to get around the issue is to break the boundary mesh points into several separate vertices—thus repeating the other attributes. This does waste memory space, so it detracts from some of the savings of the index method. However, in most large 3D models, the number of interior mesh points will greatly outnumber the boundary mesh points that you have to break up and repeat.

Unfortunately, the limitation of using glDrawElements() only with internal mesh points gives you more work to do when parsing a file. The extra work is checking each combination of attribute (3D coordinates, texture coordinates, normal vectors, and color) indices to see whether it has been used before. If it has not been used, you need to make a new entry in the attributes list.

For clarity, we're going to make up a new term: *meta-vertex*. A meta-vertex is a combination of all the attributes that can describe a vertex: 3D coordinates, texture coordinates, normal vectors, and color. Next, you're going to redo your lists using the meta-vertex concept. Please bear with the tediousness of these examples; it's important to have some concrete examples to allay confusion.

```
List 1) - faces
Face #0:  bottom face
meta-vertex 0        //the old vertex 0  / texvertex 0
meta-vertex 1        //the old vertex 1  / texvertex 1
meta-vertex 2        //the old vertex 2  / texvertex 2
meta-vertex 3        //the old vertex 3  / texvertex 3
Face #1: top face
meta-vertex 4        //the old vertex 4  / texvertex  4
meta-vertex 5        //the old vertex 5  / texvertex  5
meta-vertex 6        //the old vertex 6  / texvertex  6
meta-vertex 7        //the old vertex 7  / texvertex  7
Face #2:  front face
meta-vertex 0        //the old vertex 0  / texvertex  0
meta-vertex 3        //the old vertex 3  / texvertex  3
meta-vertex  14      //the old vertex 7  / texvertex  5
meta-vertex 4        //the old vertex 4  / texvertex  4
Face #3:  right face
meta-vertex 3        //the old vertex 3  / texvertex  3
meta-vertex 8        //the old vertex 2  / texvertex  8
meta-vertex 9        //the old vertex 6  / texvertex  9
meta-vertex  14      //the old vertex 7  / texvertex  5
Face #4:  back face
meta-vertex 8        //the old vertex  2  / texvertex   8
meta-vertex 10       //the old vertex  1  / texvertex  10
meta-vertex 11       //the old vertex  5  / texvertex  11
meta-vertex 9        //the old vertex  6  / texvertex   9
Face #5:  left face
meta-vertex 12       //the old vertex  1  / texvertex  12
meta-vertex 0        //the old vertex  0  / texvertex   0
meta-vertex 4        //the old vertex  4  / texvertex   4
meta-vertex 13       //the old vertex  5  / texvertex  13
```

You now have to repeat some 3D coordinates and add seven more entries to your 3D point list:

```
List #2) - 3D vertices
Vertex #0: (0,0,0)
Vertex #1: (0,1,0)
Vertex #2: (1,1,0)
Vertex #3: (1,0,0)
Vertex #4: (0,0,1)
Vertex #5: (0,1,1)
Vertex #6: (1,1,1)
Vertex #7: (1,0,1)
Vertex #8: (1,1,0)         //repeat of vertex 2
Vertex #9: (1,1,1)         //repeat of vertex 6
Vertex #10: (0,1,0)        //repeat of vertex 1
Vertex #11: (0,1,1)        //repeat of vertex 5
Vertex #12: (0,1,0)        //repeat of vertex 1
Vertex #13: (0,1,1)        //repeat of vertex 5
Vertex #14: (1,0,1)        //repeat of vertex 7
```

In this case, you had to add one more texvertex. For simplicity, we numbered the meta-vertices to match the first 14 texvertex numbers:

```
List #3) - 2D texture vertices
Texvertex #0: (0.25,0.67)
Texvertex #1: (0.25,1.0)
Texvertex #2: (0.5,1.0)
Texvertex #3: (0.5,0.67)
Texvertex #4: (0.25,0.33)
Texvertex #5: (0.5,0.33)
Texvertex #6: (0.5,0.0)
Texvertex #7: (0.25,0.0)
Texvertex #8: (0.75,0.67)
Texvertex #9: (0.75,0.33)
Texvertex #10: (1.0,0.67)
Texvertex #11: (1.0,0.33)
Texvertex #12: (0.0,0.67)
Texvertex #13: (0.0,0.33)
Texvertex #14: (0.5,0.33)          //repeat of texvertex 5
```

Now let's see this at work in a program. First, you will see the data from the latest representation put into the global variables cube_3d_vertex, cube_texvertex, and cube_indices. The index table has only one number for each corner; the attributes 3D vertex and texvertex lists have the same number of groups (15). The cube_3d_vertex list has 15 × 3 numbers since glVertexPointer() was called with its first parameter, 3. The cube_texvertex texvertex list has 15 × 2 numbers since glTexCoordPointer() was called with its first parameter, 2. Although the attribute lists need to have the same number of *groups*, the actual index list can be a different length. In your program, the pointer referenced in the call to glDrawElements() (cube_indices) has 24 indices.

Other than the arrangement of data in memory—statically defined global variables—the other important part of your example program is the following lines:

ModelLoading/cube_gldrawelements/cube_gldrawelements.cpp

```
//set up pointers and select texture
glEnableClientState(GL_VERTEX_ARRAY);
glEnableClientState(GL_TEXTURE_COORD_ARRAY);
glVertexPointer(3,GL_FLOAT,0,cube_3d_vertex);
glTexCoordPointer(2,GL_FLOAT,0,cube_texvertex);
glBindTexture(GL_TEXTURE_2D, cube_texID);

//set up coordinate system
glMatrixMode(GL_MODELVIEW);
glPushMatrix();
glTranslatef(25,25,0);
```

```
glRotatef(theta,0,0,1);
glTranslatef(-25,-25,0);
glScalef(50,50,50);

//call glDrawElements()
glDrawElements(GL_QUADS,24,GL_UNSIGNED_INT,cube_indices);
```

Notice that the coordinate system lines were not repeated.

Also notice how you tell OpenGL that you're going to use 3D vertex and texture vertex array pointers with the glEnableClientState() calls. You give it the attribute list pointers, with the glVertexPointer() and glTexCoordPointer() calls, before you add the call to glDrawElements() that draws the mesh. And, as you know by now, glDrawElements() is called with the index list. Figure 7.5, on the next page, shows a screenshot that demonstrates using array pointers (as with previous non-AR examples, the angle brace keys are used to rotate the model).

7.5 The OBJ File Format

Now let's dive into reading an actual Wavefront Object OBJ file into your programs. We're not going to discuss all the modes of OBJ files, just enough to get you going. Also, to simplify things, we're going to stick to one texture bitmap per OBJ file, and we're going to assume you have only positive index values (negative index values will be discussed later). In this program, we're also going to assume that the geometry is all triangles and that the texture is a PPM file.

The first thing to learn about OBJ files is that a complete model involves at least two files—three files if you have a bitmap texture. Figure 7.6, on the facing page shows the files you'll need for the Mrs. Gobble model. You'll need three files, the .obj file, the .mtl (*material*) file, and the actual texture that can be a JPG, BMP, or TGA image. OBJ and MTL files are created together when you export a model as a Wavefront OBJ file.

The OBJ file contains all the geometry, and the MTL file describes the materials. This includes the properties of the material, such as ambient, diffuse, and specular components. The OBJ file makes reference to an MTL file—if there are texture bitmap images. The MTL file references (by filename) one or more image files. In this example, there is only one image file. The arrows in Figure 7.6, on the next page, show the chain of files. A 3D model is usually referred to by the OBJ file because it is the first in the chain, and it holds all of the 3D geometry.

Figure 7.5: 3D VERTEX AND TEXTURE VERTEX ARRAY POINTERS

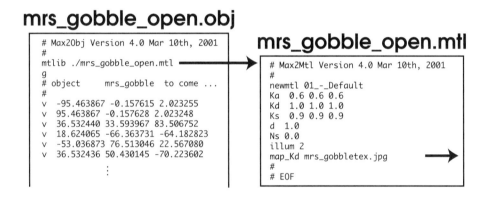

Figure 7.6: FILES YOU'LL NEED FOR THE MRS. GOBBLE MODEL

Both the OBJ and MTL files are ASCII text files, and both use the convention of # to denote the start of a comment line. When you parse an .mtl file, you can read the Ka, Kd, Ks, and other values for lighting-dependent rendering. However, we're going to use only the diffuse map_Kd property and will ignore the others. Therefore, we'll parse the MTL file looking only for the diffuse bitmap name with the map_Kd keyword.

The OBJ file contains all the geometry data (that is, the 3D vertex, normal vectors, and texture coordinates, as well as the index lists).

Here are some lines from mrs_gobble_open.obj:

```
# Max2Obj Version 4.0 Mar 10th, 2001
#
mtllib ./mrs_gobble_open.mtl
g
# object Mrs_Gobble to come ...
#
v  -95.463867 -0.157615 2.023255
v  95.463867 -0.157628 2.023248
v  36.532440 33.593967 83.506752
v  18.624065 -66.363731 -64.182823
v  -53.036873 76.513046 22.567080
.
.                 many vertex lines
.
v  79.375298 -50.379856 -15.024888
v  32.504337 109.442261 -22.071966
v  53.036877 -72.096077 35.568722
v  0.000002 -20.819765 95.224251
# 154 vertices

vt  0.315591 0.616357 0.999501
vt  0.600780 0.734480 0.382801
vt  0.315591 0.616357 0.999501
vt  0.068509 0.372733 0.195395
vt  0.981928 0.647565 0.999500
.
.               many texture coordinate lines
.
vt  0.981928 0.647565 0.999500
vt  0.981928 0.647565 0.999500
vt  0.981928 0.647565 0.999500
# 194 texture vertices

vn  0.000000 0.208260 -0.208260
vn  1.300735 -0.333096 -0.032807
vn  0.303316 0.385378 0.871483
.
.               many normal vector lines
.
vn  0.010549 0.902170 0.431251
vn  0.552676 -0.767289 0.325294
vn  -0.046327 -0.192125 0.980276
# 154 vertex normals

g Mrs_Gobble
usemtl 02_-_Default
s 1
f 134/162/134 78/103/78 95/122/95
f 90/115/90 73/99/73 116/142/116
f 79/104/79 53/72/53 153/183/153
```

Note that there are now three index integers separated by two slashes—instead of just two integers separated by one slash as in the cube model. There is one more attribute per vertex here, and this file also contains normal vectors. The first integer is the index to a 3D coordinate, the second to a texture vertex, and the third to a normal vector. In the next program, you will load but won't use the normal vectors. The normal vectors aren't necessary since you aren't setting up lighting.

Earlier in this chapter, you saw how lines beginning with v, vt, and f contain model data. Let's clearly define these line types:

- Each line starts with an ASCII character, or word, describing the line.
- Unlike C or C++ code, each line does not need a terminating character (such as ;).
- 3D vertex lines start with v and contain three floating-point numbers separated by spaces—in the order $X Z$ -Y (negative Y).
- Texture coordinate lines start with vt, followed by two or three floating-point numbers separated by spaces. We're dealing only with 2D textures, so we expect two floating-point numbers after the vt.
- Face index lines start with f and contain clusters of numbers with slash dividers. Each cluster is separated from the next with a space. These clusters contain as many numbers as attribute types. In cube.obj, we had only 3D coordinate data and texture coordinate data such that we had lines with two numbers per cluster separated by one slash (such as, "f 8/14 1/1 2/2 3/3") with two numbers per cluster. In mrs_gobble_open.obj, we have three numbers separated by two slashes because we also have normal vectors. The first number in a cluster in mrs_gobble_open.obj is the 3D coordinate, the second is the texture coordinate, and the third is the normal vector number.
- Indices in the f clusters point to the lines of attribute data in the order that they appear in the file. The first line is 1 instead of 0. For example, "f 79/104/66" says that this corner contains the 79th 3D coordinate line in this file, the 104th texture vertex coordinate, and the 66th normal vector.

Here are some more line types:

- Lines beginning with *mtllib* reference an .mtl file for the next mesh.

- Lines beginning with *g* denote the beginning of a mesh or beginning of a face index list—a name can follow that describes the following mesh. A file can contain several meshes, although we're going to ignore this keyword and assume we have only one mesh and one texture bitmap.
- Lines beginning with *usemtl* have a material name that also appears in the MTL file. Because of our assumptions, you can also ignore this line type.
- *S* lines are also ignored, as are comments.

Unfortunately, since you want to use the glDrawElements() function and you have both interior and boundary mesh points, you need to reorder this data in memory. To do this, you must convert these clusters of indices into single meta-vertex indices. Hence, you have some extra work to do. Since you want to conserve memory but still have your attribute lists line up, you need to look for previous combinations of a given cluster. This means that if you see a cluster "1/2/3" on an *f* line, you need to check whether you already have a meta-vertex that references 3D coordinate 1, texture coordinate 2, and normal vector 3. This way, you can avoid repeating the data.

You'll be using a temporary memory store for the attribute data that you free after you have loaded the file. The temporary memory store will contain your attribute lists. You don't know how large your file will be, so you will simply allocate 65536×2 or 3 floats for each list. You can use these numbers since we expect that short integers of 16 bits were used in generating this mesh. You will not do anything fancy such as using linked lists to allow you to load a file of unknown variable size. Let's chart a strategy for loading these single-mesh, single-texture models into memory:

1. Since the carriage return denotes the end of a section of data, you can simply load one ASCII line from the file at a time.
2. You start with empty attribute lists of 3D coordinate, texture coordinate, and normal vectors.
3. You will have two sets of data lists. One set is for temporary storage of the data as you load it from a file. The temporary data consists of 3D coordinate, texture coordinate, and normal vectors that you will load first when decoding *v*, *vt*, and *vn* lines. You transfer the data to a second set of lists that is used when you are actually rendering your data. The first set of lists will likely have a different number of elements in each list, whereas your second (permanent) lists will have the same number of meta-vertices with

corresponding members. The pointers to these permanent lists will be the ones used in the glVertexPointer(), glTexCoordPointer(), and glNormalPointer() function calls.

4. You will have two index lists. The first (temporary) list will simply store the ASCII cluster string, and the second (permanent) list will contain single integer elements (your meta-indices). The meta-indices will be the array used when you call glDrawElements().

5. You assume that all the attribute data (v, vt, and vn lines) will appear in the file before the f lines that reference them. When the f lines appear—carrying the meta-vertex indices—you will start populating your second, permanent set of aligned attribute data.

6. If a line starts with v, you take the subsequent three floating-point numbers and store them in a 3D coordinate list and increment your free 3D coordinate pointer.

7. If a line starts with vt, you take the subsequent two floating-point numbers, store them in a texvertex list, and increment your free texvertex pointer.

8. If a line starts with vn, you take the subsequent three floating-point numbers, store them in a normal vector list, and increment your free normal vector pointer.

9. If a line starts with f, you check each cluster (for example, 1/3/9 or 1/3) to see whether you have already assembled a meta-vertex for that combination. You will be comparing it to a temporary array of clusters kept in ASCII string form by simply doing a string compare operation.

10. If this string compare is successful, you will copy the existing meta-index number. If this cluster string is not found in your existing set, you will make a new entry in all your permanent attribute lists—pulling the appropriate attributes out of your temporary lists and copying their values. You then add the corresponding meta-index number to your final meta-index list.

11. After you reach the end of the file, you will destroy your temporary lists to free up memory.

Let's get down and code. You will use the fopen(), fgets(), and fclose() functions to access your file. Since OBJ files have data stored between carriage returns, you can use fgets() to retrieve an entire ASCII line. Note that your system may have a newer and safer version of fopen().

For easier reuse, you're going to put this all into a function—we'll call it load_model(). The function will take the filename, pointers to the attribute and meta-index lists, and a pointer to a string to hold the

PPM texture filename, and it will return the number of meta-vertices loaded. The function assumes that the pointers already have memory allocated to them. Let's set that up first. Note that we're limiting ourselves to 10KB vertex models, a reasonable assumption since we're also limiting ourselves to one texture per model.

ModelLoading/obj_gldrawelements/obj_gldrawelements.cpp

```
#define MAX_NUM_METAVERTICES 10000

// 3D/vertex
float model_3d_vertex[MAX_NUM_METAVERTICES *3];
// 2 texCoord/vertexfloat model_texvertex[MAX_NUM_METAVERTICES *2];
// 3 vector normal/vertex

float model_normal[MAX_NUM_METAVERTICES    *3];
// 3 indices/triangle
unsigned short int model_indices[MAX_NUM_METAVERTICES*3];
int model_num_metavertices;
```

Let's create some utility functions. We'll want to be case-insensitive, and we'll need to split up the cluster strings.

ModelLoading/obj_gldrawelements/obj_gldrawelements.cpp

```
//convert string to lower case
void lower_case(char *str)
{
    int i=0,diff='A'-'a';
    while((i<256)&&(str[i]!=0)) {
        if((str[i]>='A')&&(str[i]<='Z')) str[i]-=diff;
        i++;
    }
}

void split_cluster_string(char *in, int *vertex_num,
        int *texvertex_num, int *normal_num)
{
int i,num_slashes=0;
    for(i=0;i<(int)strlen(in);i++) if(in[i]=='/') num_slashes++;

    //the default is no data for each attribute type
    *vertex_num=-1; *texvertex_num=-1; *normal_num=-1;

    if(num_slashes==0) sscanf(in,"%d",vertex_num);
    else if(num_slashes==1)
        sscanf(in,"%d/%d",vertex_num,texvertex_num);
    else if(num_slashes==2)
        sscanf(in,"%d/%d/%d",
        vertex_num,texvertex_num,normal_num);
}
```

The load_model() function will be responsible for the file IO and will implement the design we have just laid out. It will create and destroy the temporary lists implicitly by having them as local variables in the function. In other words, their memory is freed just by leaving the function. One exception is *temp_cluster*, which is a large 2D array that we chose to explicitly declare (using malloc() and free()). Note that you're allocating more than a megabyte for this ASCII list alone. If you're working on a portable platform, or with little RAM, this is a piece of code that you'll want to change. Another important point is that you would want to allocate the temporary memory with new() or malloc(), instead of just declaring it on the stack as we're doing. Otherwise, this will cause a stack overflow with larger MAX_NUM_METAVERTICES settings.

ModelLoading/obj_gldrawelements/obj_gldrawelements.cpp

```cpp
unsigned short int load_model(char *obj_filename,
  float *vertex3d_list, float *texvertex_list,
  float *normal_list, unsigned short int *metaindex_list,
  char *ppm_filename)
{
  //our temporary 3D vertex storage list
  float temp_3d_xcoord[MAX_NUM_METAVERTICES];
  float temp_3d_ycoord[MAX_NUM_METAVERTICES];
  float temp_3d_zcoord[MAX_NUM_METAVERTICES];
  int num_temp_3d_coords=0;
  //our temporary 2D texvertex storage list
  float temp_texvertex_ucoord[MAX_NUM_METAVERTICES];
  float temp_texvertex_vcoord[MAX_NUM_METAVERTICES];
  int num_temp_texvertex_coords=0;
  //our temporary normal vector storage list
  float temp_normal_x[MAX_NUM_METAVERTICES];
  float temp_normal_y[MAX_NUM_METAVERTICES];
  float temp_normal_z[MAX_NUM_METAVERTICES];
  int num_temp_normals=0;
  //ascii cluster name storage
  char *temp_cluster[MAX_NUM_METAVERTICES];
  int num_temp_clusters=0;
  //output meta-indices
  int num_meta_vtx_indices=0;
  //meta_vertices
  int num_meta_vtxs=0;

  char mtl_filename[256]="";
  int i;
  FILE *objfile,*mtlfile;
  char line[256];
  float f1,f2,f3;
  char *token[8];
```

```
                  //allocate temporary cluster ASCII list
                  for( i=0; i<MAX_NUM_METAVERTICES; i++ )  {
                     temp_cluster[i]=(char*)malloc(20);
                     if(temp_cluster[i]==NULL)
                         {printf("ERROR mallocing temp_cluster\n");exit(1);}
                     strcpy(temp_cluster[i],"");
                  }

                  for( i=0; i<8; i++ )  {
                     token[i]=(char*)malloc(256);
                     if(token[i]==NULL) {printf("ERROR mallocing token\n");exit(1);}
                  }

                  objfile=fopen(obj_filename,"rb");
                  if(objfile==NULL) return -1;   //error code for problem loading file

                  //step through input file
                  while( fgets(line,256,objfile) != NULL)
                     if(line[0]!='#')  {  //skip comment lines
                        for( i=0; i<8; i++ ) strcpy(token[i],"");
                        int num_args=sscanf(line,"%s %s %s %s %s %s %s %s",token[0],token[1],
                            token[2],token[3],token[4],token[5],token[6],token[7]);
                        //turn to lower case and extract values
                        lower_case(token[0]); lower_case(token[1]); lower_case(token[2]);
                            lower_case(token[3]);
                        sscanf(token[1],"%f",&f1); sscanf(token[2],"%f",&f2);
                            sscanf(token[3],"%f",&f3);
                        //check first element on line for 'v', 'vt', 'vn', or 'f'.
                        //Ignore all other lines
                        if(strcmp(token[0],"v")==0)  {
                           //add to 3D coordinate list
                           temp_3d_xcoord[num_temp_3d_coords]=f1;
                           //rotate point about X-axis
                           temp_3d_ycoord[num_temp_3d_coords]=-f3;
                           //rotate point about X-axis
                           temp_3d_zcoord[num_temp_3d_coords]=f2;
                           num_temp_3d_coords++;
                        }
                        if(strcmp(token[0],"vt")==0)  {    //add to texvertex list
                           temp_texvertex_ucoord[num_temp_texvertex_coords]=f1;
                           //origin is in lower left
                           temp_texvertex_vcoord[num_temp_texvertex_coords]=1.0-f2;
                           num_temp_texvertex_coords++;
                        }
                        if(strcmp(token[0],"vn")==0)  {
                           //add to normal vector list
                           temp_normal_x[num_temp_normals]=f1;
                           temp_normal_y[num_temp_normals]=f2;
                           temp_normal_z[num_temp_normals]=f3;
                           num_temp_normals++;
                        }
```

```
        if(strcmp(token[0],"f")==0)  {
            if(num_args>4) num_args=4;  //limit the examination to four arguments
            for(int element=1;element<=num_args;element++)
                if(strlen(token[element])>0)  {
                    int this_meta_vtx_num=-1;
                    //for each cluster, see if string has been used before
                    for( i=0; i<num_meta_vtxs; i++ )
                    if(strcmp(token[element],temp_cluster[i])==0)
                    this_meta_vtx_num=i;  //match found
                    if(this_meta_vtx_num==-1)  {
                        int vnum,tnum,nnum;
                        //make new meta-vertex
                        split_cluster_string(token[element],&vnum,&tnum,&nnum);
                        vnum--; tnum--; nnum--;  //decrement since OBJ file starts at 1
                        if((vnum>=0)&&(vnum<num_temp_3d_coords))  {
                            vertex3d_list[num_meta_vtxs*3+0]=temp_3d_xcoord[vnum];
                            vertex3d_list[num_meta_vtxs*3+1]=temp_3d_ycoord[vnum];
                            vertex3d_list[num_meta_vtxs*3+2]=temp_3d_zcoord[vnum];
                        }
                        if((tnum>=0)&&(tnum<num_temp_texvertex_coords))  {
                            texvertex_list[num_meta_vtxs*2+0]=temp_texvertex_ucoord[tnum];
                            texvertex_list[num_meta_vtxs*2+1]=temp_texvertex_vcoord[tnum];
                        }
                        if((nnum>=0)&&(nnum<num_temp_normals))  {
                            normal_list[num_meta_vtxs*3+0]=temp_normal_x[nnum];
                            normal_list[num_meta_vtxs*3+1]=temp_normal_y[nnum];
                            normal_list[num_meta_vtxs*3+2]=temp_normal_z[nnum];
                        }
                        this_meta_vtx_num=num_meta_vtxs;
                        //add to ASCII list
                        strcpy(temp_cluster[num_meta_vtxs],token[element]);
                        num_meta_vtxs++;
                    }
                    metaindex_list[num_meta_vtx_indices++]=this_meta_vtx_num;
                }
        }
        //reference to MTL file
        if(strcmp(token[0],"mtllib")==0) strcpy(mtl_filename,token[1]);
    }
fclose(objfile);

//free temporary memory
for( i=0; i<MAX_NUM_METAVERTICES; i++ )
    if(temp_cluster[i]!=NULL) free(temp_cluster[i]);

//parse MTL file to find texture filename
strcpy(ppm_filename,"");
mtlfile=fopen(mtl_filename,"rb");
if(mtlfile==NULL) return -1;        //error, MTL file can't be loaded
while( fgets(line,256,objfile) != NULL)
    if(line[0]!='#')  {  //skip comment lines
```

```
    char arg0[256]="",arg1[256]="",arg2[256]="",arg3[256]="";
    char arg4[256]="",arg5[256]="",arg6[256]="",arg7[256]="";
    int num_args=sscanf(line,"%s %s %s %s %s %s %s %s",
        arg0,arg1,arg2,arg3,arg4,arg5,arg6,arg7);
    //turn to lower case and extract values
    lower_case(arg0); lower_case(arg1);
    if(strcmp(arg0,"map_kd")==0) strcpy(ppm_filename,arg1);
  }
 fclose(mtlfile);

 return num_meta_vtx_indices;
}
```

Have a look through load_model(), and you will see that there are actually two file-parsing blocks: a large one for the OBJ file and a smaller one for the MTL file. You need to parse the OBJ file first to find out what the filename is for the MTL file. You use fgets() to read in lines one at a time from the file. The lines are then split into shorter strings (either token or arg) by the sscanf() function. Each shorter string (token[i] in the OBJ parsing; arg0-7 in the MTL parsing) is converted to lowercase using the lower_case() function. When parsing the OBJ file, you fill up the temporary attribute lists, and when the f index lines appear, you break up the ASCII cluster strings into a set of numbers using your split_cluster_string() function.

The load_model() function is called once in the setup (in main()). If the loading was successful and the texture filename is found, then the texture is loaded.

ModelLoading/obj_gldrawelements/obj_gldrawelements.cpp

```
//load 3D model
model_num_metavertices=load_model("mrs_gobble_open.obj",
  model_3d_vertex,model_texvertex,model_normal,
  model_indices,model_texture_filename);

if((model_num_metavertices>0)&&(strlen(model_texture_filename)>0))  {
  //load bitmap texture
  texpgm=texture_read_ppm(model_texture_filename,&width,&height);
  if(texpgm!=NULL)
  glTexImage2D(GL_TEXTURE_2D, 0, GL_RGB, width, height, 0,
      GL_RGB, GL_UNSIGNED_BYTE,texpgm);
    else printf("Couldn't load %s\n",model_texture_filename);
}
```

load_model() puts the data into the global variable arrays that are referenced in the setup and call of glDrawElements(). On the next page is the opengl_draw() function.

ModelLoading/obj_gldrawelements/obj_gldrawelements.cpp

```
void opengl_draw(void)
{
  glClear(GL_COLOR_BUFFER_BIT | GL_DEPTH_BUFFER_BIT
    | GL_STENCIL_BUFFER_BIT);
  glEnable(GL_TEXTURE_2D);

  //set up pointers and select texture
  glEnableClientState(GL_VERTEX_ARRAY);
  glEnableClientState(GL_TEXTURE_COORD_ARRAY);
  //glEnableClientState(GL_NORMAL_ARRAY);
  glVertexPointer(3,GL_FLOAT,0,model_3d_vertex);
  glTexCoordPointer(2,GL_FLOAT,0,model_texvertex);
  glNormalPointer(3,0,model_normal);
  glBindTexture(GL_TEXTURE_2D, model_texID);

  //set up coordinate system
  glMatrixMode(GL_MODELVIEW);
  glPushMatrix();
  glTranslatef(25,25,0);
  glRotatef(theta,0,0,1);
  glScalef(0.3,0.3,0.3);

  //call glDrawElements()
  glDrawElements(GL_TRIANGLES,model_num_metavertices,
    GL_UNSIGNED_SHORT,model_indices);

  glPopMatrix();
  glutSwapBuffers();
}
```

Note that translate, rotate, and scale (TRS) are done to put the model at a scale we can see. If you make your own 3D model, you may have to change the scale value so that the model is the right size for your needs. As with the previous program in this chapter, the rendering is done from a fixed viewpoint (no video and no AR), and you can rotate the model with the angle braces keys. The modelview matrix is set once in the initialization and stored and retrieved every render frame with the push and pop functions.

Two good exercises for you, the developer, would be to load your own model into this program and to convert this program to run with AR. Keep in mind that you may have to change the bitmap texture to a PPM file and change its reference in the MTL file to work with this program. Try to make a program that uses a different OBJ file attached to each of the toolbars, as with 3d_augmentations.exe (aka 3d_magic_mirror.exe and 3d_magic_lens.exe).

Here are some closing notes on OBJ files. The format has more potential than we are considering, so don't expect this sample code to load all OBJ files, especially those with more than 10,000 attribute elements or those with more than one texture bitmap. A fully implemented OBJ parser would also handle multiple meshes and handle the negative index values that can appear. (Negative index values count backward into a previous mesh.) The OBJ_PARSE.C file that comes in the include\ directory of the ARTag SDK downloads handles larger models, loads separate meshes, and handles negative indexing. It is, however, not a full implementation, so it will not load some OBJ files. The goal of this chapter, and the code supplied in the SDK download, is to cover the majority of cases and to help you get your first applications running.

7.6 highgui: Reading JPEG, BMP, and TGA Textures

The previous example programs require that the texture image is in PPM format. This makes it easy for you to write code to load the file since it's basically just an uncompressed byte stream. But PPM is not the mainstream format for 3D models. Likely, the bitmap is going to be in a different format—such as JPG or TGA. Learning the JPEG standard and writing parsers for JPG files is not an undertaking to consider lightly—to explain it here would likely double the length of this book. If you use JPG files, you'll want to take some existing code off the shelf.

One convenient choice is the highgui library from OpenCV. OpenCV stands for *open computer vision*, and it is a library created by Intel to help the computer vision community. Amidst all the OpenCV functions for image processing, there are those to load and save image files. For example, you can make use of the cvLoadImage() image-loading function. To use this function, you'll need to include cv.h and highgui.h (and, if you're on Windows, link in highgui.lib). If you don't have them on your machine, these files can be found from various sources on the Web— just search for the keyword *OpenCV*.

Here are some lines you can add to your code to load JPG, BMP, and TGA (and some other) bitmaps. Note that we flip red and blue color elements to make them match the ordering when we load them into OpenGL textures. This must be done because when you have an uncompressed image, you usually just have a long linear spew of pixels as byte values. But when you have color, there are different conventions for how to list the bytes. Usually three bytes in a row contain a byte for the red, green, and blue, respectively. PPM files stored on disk and OpenGL expect different conventions, so we need to ensure that they match when we load them into textures.

```
#include "cv.h"
#include "highgui.h"
IplImage *opencv_temp;
opencv_temp=cvLoadImage(filename, 3);   //load as RGB
if(opencv_temp==NULL)
     printf("WARNING: Can't load %s\n",filename);
else
{
     int j;
     temp=(unsigned char*)opencv_temp->imageData;

     image_width=opencv_temp->width;

     image_height=opencv_temp->height;

     //flip R,B colours

     for(j=0;j<image_width*image_height*3;j+=3)

     {
        unsigned char red=temp[j+2],blue=temp[j+0];
        temp[j+0]=red; temp[j+2]=blue;
        }
}
```

7.7 VRML Files

Many of the file formats in the world are ASCII text formats. This is true not only in computer graphics but also in other disciplines that need to convey large amounts of data such as very-large-scale integration (VLSI)—which is used in silicon computer chip design and bioinformatics. Using text files may seem like a throwback to older days, or an inefficient use of space, but ASCII text files are truly platform independent and are open to less ambiguities, and you can easily view and edit the data with a common text editor. Binary file formats are usually proprietary and often have problems porting between different platforms, or even between programs written on the same platform with different compilers. For example, when entire chunks of memory are moved between memory and disk according to the memory storage conventions (such as word or long word alignment of struct elements), they may not line up between writing and reading the files. OBJ and VRML files fit into the category of files stored in ASCII format.

Another common 3D format is Virtual Reality Modeling Language (VRML), which was an attempt to create a 3D model equivalent of the Web's Hypertext Markup Language (HTML). The format suffered from intense debate during its creation. Consequently, there is more than one VRML format, and as many standards unfortunately end up, it has several different modes. The format is quite verbose and very flexible. VRML files contain more than just 3D geometry; they can contain lighting, animations, or text. It would be a multiyear effort to fully rewrite a VRML loader. That said, a subset of it is usable in 3D graphics programming. If you assume certain limitations, you can write a parser to just grab out the data you want and ignore the other keywords. Note that VRML files have a .wrl suffix.

There are VRML 1.0 and VRML 2.0 formats and X3D (http://www.web3d.org/x3d/) formats. We're going to look at a VRML 2.0 file:

```
#VRML V2.0 utf8
# 14002 vertices, 6003 triangles.

Transform { children [
    WorldInfo {   title "VRML 2 example"
    }
Viewpoint {
  position 37.499 82.4879 330.762
  orientation 0 0 1 0
}
NavigationInfo {
  avatarSize     [ 0.25, 1.6, 0.75 ]
  headlight      TRUE
  speed          5.0
  type           "EXAMINE"
  visibilityLimit 0.0
}
# Block 1
Shape {
    appearance Appearance { material
    Material {
    diffuseColor  0.8 0.8 0.8
    transparency 0
}
texture ImageTexture {
    url [ "texture_image.png" ]
  } }
geometry IndexedFaceSet {
coord
    Coordinate {
        point [   10.9876 41.0421 39.4186,
                  51.8121 43.5035 41.9862,
                  12.2345 39.6249 41.5279,
```

```
                    39.2457 41.3509 67.9943,
                    41.0147 38.5206 64.8677,
                    40.9971 41.2337 63.8268,
                          .
                          .
                          .
                    66.0233 124.751 48.5233,
                    91.2818 123.354 48.326 ]
              }
colorPerVertex FALSE
normal
Normal {
        vector [  0.789837 -0.114238 0.602584,
                  0.772743 0.0595989 0.631914,
                  0.854874 -0.00731004 0.518785,
                     .
                     .
                     .
                  0.97214 0.21904 -0.0834573,
                  0.969183 0.208614 -0.131014 ]
}
texCoord
        TextureCoordinate {
                point [   0.895508 0.69043,
                          0.895508 0.706055,
                          0.879883 0.69043,
                             .
                             .
                             .
                          0.99707 0.995117,
                          0.99707 0.999023 ]
                }
                coordIndex [0, 1, 2, -1,
                        3, 4, 5, -1,
                        6, 7, 8, -1,
                             .
                             .
                             .
                        15004, 15005, 15003, -1,
                        15006, 15007, 15003, -1 ]
                }
        }
    ] }
# End of file
```

One thing to note is that this file format, unlike OBJ files, does not separate data with carriage returns. Instead, similar to C or C++, it uses whitespace and braces. You'll need to find, or write, a function to pull out nonwhitespace strings of characters. In other words, you can't just use fgets() and work on a line-by-line basis.

Now that you have learned the concepts of indexed lists, you are able to make educated guesses about how to parse the file. First, you can see that the 3D coordinate attributes come in a list started by coordinate and point. This list is contained within square braces. Each X, Y, and Z value is separated by whitespace, and points are separated by commas. Likewise, texture vertices are similarly separated by whitespace and commas inside a point [] structure, but the point keyword follows a TextureCoordinate keyword instead. Normal vectors start with a Normal keyword but have their data contained within a vector [] structure. The meta-indices are listed after the coordIndex keyword—within square braces. The integers are separated by commas. Each attribute list has the same number of elements, and there is only one index number per corner. The data is already arranged in the meta-vertex format and does not need a temporary buffer. Finally, the texture bitmap filename can be found by looking for the ImageTexture keyword.

This example used a single large mesh; if you look at other VRML 2.0 files, you'll see several smaller meshes with different materials. Unless you stick with files from a controlled source, where you expect this format, you need to extend the memory model to have more than one mesh per object.

You can write your own parser looking for these keywords and then loading the data that you expect. It's a bit unsettling to simply ignore the other keywords and hope for the best, but it's an acceptable hack in the spirit of getting things going in a reasonable timeframe.

Similar to obj_parse.c, there is a wrl_parse.c file in the ARTag SDK download. Like the OBJ parser, it is more complex than what we have discussed in this chapter, but not a complete implementation of the standard.

If you enjoy seemingly endless and intricate file formats, you should have a look at the ASE format—another ASCII export option from 3DS-Max. The SDK download also contains an ase_parse.c file for handling these files.

7.8 Using ARTag's Mesh Manager

The *Mesh Manager* is a set of functions that your programs can use for handling 3D model files and managing memory. It also provides functionality for loading, storing, and rendering 3D textures model files. Each file contains a set of functions that you can use by including them in the top of your program (so that header files and prototypes are not needed). These four files from the ARTag SDK download constitute the Mesh Manager:

- mesh_management.c stores and renders 3D models in a mesh-based format.

- obj_parse.c loads OBJ files into the mesh_manager.

- wrl_parse.c loads VRML 1.0 and 2.0 files into the mesh_manager.

- ase_parse.c loads ASE files into the mesh_manager.

The Mesh Manager does not use the glDrawElements() function; it uses the less efficient glBegin() and glEnd() function calls instead. Upgrading it could be a good programming project for you.

Here are some excerpts from the 3d_augmentations.cpp file in the sample project directory of the download. First let's look at the include files. These include OpenCV's highgui for handling the JPG, BMP, and TGA bitmaps and the mesh_manager files. Note that you could save on the size of your executable if you include only the file format parser you plan to use.

`IntroARProg/3d_augmentations/3d_augmentations.cpp`

```
//use OpenCV highgui to load images other than PPM,PGM
#define USE_HIGHGUI
//un-define (comment out #define line) if
//you don't have or want to use OpenCV

#ifdef USE_HIGHGUI
 #include "cv.h"
 #include "highgui.h"
#endif

// The following 4 .C files were written by myself
//to help you develop AR apps, feelmfree to modify and
//improve them, or make new ones yourself.  They are n
#define OPENGL_PROJECT
//basic mesh library for manipulating and rendering meshes
#include "mesh_management.c"
//for parsing .ASE files (export option from 3D-Studio)
#include "ase_parse.c"

//for parsing .OBJ/.MTL Wavefront files from Maya
//#include "obj_parse.c"
//for parsing VRML files - basic and not complete coverage
//of the VRML standard!  Alternatively, Coin3d is recommended.
#include "wrl_parse.c"
```

The next code snippet shows the loading of model files—the model file-names have already been loaded into the model_filename element of the object structure. Note that this is part of 3d_augmentations.cpp, not mesh_manager. The suffix is separated from the filename, and according to the suffix, the correct file parser will be used. This code snippet is from the initialization code in main().

`IntroARProg/3d_augmentations/3d_augmentations.cpp`

```
for(object_num=0;object_num<objects_loaded;object_num++)  {
     char root[256],suffix[256];
     int num_meshes,num_vtxs,num_triangles,num_normals,bitmaps_loaded;

string_split_filename(object[object_num].model_filename,root,suffix);
//according to file type, import file - use #def's to determine
//what was compiled in
lower_case(suffix);
printf("Loading 3D '%s' type file <%s>\n",suffix,
     object[object_num].model_filename);
if(strcmp(suffix,"mesh")==0)
object[object_num].meshman_model_num=mesh_management_read_mesh(
     object[object_num].model_filename,
     MAX_EXPECTED_MATERIALS,&num_meshes,&num_vtxs,&num_triangles,
     &num_normals,&bitmaps_loaded);
#ifdef _WRL_PARSE_C_
if(strcmp(suffix,"wrl")==0)
     object[object_num].meshman_model_num=wrl_parse(
     object[object_num].model_filename,
     MAX_EXPECTED_MATERIALS,&num_meshes,&num_vtxs,&num_triangles,
     &num_normals,&bitmaps_loaded);
#endif
#ifdef _ASE_PARSE_C_
if(strcmp(suffix,"ase")==0)
     object[object_num].meshman_model_num=ase_parse(
     object[object_num].model_filename,
     MAX_EXPECTED_MATERIALS,&num_meshes,&num_vtxs,&num_triangles,
     &num_normals,&bitmaps_loaded);
#endif
#ifdef _OBJ_PARSE_C_if(strcmp(suffix,"obj")==0)
     object[object_num].meshman_model_num=obj_parse(
     object[object_num].model_filename,
     MAX_EXPECTED_MATERIALS,&num_meshes,&num_vtxs,&num_triangles,
     &num_normals,&bitmaps_loaded);
#endif
     }//for(object_num=0;object_num<objects_loaded;object_num++)
```

Now that the models are loaded into memory, let's render them. Here is a simplified version of the opengl_draw() function. This code shows the modelview matrix being set with ARTag for each image frame. You can ignore some of the extra details such as the potential mirroring of the display image (for magic mirror vs. magic lens systems) and the automatic resizing and rotation removal options.

```cpp
void opengl_draw(void)
{
    int object_num;

    glClear(GL_COLOR_BUFFER_BIT | GL_DEPTH_BUFFER_BIT | GL_STENCIL_BUFFER_BIT);

    //turn off back face culling for camera texture
    glDisable(GL_CULL_FACE);

    // draw a quad for the background video
    glLoadIdentity();
    glDisable(GL_LIGHTING);
    glEnable(GL_TEXTURE_2D);
    glBindTexture(GL_TEXTURE_2D, camera_texID);
    glBegin(GL_QUADS);
    glColor3f(1.0f, 1.0f, 1.0f);
    //draw camera texture, set with offset to aim only at cam_width x
    //cam_height upper left bit
    //assign texture coordinates according to mirror mode so that
    //video is flipped or un-flipped
    if(mirror_on==0)  {
        //normal operation (magic mirror off)
        glTexCoord2f(0.0f, (float)cam_height/1024.0);
        glVertex3f(camera_opengl_dLeft, camera_opengl_dBottom, -1024);
        glTexCoord2f(0.0f, 0.0f);
        glVertex3f(camera_opengl_dLeft, camera_opengl_dTop, -1024);
        glTexCoord2f((float)cam_width/1024.0, 0.0f);
        glVertex3f(camera_opengl_dRight, camera_opengl_dTop, -1024);
        glTexCoord2f((float)cam_width/1024.0, (float)cam_height/1024.0);
        glVertex3f(camera_opengl_dRight, camera_opengl_dBottom, -1024);
    }
    else {
        //flip background image for "magic mirror" effect
        glTexCoord2f(0.0f, (float)cam_height/1024.0);
        glVertex3f(camera_opengl_dRight, camera_opengl_dBottom, -1024);
        glTexCoord2f(0.0f, 0.0f);
        glVertex3f(camera_opengl_dRight, camera_opengl_dTop, -1024);
        glTexCoord2f((float)cam_width/1024.0, 0.0f);
        glVertex3f(camera_opengl_dLeft, camera_opengl_dTop, -1024);
        glTexCoord2f((float)cam_width/1024.0, (float)cam_height/1024.0);
        glVertex3f(camera_opengl_dLeft, camera_opengl_dBottom, -1024);
    }
    glEnd();
```

```
//enable back face culling - set CW,CCW definition of a front face
//according to mirror mode so that wrong face won't be rendered
//in mirror mode
if(mirror_on==0) glFrontFace(GL_CCW);
else  glFrontFace(GL_CW);
glEnable(GL_CULL_FACE);  //turn off back face culling for camera texture

//draw objects: see if their marker or array is visible, set OpenGL matrix,
//and render
for(object_num=0;object_num<objects_loaded;object_num++)  {
   if(object[object_num].valid)  {
      int artag_object_id=object[object_num].artag_object_id;
      if(artag_is_object_found(artag_object_id))  {
         //optional disabling of object rotation
         if(object[object_num].no_rotate)
           artag_remove_object_rotation(artag_object_id);

         //set MODELVIEW matrix from camera pose
         int artag_object_id=object[object_num].artag_object_id;
         artag_set_object_opengl_matrix(artag_object_id,mirror_on);

         //adjust object-dependent OpenGL parameters
         if(object[object_num].render_with_lighting_on)
             glEnable(GL_LIGHTING);
         else
             glDisable(GL_LIGHTING);
         // render world objects
         meshman_render_opengl(object[object_num].meshman_model_num,1,0);
      }
   }
}

glutSwapBuffers();
```

The big thing to note in this code is the meshman_render_opengl() function. This function simply renders the model for you. You just need to provide it with a handle number (obtained from the original parse file function calls) and some options. It is assumed that you have set the modelview matrix, with translation, rotation, and scale operations for a non-AR application, or you are using the ARTag modelview pose setting function artag_set_object_opengl_matrix().

7.9 Conclusions

Congratulations if you made it through all, or most, of the material in this chapter. Because of the unfortunate complexities of the 3D files formats and the necessity to reorganize the data, it required more convoluted programming and data handling than previous chapters.

In this chapter, you learned the benefits of storing 3D geometry data for models in separate lists with integer indices to reference them. You learned how a vertex inside a model has the attributes of 3D coordinate data (three floating-point numbers) and may also have texture vertex data (two floating-point numbers), normal vector data for lighting (three floating-point numbers), and color data. You also learned the convention of separating them into different lists and referring to them by index instead of their absolute values.

Furthermore, you learned that the optimal solution is to avoid repeating any data and for every vertex in the model to have separate indices for each attribute. You also learned that some formats repeat some data—such as how the memory must be set up for OpenGL's efficient glDrawElements(). glDrawElements() requires that all the lists have their elements lined up so that only one integer (which we called a *meta-vertex index*) can reference all of the attribute types. The concept of what we termed *internal mesh points* and *boundary mesh points* shows the difference between model vertices that need to repeat data and those that don't. You also saw how the boundary points take away a bit from the data savings that the index methodology gives, and you also suffered through a complex function load_model() that performed the reordering for OBJ files.

You were also introduced to a functional subset of Wavefront Object files (with .obj suffixes) and VRML 2.0 files (.wrl) and loaded a model from an OBJ file into a memory structure that glDrawElements() can render. And you learned how to use the Mesh Manager functions to save some of this programming work.

In summary, this chapter gave you the capability of loading complex 3D models that can be found on the Web or exported from popular 3D design packages such as 3DSMax, Softimage, Maya, and Cinema4D. Note that we did not cover the full standard for modeling formats, only enough to allow you to read in 3D textured geometry. Now you are able to use the typical game or animation design flow: creating content in external 3D and 2D programs, programming the behavior and interactions, and using the graphics acceleration of OpenGL to render your content.

Chapter 8

Your Own AR Game

Now that you understand AR, OpenGL, and ARTag, you've seen how to load 3D models, and you have some experience developing AR applications, let's put everything together into a fun AR project. In this chapter, you will learn how to create a 3D AR video game. This isn't a book about game programming, so this chapter is not a comprehensive summary of the subject, but after reading through this chapters, you will understand how to create a working AR video game.

Before you read on, you may want to take a look at the twars demo that inspired the game shown in this chapter (see Figure 8.1, on the following page, and Figure 8.2, on page 197). This game looks best if you print the table.gif pattern large enough to cover most of a coffee table. If you have any issues with the demo, try running the utility twars_magic_lens_image_test.exe (code\YourARGame\twars_compiled\). This version of the program uses a screenshot of the table.gif image instead of camera input.

Using all of the knowledge you've acquired in previous chapters, plus some basic game engine design skills, you're now going to build an AR video game. The simulation will include tanks driving within a city model—it is creatively called Tank Wars. Figure 8.3, on page 198, shows a screenshot of the Tank Wars implementation.

Figure 8.4, on page 199, shows a zoomed-in view of Tank Wars—a tank on the blue team is destroying an enemy green tank.

Through the course of this chapter, you'll see Tank Wars gradually being put together into a working system. You'll start with a basic ARTag OpenGL AR program and then add some simple physics.

Figure 8.1: THE FULL TWARS VERSION OF THE GAME

Eventually, you will expand the game so that it includes a behavioral model and path planning for your robot tanks.

Here are the steps you're going to see in the development of Tank Wars:

1. Set up a basic ARTag OpenGL AR program with a single texture on the ground (twars_1_map_base.cpp).

2. Add some walls to make a maze (twars_2_maze_walls.cpp).

3. Add a keyboard controlled tank (twars_3_keyboard_tank.cpp).

4. Extend to multiple tanks, add simple animations, and add the *Request-Simulate* architecture (twars_4_multi_tanks.cpp).

5. Prevent tanks from driving through walls (twars_5_walls.cpp).

6. Add flying missiles (twars_6_missiles.cpp).

7. Bring in some robot tanks, and give them *vision* to detect other tanks (twars_7_vision.cpp).

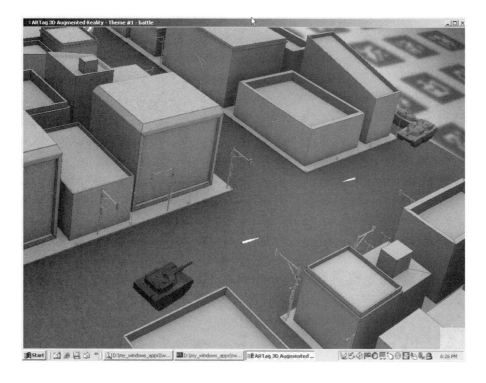

Figure 8.2: A TWARS STREET BATTLE

8. Add behavior #1: firing a missile (twars_8_vision.cpp).

9. Add behavior #2: responding to attack (twars_9_face.cpp).

10. Add behavior #3: rotating to face the enemy (twars_10_rotate.cpp).

11. Add behavior #4: moving agents (twars_11_travel.cpp).

12. Plan your path: how to get from A to B (twars_12_path_plan.cpp).

13. Create your robot tanks' *behavior tree*, and learn how to combine multiple behaviors into a semi-intelligent agent.

14. Add behavior #6: patrolling (twars_13_patrol.cpp). Behavior 6 comes before behavior 5 simply because it will be easier to discuss them in this order. The robot tanks will process the behaviors in their numerical order.

15. Add behavior #5: helping (twars_14_help.cpp).

Figure 8.3: THE TANK WARS AR GAME

16. Watch the mayhem! Bring it all together, and unleash armies of robot tanks on each other (twars_15_final.cpp).

Your programs will be named twars_X_description where X is a heading number and description is a word or two. As usual, you can obtain these programs from the book's downloads.

8.1 Basic ARTag OpenGL AR Program

First, you'll see a basic setup; this is the program you're going to build upon. It simply places a map image over the *base0* marker array. In the map, black represents free space—where our game elements (tanks) can move—and white represents barriers (walls and buildings) that the elements cannot move through, see through, or shoot through. twars_1_map_base.cpp includes the base program that will be used for all of the Tank Wars examples.

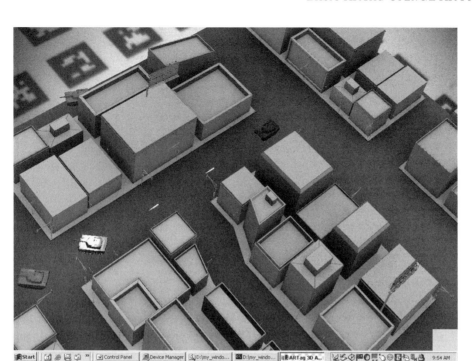

Figure 8.4: A ZOOMED-IN VIEW OF TANK WARS

Aligning and Scaling Three Coordinate Systems

When setting up your own game (or animation) with a map image, you'll need to align three coordinate systems. First, there is the coordinate system that the game engine uses—we'll call this the *world coordinate system*. The location of the tanks and the scale of the models will be in this world coordinate system. Second, you need to consider the coordinate system of your marker array—this will tell you where your origin is, what direction the axes are, and the scale. Finally, since you're using a map image—which in the general case may be a different scale than the world coordinate system—you need to consider how the units in the map correspond to the units in the world. A fourth quasicoordinate system is in the image manipulation program, which will usually mean that you have to flip the image vertically.

We'll call the world coordinates of a point (that is, X_{w_1}, Y_{w_1}, Z_{w_1}) the *marker array coordinates* (X_{a_1}, Y_{a_1}, Z_{a_1}) and the *map image coordinates* (X_{m_1}, Y_{m_1}, Z_{m_1}). Now here's a mental exercise for you: which one will you use in the opengl_draw() function? It's good to think this question through.

The answer is $(X_{a_1}, Y_{a_1}, Z_{a_1})$, because the OpenGL modelview matrix is set in the coordinates of the physical world points (the marker corners).

In any AR application, you need to correlate the world coordinate system with the physical coordinates in the real world. In the case of Tank Wars, the units of the physical coordinate system are as long as one unit of the printed array file. You don't need to work in real units, such as millimeters or inches.

You will have to create a mapping between the X, Y, Z coordinates in your array file (panel_set.cf) and your game coordinate system. Figure 8.5, on the facing page, shows the axis in the *base0* pattern that you'll be using for your game. This image was created by running artag_viewer_image.exe with the camera_image.pgm image. If you look in the array file (panel_set.cf), you see that Z = 0 for all points and that X and Y both range from positive 80 to negative 80. The origin is in the center.

For this example, you'll make the world 320 units wide by 320 units deep (world coordinates). This has to span over 160 by 160 units for the *base0* array (marker array = physical world coordinates), and it has to correspond to your 32 by 32 square map image.

The following equations give you your mappings:

$$X_a = 0.5 * X_w - 80 \quad Y_a = 0.5 * Y_w - 80 \quad Z_a = 0.5 * Z_w \tag{8.1}$$

$$X_m = 0.1 * X_w - 80 \quad Y_m = 0.1 * Y_w - 80 \quad Z_m = 0.1 * Z_w \tag{8.2}$$

You'll start with the world coordinates—the units your game engine will work in—and you'll convert these to array coordinates when drawing in opengl_draw(). The conversion is done using equation 8.1. When you want to know where something is located in the map, you'll need to convert from world coordinates to map coordinates using equation 8.2.

Note that in the twars_1_map_base.cpp program, you set the map image to X_a, Y_a = +/-80 with the texture coordinates of 0.0 and 1.0. You do this because texture coordinates are from 0–1 regardless of the measurement of the bitmap in pixels. The vertical (V axis) values for the texture vertices are flipped because OpenGL considers the origin to be in the lower left.

Figure 8.5: THE *base0* PATTERN STRETCHES FROM +/- 80.0 ON BOTH
THE X- AND Y-AXES.

Now let's discuss the map image. You must get your coordinate system
straight. For your game, you want a *right-handed* coordinate system,
where X and Y form the horizontal plane and Z is up. It is possible to
create a system that works the opposite way (left-handed), but right-
handed coordinate systems are the de facto standard for video games.

Right-handed systems can be described in this way. First, hold out
your right hand so that your thumb is at a 90-degree angle to your
index finger. With your right hand held palm up, your thumb is the X-
axis, your index finger is the Y-axis, and your middle finger points up
for the Z-axis.

In image manipulation programs, the origin is usually in the upper-left,
and the Y coordinate increases as you go down. This is why you will
need to flip the image vertically before saving it in your image program
(for example, Microsoft Paint, Corel Paint Shop Pro, or Adobe Photoshop). Figure 8.6, on the next page, shows the map that you want on

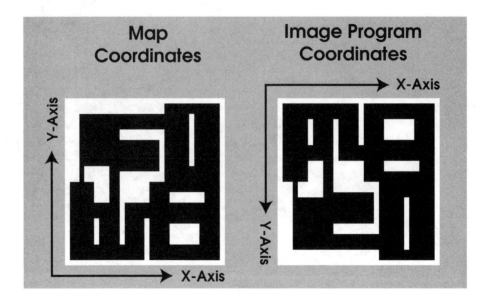

Figure 8.6: The world map

the left and how it looks in an image manipulation program on the right. The easiest thing to do is to design your world so that it looks like the image on the left and do a vertical flip before saving it. Remember to save your map as a binary PPM file so that your AR code can load it. PPM files were discussed in detail earlier in Chapter 5.

With these coordinate systems in mind, have a look at the screen capture from twars_1_map_base.cpp in Figure 8.7, on the facing page.

8.2 Add Some Walls to Make a Maze

Now you're going to add some height to the maze walls. In the final game, you will use some building models from a 3D design program— these are just temporary walls. To make things easier, you're going to reuse the cube you made in Chapter 8, with glDrawElements(). Figure 8.8, on page 204, shows a screenshot of the result.

To make the walls stand out, you will simulate a light source (above the array) by shading the sides of the walls (see Figure 8.9, on page 205). In Figure 8.8, on page 204, you can see a the texture from the cube_gldrawelements.cpp program (from the previous chapter).

Figure 8.7: The world map in AR

In this screenshot, you can see some shading was added to give the illusion of light. The light source is above and off to one side.

The file twars_2_maze_walls.cpp has the cube definitions (in the global variables) copied from cube_gldrawelements.cpp—to save space, they're not repeated. The pointers are set up in main() so that you only need to call glDrawElements() in the loop. The new global variables for the cube texture image and the map width and height are as follows:

YourARGame/Tank Wars Projects/twars_2_maze_walls/twars_2_maze_walls.cpp

```
#define MAP_BITMAP_NAME "map.ppm"
#define MAP_WIDTH 32
#define MAP_HEIGHT 32
#define CUBE_BITMAP_NAME "cube_texture.ppm"

//cam_image is cam_width*cam_height from camera,
//cam_tex_img is 1024*1024
unsigned char *cam_image,*cam_tex_img;
//1=RGB, 0=greyscalechar rgb_greybar;

int cam_width, cam_height;
unsigned char *screen_image;
int artag_object_id;   //artag object # for array
```

Figure 8.8: TWARS_2_MAZE_WALLS.CPP WITH 3D CUBE WALLS BUILT UP FROM THE MAP

```
//camera params ("K" matrix) - perfect
//(no radial ,etc distortion) pinhole model
float camera_cx,camera_cy;  //camera pa
//rams

//variables for OpenGL for camera image
GLuint camera_texID;  //handle to camera image texture
double camera_opengl_dRight,camera_opengl_dLeft,
    camera_opengl_dTop,camera_opengl_dBottom;
GLuint map_texID,cube_texID;
unsigned char *texmap,*texcube;
int cubetex_width,cubetex_height;
```

Next, let's look at the additions to the initialization in main(). These changes take care of loading and setting up the new texture and setting up the pointers for glDrawElements().

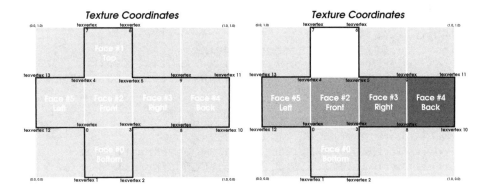

Figure 8.9: CUBE TEXTURE FROM CHAPTER 7 (LEFT) AND MODIFIED TEX-
TURE TO SIMULATE LIGHTING (RIGHT)

```
YourARGame/Tank Wars Projects/twars_2_maze_walls/twars_2_maze_walls.cpp
```

```cpp
//load coordframe file
if(load_array_file(ARRAY_FILENAME))
        printf("ERROR loading <%s>\n",ARRAY_FILENAME);else
        printf("Loaded array file <%s>\n",ARRAY_FILENAME);

//associate object with array named "base0"
artag_object_id=artag_associate_array("base0");

//set viewing frustrum to match camera FOV
glMatrixMode (GL_PROJECTION);
glLoadIdentity ();
camera_opengl_dRight = (double)cam_width / (double)(2.0 * DEFAULT_FX);
camera_opengl_dLeft = -camera_opengl_dRight;
camera_opengl_dTop = (double)cam_height / (double)(2.0 * DEFAULT_FY);
camera_opengl_dBottom = -camera_opengl_dTop;
glFrustum(camera_opengl_dLeft, camera_opengl_dRight,
     camera_opengl_dBottom, camera_opengl_dTop, 1.0, 102500.0);
camera_opengl_dLeft *= 1024;
camera_opengl_dRight *= 1024;
camera_opengl_dBottom *= 1024;
camera_opengl_dTop *= 1024;
glMatrixMode(GL_MODELVIEW);
glLoadIdentity();

//rgb image
cam_image=(unsigned char*)malloc(cam_width*cam_height*4+100);
if(cam_image==NULL) {printf("failed malloc\n");exit(1);}

//camera texture
cam_tex_img=(unsigned char*)malloc(1024*1024*4+100);
if(cam_tex_img==NULL) {printf("failed malloc\n");exit(1);}
```

```
// make a texture for the video
glGenTextures(1, &camera_texID);
glBindTexture(GL_TEXTURE_2D, camera_texID);
glTexParameteri(GL_TEXTURE_2D,GL_TEXTURE_MAG_FILTER,GL_LINEAR);
glTexParameteri(GL_TEXTURE_2D,GL_TEXTURE_MIN_FILTER,GL_LINEAR);

//load map file PPM image
glGenTextures(1, &map_texID);
glBindTexture(GL_TEXTURE_2D, map_texID);
glTexParameteri(GL_TEXTURE_2D,GL_TEXTURE_MAG_FILTER,GL_LINEAR);
glTexParameteri(GL_TEXTURE_2D,GL_TEXTURE_MIN_FILTER,GL_LINEAR);

texmap=texture_read_ppm(MAP_BITMAP_NAME,&width,&height);
if (texmap!=NULL)
    glTexImage2D(GL_TEXTURE_2D, 0, GL_RGB, width, height, 0, GL_RGB,
                GL_UNSIGNED_BYTE,texmap);
else {printf("Couldn't load <%s>\n",MAP_BITMAP_NAME);exit(1);}
if((width!=MAP_WIDTH)||(height!=MAP_HEIGHT))
    {printf("ERROR: map width,height=%d,%d  expecting %d,%d\n",
        width,height,MAP_WIDTH,MAP_HEIGHT);exit(1);}

//load cube texture PPM image
glGenTextures(1, &cube_texID);
glBindTexture(GL_TEXTURE_2D, cube_texID);
glTexParameteri(GL_TEXTURE_2D,GL_TEXTURE_MAG_FILTER,GL_LINEAR);
glTexParameteri(GL_TEXTURE_2D,GL_TEXTURE_MIN_FILTER,GL_LINEAR);
texcube=texture_read_ppm(CUBE_BITMAP_NAME,&cubetex_width,&cubetex_height);
if (texcube!=NULL)
    glTexImage2D(GL_TEXTURE_2D, 0, GL_RGB, cubetex_width,
                cubetex_height, 0, GL_RGB, GL_UNSIGNED_BYTE,texcube);
else {printf("Couldn't load <%s>\n",CUBE_BITMAP_NAME);exit(1);}

//cube points - set up pointers, since we only have one
//pointer set we do this in setup
glEnableClientState(GL_VERTEX_ARRAY);
glEnableClientState(GL_TEXTURE_COORD_ARRAY);
glVertexPointer(3,GL_FLOAT,0,cube_3d_vertex);
glTexCoordPointer(2,GL_FLOAT,0,cube_texvertex);
```

The next addition is the code added to opengl_draw(). Notice how you'll step through each map square to determine whether it's full (whether the blue color channel is above 50/255) and draw the cube only if this check is true. We use the inverse of equation 8.2, on page 200, to transfer from map to world coordinates and then apply equation 8.1, on page 200, to map from world to array coordinates. You'll add a scale factor of five since the cube is only 1 unit wide, whereas a map square (pixel) corresponds to 10 world units and the scale to array units is 0.5 (equation 8.1, on page 200). Note how the cubes sit on top of the white squares in the map.

```
void opengl_draw(void)
{
    glClear(GL_COLOR_BUFFER_BIT | GL_DEPTH_BUFFER_BIT | GL_STENCIL_BUFFER_BIT);

    // draw a quad for the background video
    glLoadIdentity();
    glDisable(GL_LIGHTING);
    glEnable(GL_TEXTURE_2D);
    glBindTexture(GL_TEXTURE_2D, camera_texID);
    glBegin(GL_QUADS);
    glColor3f(1.0f, 1.0f, 1.0f);

    //draw camera image as background texture
    glTexCoord2f(0.0f, (float)cam_height/1024.0);
    glVertex3f(camera_opengl_dLeft, camera_opengl_dBottom, -1024);
    glTexCoord2f(0.0f, 0.0f);
    glVertex3f(camera_opengl_dLeft, camera_opengl_dTop, -1024);
    glTexCoord2f((float)cam_width/1024.0, 0.0f);
    glVertex3f(camera_opengl_dRight, camera_opengl_dTop, -1024);
    glTexCoord2f((float)cam_width/1024.0, (float)cam_height/1024.0);
    glVertex3f(camera_opengl_dRight, camera_opengl_dBottom, -1024);
    glEnd();

    //draw map on X-Y plane
    if(artag_is_object_found(artag_object_id))  {
    artag_set_object_opengl_matrix(artag_object_id,0);

    //set the map image on the X-Y plane stretching from Xa,Ya=-80 to 80
    glEnable(GL_TEXTURE_2D);
    glBindTexture(GL_TEXTURE_2D, map_texID);
    glBegin(GL_QUADS);
    glColor3f(1.0f, 1.0f, 1.0f);
    glTexCoord2f(0.0f, 1.0f);  glVertex3f(-80, 80,0);
    glTexCoord2f(1.0f, 1.0f);  glVertex3f( 80, 80,0);
    glTexCoord2f(1.0f, 0.0f);  glVertex3f( 80,-80,0);
    glTexCoord2f(0.0f, 0.0f);  glVertex3f(-80,-80,0);
    glEnd();

    //draw walls
    glBindTexture(GL_TEXTURE_2D, cube_texID);
    int xm,ym;      //map coordinates
    float xw,yw;  //world coordinates
    float xa,ya;  //array=physical=rendering coordinates

    for(ym=0;ym<MAP_HEIGHT;ym++)
      for(xm=0;xm<MAP_WIDTH;xm++)
      //just check one color channel
      if(texmap[(xm+ym*MAP_WIDTH)*3]>50)  {
      glPushMatrix();  //save modelview matrix for next iteration
```

```
//convert from xm,ym to world coords xw,ys.
//Inverse of Eqn. 2 in chapter 9
xw=(float)xm*10.0; yw=(float)ym*10.0;
//convert from world coords to marker coords.
//Eqn. 1 in chapter 9
xa=0.5*xw-80.0; ya=0.5*yw-80.0;
glTranslatef(xa,ya,0.0);
glScalef(5,5,5);
glDrawElements(GL_QUADS,24,GL_UNSIGNED_INT,cube_indices);
glPopMatrix();
    }
}
```

8.3 Add a Keyboard-Controlled Tank

You're now going to bring in a tank model using OBJ_PARSE.C and render it using MESH_MANAGMENT.C. You're also going to add some simple controls for the tank: the J and K keys will rotate your tank, and the I and M keys will drive it forward and backward. Note that you're not going to try to stop the tank from going through walls or out of bounds; you'll be able to drive the tank right off the pattern if you want. Later in this chapter, you'll add the physics required to keep the tank inside the borders of the map.

The next code block shows the define and include statements as well as the global variables for tank position and tank2_model_num, which is a handle used to refer to the model when you're using mesh_manager. You're labeling this tank type as *2* to fit in with a later version of the program—where team 1 is composed of blue tanks and team 2 is green.

YourARGame/Tank Wars Projects/twars_3_keyboard_tank/twars_3_keyboard_tank.cpp

```
//use OpenCV highgui to load images other than PPM,PGM
//un-define (comment out #define line) if you don't have
//or want to use OpenCV
#define USE_HIGHGUI

#ifdef USE_HIGHGUI
 #include "cv.h"
 #include "highgui.h"
#endif

#define OPENGL_PROJECT
//basic mesh library for manipulating and rendering meshes
#include "mesh_management.c"
//for parsing .OBJ/.MTL Wavefront files
#include "obj_parse.c"
```

```
#define TANK2_MODEL_NAME "green_tank.obj"
//maximum number of materials expected in a 3D model file
#define MAX_EXPECTED_MATERIALS 1500
int tank2_model_num;
float tank_xw, tank_yw, tank_angle;
```

Next comes the code to load your green_tank.obj 3D model. You first have to initialize mesh_manager, load the model with obj_parse(), and then load all the bitmaps. You will load the bitmaps after all the models have been loaded. This is a good idea in case more than one model references the same bitmap.

YourARGame/Tank Wars Projects/twars_3_keyboard_tank/twars_3_keyboard_tank.cpp

```
//mesh manager initialization
//100 object_models, 2000 meshes, 1000 materials,
//1,500,000 polys,
//1,500,000 points
//init_mesh_management(100,2000,1000,1500000,1500000);

//load tank model
int num_meshes,num_vtxs,num_triangles,num_normals,bitmaps_loaded;
tank2_model_num=obj_parse(TANK2_MODEL_NAME,
      MAX_EXPECTED_MATERIALS,&num_meshes,&num_vtxs,&num_triangles,
      &num_normals,&bitmaps_loaded);
printf("loaded tank model=<%s> tank2_model_num=%d\n",
      TANK2_MODEL_NAME,tank2_model_num);

//load bitmaps
printf("loading bitmaps\n");
bitmaps_loaded=mesh_management_load_bitmaps();
printf("Successfully loaded %d of %d bitmaps\n",
      bitmaps_loaded,meshman_bitmap_ptr);

//initial tank position and orientation
tank_xw=30.0; tank_yw=30.0; tank_angle=0.0;
```

The mesh_manager—which is the code from mesh_management.c—handles a lot of the work for you. Notice how simply the model is rendered from just one function call in opengl_draw(). Also note that you use the handle that you got when you loaded the OBJ file.

YourARGame/Tank Wars Projects/twars_3_keyboard_tank/twars_3_keyboard_tank.cpp

```
void opengl_draw(void)
{
   glClear(GL_COLOR_BUFFER_BIT | GL_DEPTH_BUFFER_BIT | GL_STENCIL_BUFFER_BIT);

   // draw a quad for the background video
   glLoadIdentity();
   glDisable(GL_LIGHTING);
```

```
glEnable(GL_TEXTURE_2D);
glBindTexture(GL_TEXTURE_2D, camera_texID);
glBegin(GL_QUADS);
glColor3f(1.0f, 1.0f, 1.0f);

//draw camera image as background texture
glTexCoord2f(0.0f, (float)cam_height/1024.0);
glVertex3f(camera_opengl_dLeft, camera_opengl_dBottom, -1024);
glTexCoord2f(0.0f, 0.0f);
glVertex3f(camera_opengl_dLeft, camera_opengl_dTop, -1024);
glTexCoord2f((float)cam_width/1024.0, 0.0f);
glVertex3f(camera_opengl_dRight, camera_opengl_dTop, -1024);
glTexCoord2f((float)cam_width/1024.0, (float)cam_height/1024.0);
glVertex3f(camera_opengl_dRight, camera_opengl_dBottom, -1024);
glEnd();

//draw map on X-Y plane
if(artag_is_object_found(artag_object_id))  {
artag_set_object_opengl_matrix(artag_object_id,0);

//set the map image on the X-Y plane stretching from Xa,Ya=-80 to 80
glEnable(GL_TEXTURE_2D);
glBindTexture(GL_TEXTURE_2D, map_texID);
glBegin(GL_QUADS);
glColor3f(1.0f, 1.0f, 1.0f);
glTexCoord2f(0.0f, 1.0f);  glVertex3f(-80, 80,0);
glTexCoord2f(1.0f, 1.0f);  glVertex3f( 80, 80,0);
glTexCoord2f(1.0f, 0.0f);  glVertex3f( 80,-80,0);
glTexCoord2f(0.0f, 0.0f);  glVertex3f(-80,-80,0);
glEnd();

//draw walls
glBindTexture(GL_TEXTURE_2D, cube_texID);
int xm,ym;      //map coordinates
float xw,yw;  //world coordinates
float xa,ya;  //array=physical=rendering coordinates

for(ym=0;ym<MAP_HEIGHT;ym++)
  for(xm=0;xm<MAP_WIDTH;xm++)
    //just check one color channel
    if(texmap[(xm+ym*MAP_WIDTH)*3]>50)  {
      //save modelview matrix for next iteration
      glPushMatrix();
      //convert from xm,ym to world coords xw,ys.
      //Inverse of Eqn. 2 in chapter 9
      xw=(float)xm*10.0; yw=(float)ym*10.0;
      //convert from world coords to marker coords.
      //Eqn. 1 in chapter 9
      xa=0.5*xw-80.0; ya=0.5*yw-80.0;
      glTranslatef(xa,ya,0.0);
      glScalef(5,5,5);
```

```
        glDrawElements(GL_QUADS,24,GL_UNSIGNED_INT,cube_indices);
        glPopMatrix();
      }
      //draw tank
      glDisable(GL_LIGHTING);
      //convert from world coords to marker coords.
      //Eqn. 1 in chapter 9
      xa=0.5*tank_xw-80.0; ya=0.5*tank_yw-80.0;
      glTranslatef(xa,ya,0.0);
      glRotatef(tank_angle,0,0,1);
      meshman_render_opengl(tank2_model_num,1,0);
  }
```

The keyboard controls for the tank are quite simple; the tank simply lurches ahead or rotates by 10 degrees. But don't worry, you'll see smoother operation in the next section.

YourARGame/Tank Wars Projects/twars_3_keyboard_tank/twars_3_keyboard_tank.cpp

```cpp
void opengl_key_down(unsigned char k, int x, int y)
{
//escape key exits program
    if(k==27)  exit(0);
    else if(k=='j') tank_angle+=10.0;
    else if(k=='k') tank_angle-=10.0;
    else if(k=='i')  {
        tank_xw+=3.0*cos(tank_angle*M_PI/180.0);
        tank_yw+=3.0*sin(tank_angle*M_PI/180.0);
    }
    else if(k=='m')  {
        tank_xw-=3.0*cos(tank_angle*M_PI/180.0);
        tank_yw-=3.0*sin(tank_angle*M_PI/180.0);
    }
}
```

Figure 8.10, on the next page, shows a tank model loaded from the OBJ file, rendered with mesh_manager, and then moved around using keyboard control. This is the twars_3_keyboard_tank.cpp version of Tank Wars.

Notice the *augmented* fun you can have driving the tank off the marker array pattern and onto your desktop.

8.4 Multiple Tanks, Simple Animations, and the Request-Simulate Architecture

One drawback to twars_3_keyboard_tank.cpp is that the tank motion is awkward. You're going to fix this problem with a velocity/acceleration model for speed and a steering wheel model for the rotation. You will

Figure 8.10: TANK MODEL LOADED FROM OBJ FILE

also change the global variables for position and orientation of your single tank (tank_xw, tank_yw, tank_angle) into an array. This array will include structure, velocity, and status. After adding the array, you'll be able to add ten tanks instead of just one! The status variable will indicate whether a tank is alive or destroyed and how badly damaged it is. To change control of which tank you're driving, you'll press the 0 through 9 keys.

In addition, you're going to load more than just one OBJ tank model—as you did in twars_3_keyboard_tank.cpp. You will have two sets of four tank models. The two sets of tanks will represent the two *teams*. The four models are the regular tank, two exploding tanks, and a destroyed tank. Team 0 will be blue, and team 1 will be green.

The tank model displayed will be a function of the status and damage of the tank. Since you don't want the tanks shooting yet, you'll be able to destroy a tank by selecting it and pressing the D key.

Let's first look at the tank data structure. This structure contains all of the information that will be used by both your current manual tanks and your future robot tanks. Note here that the variables tank_xw, tank_yw, and tank_angle are replaced by elements within the structure X, Y, Z, and angle (Z = 0 for your game).

YourARGame/Tank Wars Projects/twars_4_multi_tanks/twars_4_multi_tanks.cpp

```
//float tank_xw,tank_yw,tank_angle;
struct tank_s
      {
      //current position
      float x,y,z,angle;
      //last position
      float last_x,last_y,last_z,last_angle;
      //translational and rotational velocity
      float velocity,dangle;
      //reset all movement requests
      bool move_cw,move_ccw,move_fast,move_slow,move_fire;
      //physics setting for this tank
      float max_rot_rate,max_speed;
      //status and actions
      //true=AI controlled, false=user controlled
      bool robot;

      bool request_fire;
      int team;
      int damage;
      //true=active, false=destroyed
      bool status;
      //true for one time tick after collision with wall or bullet
      bool crash;
      };
struct tank_s tank[NUM_TANKS];
int current_tank_num;
```

Next, let's take a closer look at your keyboard control. This time, instead of directly controlling the tank's position and orientation within the opengl_key_down() function, you'll merely set *requests* to accelerate or turn. Notice that you're also adding the—currently inactive—code to fire a missile with the spacebar.

The current_tank_num variable holds an integer that corresponds to the tank you're driving. As before, use the 0–9 keys to switch to a different tank, and a temporary line of code destroys the current tank when you press D.

YourARGame/Tank Wars Projects/twars_4_multi_tanks/twars_4_multi_tanks.cpp

```
void opengl_key_down(unsigned char k, int x, int y)
{
    //escape key exits program
    if(k==27)  exit(0);
    else if(k=='j') tank[current_tank_num].move_ccw=true;
    else if(k=='k') tank[current_tank_num].move_cw=true;
    //speed up
    else if(k=='i') tank[current_tank_num].move_fast=true;
    //slow down or go backwards
    else if(k=='m') tank[current_tank_num].move_slow=true;
    //want to fire a missile
    else if(k==' ') tank[current_tank_num].move_fire=true;
    else if((k>='0')&&(k<='9')) current_tank_num=k-'0';
    //temporary code, destroy tank
    else if(k=='d') tank[current_tank_num].status=false;
}
```

Let's see the initialization of the tank structures in main()—after the model loading. The initial positions of the tanks were determined by simply looking for suitable spots in the map.ppm file.

YourARGame/Tank Wars Projects/twars_4_multi_tanks/twars_4_multi_tanks.cpp

```
//initial tank position and orientation: tank_xw=30.0; tank_yw=30.0; tank_angle=0.0;
//old code from twars_3; choose tank positions manually on map image
        tank[0].x= 30.0; tank[0].y= 30.0; tank[0].z=0.0; tank[0].angle=0.0;
        tank[1].x= 30.0; tank[1].y=100.0; tank[1].z=0.0; tank[1].angle=0.0;
        tank[2].x= 80.0; tank[2].y= 30.0; tank[2].z=0.0; tank[2].angle=0.0;
        tank[3].x= 80.0; tank[3].y=100.0; tank[3].z=0.0; tank[3].angle=0.0;
        tank[4].x=130.0; tank[4].y= 30.0; tank[4].z=0.0; tank[4].angle=0.0;
        tank[5].x=220.0; tank[5].y=160.0; tank[5].z=0.0; tank[5].angle=0.0;
        tank[6].x=220.0; tank[6].y=270.0; tank[6].z=0.0; tank[6].angle=0.0;
        tank[7].x=280.0; tank[7].y=160.0; tank[7].z=0.0; tank[7].angle=0.0;
        tank[8].x=280.0; tank[8].y=270.0; tank[8].z=0.0; tank[8].angle=0.0;
        tank[9].x=150.0; tank[9].y=270.0; tank[9].z=0.0; tank[9].angle=0.0;

    for(int tank_num=0;tank_num<NUM_TANKS;tank_num++)  {
      tank[tank_num].dangle=0.0;
      //tank "performance" settings
      tank[tank_num].max_rot_rate=15.0; tank[tank_num].max_speed=5.0;
      //initial status and action settings
      tank[tank_num].robot=false;   //set all tanks to manually controlled
      tank[tank_num].team=tank_num/5; tank[tank_num].status=true;
      tank[tank_num].crash=false; tank[tank_num].request_fire=false;
      tank[tank_num].damage=10;     //for later development
      //reset all movement requests
      tank[tank_num].move_cw=false; tank[tank_num].move_ccw=false;
      tank[tank_num].move_fast=false; tank[tank_num].move_slow=false;
      tank[tank_num].move_fire=false;
        }
    current_tank_num=0;
```

This is a good time to introduce the game_engine_physics() function. As always, it's useful to separate the game/animation behavior from the graphics and other code. This loose coupling helps with portability and makes for easier reading and debugging. It's also beneficial to separate the gamer's or AI element's (robot tank's) desired actions from the physics of motion. We'll call this the *Request-Simulate* architecture. A manual user, or an AI routine, requests an action, and a central function performs the actual changes to the game state. Neither the manual code nor the AI code is going to directly change the position or orientation of any game element.

The central function game_engine_physics() is called inside your opengl_tick() routine. This function interprets manual inputs—such as increasing the velocity when the user presses the I key—and updates the position and orientation of the tanks. Note that you are able to accelerate a tank, switch to another tank, and control the new one while the first one slows down.

You may need to tweak the rotational and translational components, as well as the dampening coefficients for speed. This will make the tanks easier to control on your machine. The *feel* of the movement will be affected by your computer and camera speed. Note that there is a possible improvement here. Have you ever tried running a really old video game on a modern-day computer? If so, you've probably seen games that run much faster than they were intended to run—even the slowest animation setting in the Windows version of Hearts suffers from this problem. With these games, the opposite can also happen (that is, on slower machines, they run way too slow). The reason for this problem is that these games rely upon CPU cycles instead of actual time. To correct this problem, you could set a callback function to happen every few milliseconds. This makes the game run at the same speed on all machines, and therefore, the feel is independent of the machine and camera. We won't delve into adding proper timers in this book, but it's an improvement that you could add on your own.

Here is a brief code snippet showing the game_engine_physics() function being called from opengl_tick():

```
YourARGame/Tank Wars Projects/twars_4_multi_tanks/twars_4_multi_tanks.cpp
```

```
//update game
game_engine_physics();

glutPostRedisplay();
```

Now let's look at the game_engine_physics() function. Notice that we first process the manual tank's movement requests and then update all of the tank positions. Of course, it's possible to add manual controls for more than one tank at once. An exercise for you would be to learn some socket programming and then change the code to allow multiple players—on different computers—to operate manual tanks.

```
YourARGame/Tank Wars Projects/twars_4_multi_tanks/twars_4_multi_tanks.cpp
void game_engine_physics(void)
{
    //---------------    update game    ----------------//
    int tank_num;

    //update control inputs to tanks
    for(tank_num=0;tank_num<NUM_TANKS;tank_num++)
    {
    if(tank[tank_num].status)  {
    //rotate ccw
    if((tank[tank_num].move_ccw) &&
      (tank[tank_num].dangle<tank[tank_num].max_rot_rate))
      tank[tank_num].dangle+=2.0;
    //rotate cw
    if((tank[tank_num].move_cw) &&
      (tank[tank_num].dangle>-1.0*tank[tank_num].max_rot_rate))
      tank[tank_num].dangle-=2.0;
    //speed up
    if((tank[tank_num].move_fast) &&
      (tank[tank_num].velocity<tank[tank_num].max_speed))
      tank[tank_num].velocity+=0.8;
    //slow down
    if((tank[tank_num].move_slow) &&
      (tank[tank_num].velocity>-1.0*tank[tank_num].max_speed))
      tank[tank_num].velocity-=0.8;
    //fire button
    if((tank[tank_num].status) && (tank[tank_num].move_fire))
            tank[tank_num].request_fire=true;
          }
    //dampen movements if no manual input present
    tank[tank_num].dangle*=0.80;
    if(tank[tank_num].move_fast==false)
      tank[tank_num].velocity*=0.90;
    //stop tanks from drifting slowly
    if(fabs(tank[tank_num].velocity)<0.1)
      tank[tank_num].velocity=0.0;
    else if(fabs(tank[tank_num].dangle)<0.5)
     tank[tank_num].dangle=0.0;
    //reset all movement requests
    tank[tank_num].move_cw=false;
    tank[tank_num].move_ccw=false;
    tank[tank_num].move_fast=false;
```

```
    tank[tank_num].move_slow=false;
    tank[tank_num].move_fire=false;
    }

    //update all tank positions
    for(tank_num=0;tank_num<NUM_TANKS;tank_num++)
      if(tank[tank_num].status)  {
            //update angle
        tank[tank_num].angle+=tank[tank_num].dangle;
            //keep angle within limits +/-180 degrees
        while(tank[tank_num].angle<-180.0)
          tank[tank_num].angle+=360.0;
        while(tank[tank_num].angle>=180.0)
          tank[tank_num].angle-=360.0;
            //update position
        tank[tank_num].x+=tank[tank_num].velocity *
          cos(tank[tank_num].angle*M_PI/180.0);
        tank[tank_num].y+=tank[tank_num].velocity *
          sin(tank[tank_num].angle*M_PI/180.0);
      }
}
```

Finally, let's look at the code loading our new tank models. In this program, you will see the healthy and destroyed tank models, but you'll have to wait until the next section to see the fire animation for tanks in the process of being destroyed.

Your tank model names, and global variables for model handles used by the mesh manager, are defined at the top as follows:

YourARGame/Tank Wars Projects/twars_4_multi_tanks/twars_4_multi_tanks.cpp

```
#define TANK1_MODEL_NAME "blue_tank.obj"
#define TANK1_BURNING1_MODEL_NAME "blue_tank_hit1.obj"
#define TANK1_BURNING2_MODEL_NAME "blue_tank_hit2.obj"
#define TANK1_DESTROYED_MODEL_NAME "blue_tank_destroyed.obj"
#define TANK2_MODEL_NAME "green_tank.obj"
#define TANK2_BURNING1_MODEL_NAME "green_tank_hit1.obj"
#define TANK2_BURNING2_MODEL_NAME "green_tank_hit2.obj"
#define TANK2_DESTROYED_MODEL_NAME "green_tank_destroyed.obj"
//alive tanks models
int tank1_model_num,tank2_model_num;
//burning step 1 tanks models
int tank1_burning1_model_num,tank2_burning1_model_num;
//burning step 2 tanks models
int tank1_burning2_model_num,tank2_burning2_model_num;
//destroyed tanks models
int tank1_destroyed_model_num,tank2_destroyed_model_num;
```

You load the models like this:

YourARGame/Tank Wars Projects/twars_4_multi_tanks/twars_4_multi_tanks.cpp

```
//load tank models
int num_meshes,num_vtxs,num_triangles,num_normals,bitmaps_loaded;
//alive tanks models
tank1_model_num=obj_parse(TANK1_MODEL_NAME,
    MAX_EXPECTED_MATERIALS,&num_meshes,
    &num_vtxs,&num_triangles, &num_normals,&bitmaps_loaded);
printf("name=<%s>  tank1_model_num=%d\n",
    TANK1_MODEL_NAME,tank1_model_num);
tank2_model_num=obj_parse(TANK2_MODEL_NAME,
    MAX_EXPECTED_MATERIALS,&num_meshes,&num_vtxs,&num_triangles,
    &num_normals,&bitmaps_loaded);
printf("name=<%s>  tank2_model_num=%d\n",
    TANK2_MODEL_NAME,tank2_model_num);


//burning animation stage1 tanks models
tank1_burning1_model_num=obj_parse(TANK1_BURNING1_MODEL_NAME,
    MAX_EXPECTED_MATERIALS,&num_meshes,&num_vtxs,&num_triangles,
    &num_normals,&bitmaps_loaded);
printf("name=<%s>  tank1_burning1_model_num=%d\n",
    TANK1_BURNING1_MODEL_NAME, tank1_burning1_model_num);
tank2_burning1_model_num=obj_parse(TANK2_BURNING1_MODEL_NAME,
    MAX_EXPECTED_MATERIALS,&num_meshes,&num_vtxs,&num_triangles,
&num_normals,&bitmaps_loaded);
printf("name=<%s>  tank2_burning1_model_num=%d\n",
    TANK2_BURNING1_MODEL_NAME,tank2_burning1_model_num);


//burning animation stage2 tanks models
tank1_burning2_model_num=obj_parse(TANK1_BURNING2_MODEL_NAME,
    MAX_EXPECTED_MATERIALS,&num_meshes,&num_vtxs,&num_triangles,
    &num_normals,&bitmaps_loaded);
printf("name=<%s>  tank1_burning2_model_num=%d\n",
    TANK1_BURNING2_MODEL_NAME,
tank1_burning2_model_num);
tank2_burning2_model_num=obj_parse(TANK2_BURNING2_MODEL_NAME,
    MAX_EXPECTED_MATERIALS,&num_meshes,&num_vtxs,&num_triangles,
    &num_normals,&bitmaps_loaded);
printf("name=<%s>  tank2_burning2_model_num=%d\n",
    TANK2_BURNING2_MODEL_NAME,tank2_burning2_model_num);


//destroyed tanks models
tank1_destroyed_model_num=obj_parse(TANK1_DESTROYED_MODEL_NAME,
MAX_EXPECTED_MATERIALS,&num_meshes,&num_vtxs,&num_triangles,
&num_normals,&bitmaps_loaded);
printf("name=<%s>  tank1_destroyed_model_num=%d\n",
    TANK1_DESTROYED_MODEL_NAME,tank1_destroyed_model_num);
tank2_destroyed_model_num=obj_parse(TANK2_DESTROYED_MODEL_NAME,
    MAX_EXPECTED_MATERIALS,&num_meshes,&num_vtxs,&num_triangles,
    &num_normals,&bitmaps_loaded);
```

The next code fragment shows the status, crash, and damage elements of the tank_s structure—this determines which version of the tank model to display:

```
YourARGame/Tank Wars Projects/twars_4_multi_tanks/twars_4_multi_tanks.cpp
for(int tank_num=0;tank_num<NUM_TANKS;tank_num++)  {
int model_num;
//--------assign model according to tank team and state--------
if(tank[tank_num].team==0)  {
    //BLUE Tanks = Team 0
    if(tank[tank_num].crash)
    {model_num=tank1_burning1_model_num; tank[tank_num].crash=0;}
    else if(tank[tank_num].status)
    model_num=tank1_model_num;  //alive tank
    else if((tank[tank_num].status==0)&&(tank[tank_num].damage<0))
    {
        if(abs(tank[tank_num].damage)%2==0)
        //burning tank stage 1
        model_num=tank1_burning1_model_num;
        else
        model_num=tank1_burning2_model_num;
        //burning tank stage 2
        }
    else
        //destroyed tank
        model_num=tank1_destroyed_model_num;
        }
    else if(tank[tank_num].team==1)  {
     //GREEN Tanks = Team 1
     if(tank[tank_num].crash)
     {model_num=tank2_burning1_model_num; tank[tank_num].crash=0;}
     else if(tank[tank_num].status)
     model_num=tank2_model_num;  //alive tank
     else if((tank[tank_num].status==0)&&(tank[tank_num].damage<0))
     {
        if(abs(tank[tank_num].damage)%2==0)
        //burning tank stage 1
                model_num=tank2_burning1_model_num;
    else
        //burning tank stage 2
        model_num=tank2_burning2_model_num;
         }
    else
        //destroyed tank
        model_num=tank2_destroyed_model_num;
        }

    //--------adjust tank pose and render--------
    //save modelview matrix for next iteration
    glPushMatrix();
```

Figure 8.11: MULTIPLE TANKS OF TWO TEAMS, SOME DESTROYED, FROM
TWARS_4_MULTI_TANKS.CPP

```
//convert from world coords to marker coords.
//Eqn. 1 in chapter 9
xa=0.5*tank[tank_num].x-80.0; ya=0.5*tank[tank_num].y-80.0;
glTranslatef(xa,ya,0.0);
glRotatef(tank[tank_num].angle,0,0,1);
meshman_render_opengl(model_num,1,0);
glPopMatrix();
        }
    }
```

It feels like the time for another screen capture. Figure 8.11 shows
some tanks after they have been moved around and some have been
destroyed (with the self-destruct D key).

8.5   Preventing Tanks from Driving Through Walls

As already mentioned, there's nothing to stop the tank from driving through walls—which is cool to play with because you can drive tanks onto your desktop. Obviously, your game should really have walls that the robot tanks cannot drive through.

Your current game engine updates each tank's X_w and Y_w position (world coordinates). How do you stop the tank from going into a place in the world that corresponds to a blocked map position? You can prevent the tank from going to an incorrect (X_w, Y_w) position (by considering where the tank will be moving), or you can keep track of the last position and revert to it if the current position is on a blocked map square. In this example, you'll do that latter.

The steps to add this functionality are as follows:

1. Use the velocity to update the position (X_w, Y_w).

2. Map (X_w, Y_w) to (X_m, Y_m) to see whether the position is a valid map square (using equation 8.2, on page 200).

3. If the tank is on an invalid map square, revert to the last (X_w, Y_w) position and report a collision.

4. If a collision is reported, decrement the tank's damage points (10 = new tank, 0 or less is a destroyed tank), and check whether this means the tank is destroyed.

5. Update the last (X_w, Y_w) position for use in the next iteration (using the tank[tank_num].last_x and y variables).

This section is fairly short. The next logical step in the subject of damage and tank destruction, that of missiles, will be in a different section. Here are the additions to your game_engine_physics() function:

YourARGame/Tank Wars Projects/twars_5_walls/twars_5_walls.cpp

```
//check for collision with walls
for(tank_num=0;tank_num<NUM_TANKS;tank_num++)
    if(tank[tank_num].status)  {
    int xm,ym;      //map coordinates
    //convert from world coordinates (in tank struct)
    //to map coordinates using Eqn. 2 in chapter 9
    xm=(int)(0.1*tank[tank_num].x);
    ym=(int)(0.1*tank[tank_num].y);
    //just check one color channel
    if(texmap[(xm+ym*MAP_WIDTH)*3]>50)  {
```

Figure 8.12: A TANK BLOWING UP AFTER HITTING A WALL TOO MANY TIMES

```
//collision with wall occurred - revert to last position
tank[tank_num].x=tank[tank_num].last_x;
tank[tank_num].y=tank[tank_num].last_y;
tank[tank_num].damage-=abs((int)(0.5*tank[tank_num].velocity));
//make tank bounce back
tank[tank_num].velocity*=-0.3;
//flag for rendering to use flashing model
```

We hate to ask you to do this, but please crash your tank repeatedly into the walls until it's destroyed. This will test your code.

Figure 8.12 shows a tank exploding as it runs out of damage points. If you tried this, you probably noticed that the tank was half inside the wall. This is because your game engine considers only where the center of the tank is and stops it from going into a map square that is a boundary wall. To reduce this ugly visual effect, you need to set your 3D model of the buildings back about half a tank width. This will keep the boundary at the same position, but the visual cue (the wall or building) will be slightly farther away.

8.6 Add Flying Missiles

Warning: this section may disturb you if you find augmented war disturbing. In this section, you're now going to add flying missiles so that tanks can destroy one another. Hey, they're tanks—what did you think was going to happen?

Missiles are going to be similar to tanks in that they are both game elements; their existence needs to be tracked in your game engine, and a model needs to be rendered. Thus, you need to add code to both your game engine and the rendering code in opengl_draw().

First let's add some elements to the tank_s structure to deal with your missiles:

```
YourARGame/Tank Wars Projects/twars_6_missiles/twars_6_missiles.cpp
struct tank_s
    {
    //current position
    float x,y,z,angle;
    //last position
    float last_x,last_y,last_z,last_angle;
    //translational and rotational velocity
    float velocity,dangle;
    //reset all movement requests
    bool move_cw,move_ccw,move_fast,move_slow,move_fire;
    //physics setting for this tank
    float max_rot_rate,max_speed;
    //status and actions
    //true=AI controlled, false=user controlled
    bool robot;
    int team;
    int damage;
    //true=active, false=destroyed
    bool status;
    //true for one time tick after collision with
    //wall or missile
    bool crash;
    //missile info
    bool request_fire;
    //time in frames since tank last fired
    int reload_time;
    //reload time setting
    int time_to_reload;
    //info on incoming missiles that recently hit tank
    //true if tank has been hit
    bool recently_hit;
    float hit_angle;
    };
```

You'll also set up an array of structures to contain all the data for the missiles.

```
#define SHOTS_PER_TANK 3
#define MISSILE_SPEED 8.0

struct missile_s
      {
      float x,y,z,angle;
      //how much damage will missile give
      int damage;
      //true=missile active and flying, false=not in existence
      int status;
      };
struct missile_s missile[NUM_TANKS*SHOTS_PER_TANK];
```

In the initialization, you need to set all undeclared data—in this case, the extra Boolean flags for the new tank, and missile data and the reload time for the tanks.

```
#define SHOTS_PER_TANK 3
#define MISSILE_SPEED 8.0

struct missile_s
      {
      float x,y,z,angle;
      //how much damage will missile give
      int damage;
      //true=missile active and flying, false=not in existence
      int status;
      };
struct missile_s missile[NUM_TANKS*SHOTS_PER_TANK];
```

Now let's get into the real action: the game_engine_physics() function. We'll look at the code in sections; each is a loop through the tank or missile structures.

First is the missile launch loop. The request_fire member you added to tank_s in twars_4_multi_tanks.cpp is now going to be read. If this variable is true, then a missile is launched from just outside the tank's location. (The missile can't be launched at the tank location, because this would result in an immediate missile-tank collision.)

Note that you will assign the tank's angle to the missile, give the missile a damage number (a value to subtract from the hapless target's damage level), and set the missile's status element to Boolean true.

Next, you loop through the tanks and decrement the reload_time element of the tank structure; this prevents the tank from immediately releasing another missile. The next step is to update the missile locations—according to their angle. In this step, only missiles with status = true are considered.

The last two loops check for collisions between missiles and walls and between missiles and tanks. You use equation 8.2, on page 200, to convert missile world coordinates into map coordinates—as you did for the tank to wall collisions—to see whether the missiles should be deactivated. For collisions between the missiles and the tanks, you declare a collision if they pass within three world units of each other. You thereby approximate the tank as a circular object (of radius three) for the collision detection.

YourARGame/Tank Wars Projects/twars_6_missiles/twars_6_missiles.cpp

```
void game_engine_physics(void)
{
   //-----  update game -------//
   int i,tank_num;



   //update control inputs to tanks
   for(tank_num=0;tank_num<NUM_TANKS;tank_num++)  {
      if(tank[tank_num].status)  {
         //rotate ccw
   if((tank[tank_num].move_ccw) &&
      (tank[tank_num].dangle<tank[tank_num].max_rot_rate))
      tank[tank_num].dangle+=2.0;
   //rotate cw
   if((tank[tank_num].move_cw) &&
      (tank[tank_num].dangle>-1.0*tank[tank_num].max_rot_rate))
      tank[tank_num].dangle-=2.0;
   //speed up
   if((tank[tank_num].move_fast) &&
      (tank[tank_num].velocity<tank[tank_num].max_speed))
      tank[tank_num].velocity+=0.8;
   //slow down
   if((tank[tank_num].move_slow) &&
      (tank[tank_num].velocity>-1.0*tank[tank_num].max_speed))
      tank[tank_num].velocity-=0.8;
   //fire button
   if((tank[tank_num].status) &&
     (tank[tank_num].move_fire))
           tank[tank_num].request_fire=true;
              }
```

```
        //dampen movements if no manual input present
        tank[tank_num].dangle*=0.80;
        if(tank[tank_num].move_fast==false)
          tank[tank_num].velocity*=0.90;
        //stop tanks from drifting slowly
        if(fabs(tank[tank_num].velocity)<0.1)
          tank[tank_num].velocity=0.0;
        else if(fabs(tank[tank_num].dangle)<0.5)
          tank[tank_num].dangle=0.0;
        //reset all movement requests
        tank[tank_num].move_cw=false;
        tank[tank_num].move_ccw=false;
        tank[tank_num].move_fast=false;
        tank[tank_num].move_slow=false;
        tank[tank_num].move_fire=false;
      }

//update all tank positions
for(tank_num=0;tank_num<NUM_TANKS;tank_num++)
  if(tank[tank_num].status)  {
        //update angle
    tank[tank_num].angle+=tank[tank_num].dangle;
        //keep angle within limits +/-180 degrees
    while(tank[tank_num].angle<-180.0)
      tank[tank_num].angle+=360.0;
    while(tank[tank_num].angle>=180.0)
      tank[tank_num].angle-=360.0;
        //update position
    tank[tank_num].x+=tank[tank_num].velocity *
      cos(tank[tank_num].angle*M_PI/180.0);
    tank[tank_num].y+=tank[tank_num].velocity *
      sin(tank[tank_num].angle*M_PI/180.0);
  }

//check for tank collision with walls
for(tank_num=0;tank_num<NUM_TANKS;tank_num++)
  if(tank[tank_num].status)  {
      int xm,ym;      //map coordinates
      //convert from world coordinates (in tank struct)
      //to map coordinates using Eqn. 2 in chapter 9
      xm=(int)(0.1*tank[tank_num].x);
      ym=(int)(0.1*tank[tank_num].y);
      //just check one color channel
      if(texmap[(xm+ym*MAP_WIDTH)*3]>50)  {
        //collision with wall occurred - revert to last position
        tank[tank_num].x=tank[tank_num].last_x;
        tank[tank_num].y=tank[tank_num].last_y;
        tank[tank_num].damage-=abs((int)(0.5*tank[tank_num].velocity));
        tank[tank_num].velocity*=-0.3;  //make tank bounce back
        //flag for rendering to use flashing model
        tank[tank_num].crash=true;
```

```
printf("tank[%d].damage=%d\n",tank_num,tank[tank_num].damage);
        }
    }

//launch missiles for each tank that wishes to fire
//if any missiles available, and reload time ok create a new missile
for(tank_num=0;tank_num<NUM_TANKS;tank_num++)  {
  if(tank[tank_num].request_fire)  {
  for(i=0;i<SHOTS_PER_TANK;i++)  {
  int shot=tank_num*SHOTS_PER_TANK+i;
  if((missile[shot].status==false)&&(tank[tank_num].reload_time==0))  {
       missile[shot].angle=tank[tank_num].angle;
       missile[shot].x=tank[tank_num].x+8.0 *
         cos(tank[tank_num].angle*M_PI/180.0);
       missile[shot].y=tank[tank_num].y+8.0 *
         sin(tank[tank_num].angle*M_PI/180.0);
       missile[shot].damage=4;
       missile[shot].status=true;
       tank[tank_num].reload_time=tank[tank_num].time_to_reload;
       printf("missile %d launched from tank %d\n",i,tank_num);
       }
     }
   }
   tank[tank_num].request_fire=0;
}

//tank reload time status
for(tank_num=0;tank_num<NUM_TANKS;tank_num++)
   if((tank[tank_num].reload_time>0)&&(tank[tank_num].status))
      tank[tank_num].reload_time--;

//update missile locations
for(i=0;i<NUM_TANKS*SHOTS_PER_TANK;i++)
   if(missile[i].status)  {
      missile[i].x+=MISSILE_SPEED*cos(missile[i].angle*M_PI/180.0);
      missile[i].y+=MISSILE_SPEED*sin(missile[i].angle*M_PI/180.0);
      printf("missile %d (x,y,z)=%f,%f,%f\n",i,missile[i].x,
        missile[i].y,missile[i].z);
   }

//check for missiles hitting walls
for(i=0;i<NUM_TANKS*SHOTS_PER_TANK;i++)
   if(missile[i].status)  {
      int xm,ym;      //map coordinates
      //convert from world coordinates
      //(in tank struct) to map coordinates
      //using Eqn. 2 in chapter 9
      xm=(int)(0.1*missile[i].x);
      ym=(int)(0.1*missile[i].y);
      //check if map square is free
      if(texmap[(xm+ym*MAP_WIDTH)*3]>50)  {
```

```
            //simply deactivate missile if on obstacle square
               missile[i].status=0;
               printf("missile %d hits wall and is deactivated\n",i);
            }
      }

      //check for collisions between tanks and missiles
      for(tank_num=0;tank_num<NUM_TANKS;tank_num++)
         for(i=0;i<NUM_TANKS*SHOTS_PER_TANK;i++)
            if(missile[i].status)  {
               float dist_x=tank[tank_num].x-missile[i].x;
               float dist_y=tank[tank_num].y-missile[i].y;
               float dist_z=tank[tank_num].z-missile[i].z;
               //check if missile comes within 3 units of tank center
               if(sqrt(dist_x*dist_x+dist_y*dist_y+dist_z*dist_z)<9.0)
               {
                  missile[i].status=0;
                  tank[tank_num].damage-=missile[i].damage;
                  tank[tank_num].recently_hit=true;
                  tank[tank_num].hit_angle=missile[i].angle;
                  tank[tank_num].hit_angle+=M_PI;
                  if(tank[tank_num].hit_angle>2.0*M_PI)
                     tank[tank_num].hit_angle-=2.0*M_PI;
                  //so recipient tank flashes
                  tank[tank_num].crash=true;
                  printf("missile %d collided with tank %d\n",i,tank_num);
               }
            }
      }
```

As with the tanks, you are going to use an external 3D model file for our missile model—although it's just one polygon in this example.

The following three code fragments define variables, load the missile model with obj_parse(), and render the model inside opengl_draw():

```
YourARGame/Tank Wars Projects/twars_6_missiles/twars_6_missiles.cpp
#define MISSILE_MODEL_NAME "missile.obj"
//alive tanks models
int tank1_model_num,tank2_model_num;
//burning step 1 tanks models
int tank1_burning1_model_num,tank2_burning1_model_num;
//burning step 2 tanks models
int tank1_burning2_model_num,tank2_burning2_model_num;
//destroyed tanks models
int tank1_destroyed_model_num,tank2_destroyed_model_num;
//missile model
int missile_model_num;
```

YourARGame/Tank Wars Projects/twars_6_missiles/twars_6_missiles.cpp

```
missile_model_num=obj_parse(MISSILE_MODEL_NAME,
    MAX_EXPECTED_MATERIALS,&num_meshes,&num_vtxs,&num_triangles,
    &num_normals,&bitmaps_loaded);
printf("name=<%s>  missile_model_num=%d\n",MISSILE_MODEL_NAME,missile_model_num);
for(int tank_num=0;tank_num<NUM_TANKS;tank_num++)  {
tank[tank_num].dangle=0.0;
//tank "performance" settings
tank[tank_num].max_rot_rate=15.0; tank[tank_num].max_speed=5.0;
//initial status and action settings
tank[tank_num].robot=false;  //set all tanks to manually controlled
tank[tank_num].team=tank_num/5; tank[tank_num].status=true;
tank[tank_num].crash=false; tank[tank_num].move_fire=false;
tank[tank_num].damage=10;
//reset all movement requests
tank[tank_num].move_cw=false; tank[tank_num].move_ccw=false;
tank[tank_num].move_fast=false; tank[tank_num].move_slow=false;
tank[tank_num].request_fire=false;
//missile related struct elements
tank[tank_num].reload_time=0;        //time in frames since tank last fired
tank[tank_num].time_to_reload=4;     //reload time setting
tank[tank_num].recently_hit=false;   //indicates if tank has recently been hit
}
current_tank_num=0;

//reset all missiles
for(int i=0;i<NUM_TANKS*SHOTS_PER_TANK;i++)
missile[i].status=false;
```

YourARGame/Tank Wars Projects/twars_6_missiles/twars_6_missiles.cpp

```
//update missile locations and check for missiles hitting walls
for(int i=0;i<NUM_TANKS*SHOTS_PER_TANK;i++)
   if(missile[i].status)
     {
            //array=physical=rendering coordinates
     float xa,ya;
     //save modelview matrix for next iteration
     glPushMatrix();
     //convert from world coords to marker coords.  Eqn. 1 in chapter 9
     xa=0.5*missile[i].x-80.0; ya=0.5*missile[i].y-80.0;
     glTranslatef(xa,ya,1.25);
     glRotatef(missile[i].angle,0,0,1);
     meshman_render_opengl(missile_model_num,1,0);
     glPopMatrix();
     }
```

Figure 8.13, on the following page, shows your missiles flying.

Figure 8.13: MISSILES IN ACTION

8.7 Summary

Let's take a brief break and analyze what you've seen so far. You've been building up your Tank Wars game using the model loading and rendering code supplied with the ARTag download (that is, obj_parse.c and mesh_management.c), and you have created your game_engine_physics() function. The game_engine_physics() function contains all your game functionality, that is, the elements that are changing from one instant in time to another.

The game engine is a *state machine*: a system that depends both on inputs and on its last known state. The existence, status, and position of all the tanks and missiles is stored in the world state. The state evolves as a function of its last state and any new inputs. The map.ppm image is a constant for the game engine; it is used to define obstacles that stop tanks and missiles.

The user keyboard presses can be considered input to the game engine, and the rendering inside opengl_draw() can be considered to be the output. We've structured things so that the AI of the robot tanks will be input to the world in the same way as the user input. By changing the velocity and steering angle and requesting that a missile be fired, both the human user and the AI control the tanks through the same interface—the tank structure.

So far, your only game engine feature has been the *physics* of the game state—it was encapsulated in the game_engine_physics() function. Another element of our growing game engine is coming up: the robot tank behaviors.

Chapter 9

Enhancing Your AR Game

This chapter builds upon the game you started to build in the previous chapter. Now that you have the basics of your game, it's time to add some artificial intelligence (AI) and complete the tank behaviors. The AI of a game is often the most challenging part; even simple behaviors require careful thought and often require a great deal of code. But it's also true that the element that distinguishes one game as more fun and intriguing to play from another is often the quality of the AI. It's extremely difficult to program AI that is as interesting as human opponents. This book is about AR, not AI, so you will create a simple AI system.

9.1 AI for Robot Tanks

An integral part of many video games is some quasi-intelligent behavior of various game elements—usually the bad guys. This sort of AI ranges from the ghosts in Mrs. Gobble to the worker and army units in real-time strategy (RTS) games. Often, as in your tank game, the robot elements need only a minimal level of intelligence. In others, such as an RTS—or in the extreme case, a chess game—the AI is what makes the game.

Regardless of how involved the AI is, it needs to be well thought out. Without sufficient planning, the robot behavior can turn out to be far different from what you expected. Also, poor planning can lead to many ad hoc changes and "repairs" that make your code undesirable. Not to suck the fun out of programming a video game, but game AI quickly becomes a complex state machine, and too much interactivity between behaviors can lead to complex feedback paths.

Trying to fix one thing can end up causing something else in turn to act strangely, and after a while, the programmer has to admit that she does not understand the system she has created.

It may sound exciting to have unexpected robot behavior, but unexpected behavior usually means that the robot tanks just sit around, clump together in traffic jams, or inexplicably drive through walls. Unexpected robot behavior usually means a frustrating programming experience—not the robots becoming self-aware.

> "A problem clearly stated is a problem half solved."
> —Dorothea Brande

The more clearly you describe what you want your AI game elements to do, the greater the chance you will end up making a system that works. You should first plan things from a system's viewpoint and then make concrete plans for various parts. Obviously, you should do this before you start coding. If there are any contradictions or undesired outcomes, you'll have to face them at some point, and it's usually easier to do so before you start coding.

There are many ways to plan your game AI behavior. Similar to a chess game, you could examine a number of possible next moves and then for each consider several different behaviors. Then, for each option, examine a number of possible moves. This expands in an exponentially growing tree of possibilities, so it is more suited to a strategy game than your tank game.

An alternate AI system architecture is to design a set of behaviors the agent (tank) can be doing one at a time. Since only one behavior can be acted upon at a time, these behaviors are prioritized. A behavior is activated by some conditions—if active, each behavior suppresses behaviors lower on the priority list. Also, the lower priority behaviors should somehow move the system to a state where the higher-priority behaviors kick in. Imagine a simplified animal behavior: avoiding a predator is an overriding behavior to finding food and water, which itself is an overriding behavior to finding some entertainment. For example, a wombat's boredom behavior is quickly replaced by predator avoidance behaviors if a hungry fox suddenly appears.

You're going to adopt this architecture of prioritized behaviors in your Tank Wars game. Now you have an architecture framework. The next step is to design a set of behaviors and prioritize them.

Let's clarify how your tanks should behave. They should have the ability to *see* opponent tanks and should try to fire shells at them. The tanks should not be able to see through walls, but they should be able to distinguish friend from foe. Since the missiles don't change trajectory, the tanks need to be able to turn and face the enemy before shooting. Based on these points, let's set down some behavior rules and their priority:

Behavior #1: If a robot tank sees an enemy tank and is lined up with it, it should launch a missile.

Behavior #2: If a robot tank sees an enemy tank, it should rotate to line up with it.

Behavior #1 overrides behavior #2. The easy way to implement priority is to set up an "if, else if, else" structure with the higher (lower priority #) behaviors higher in the "if, else if, else" code. Note that you should be careful what priority you assign to each behavior. For example, if you put the rotate behavior first, then even if a tank had an enemy lined up, it may rotate away to face another. Putting the firing behavior first is logical—if the tank can take a shot, it should fire.

If you give your tanks a limited field of view—as in your game—a robot may not see an enemy tank that is aiming in its direction. In this case, the robot tank should do something when it gets hit by an incoming missile; this is behavior #3.

Behavior #3: If a robot tank gets hit by a missile, it will rotate to face the direction of the oncoming missile.

These three behaviors act in a chain reaction from low to high priority. If a tank is minding its own business and a missile suddenly hits it, behavior #3 activates, and it turns to face the threat; perhaps it should run away, but that's more complex. Once the tank rotates far enough to see the enemy tank that fired, behavior #2 kicks in, and it keeps rotating to line up with the aggressor (which may be a different angle, if the enemy has moved since it fired the original missile). Once a tank has its turret lined up with the enemy, behavior #1 activates, and it fires. The first few stages in the next section will help you implement these three behaviors.

You can simplify the situation by having the first three behaviors happen when the tank is not moving, so let's declare that the tank will brake if it's moving and wants to perform behavior #1, #2, or #3.

So far, you have basically added the behavior of a gun turret, so now you will add some motion. What should a tank do if not immediately in a battle (behaviors #1–#3)? A logical behavior would be to go help another tank on its team, but how do you define help? Remember that you don't want to directly battle the enemies with his lower-priority behavior; you only want this behavior to bring about a situation that invokes the higher-priority behaviors—the ones responsible for battle. With this in mind, let's define helping a fellow tank that is in a battle:

Behavior D: A robot tank will drive to the (X, Y) coordinates of a team member that currently sees an enemy.

Note the switch from numbered behaviors to letters; you're going to renumber the ones with letters later in this chapter. Also note that you don't need to preface the behavior rule by "If a robot is just sitting around doing nothing, then..." because this is implicit in our priority architecture.

You can imagine that these behaviors could still result in some strange results. The default behavior—if conditions don't trigger behaviors #1 to #3 or D—is to sit still. This means the game can get stuck in a state where all tanks are just sitting still in different parts of the map. Therefore, you will add patrolling as the final behavior. If none of the tanks on a team is in battle, then they'll all drive around until one finds an enemy. This will trigger behavior D, and the rest of the tanks will roll over.

Patrolling, like *helping*, is a vague concept, so you need to clarify it into a simple and precise behavior. In Tank Wars, you'll implement searching by picking a semirandom destination in the map and driving toward it. Specifically, you'll have a list of *waypoints* for each team, and each "bored" tank will pull a waypoint off the list and navigate to it. The next bored tank will pull the next waypoint off the list. The list of waypoints will be chosen so that the tanks fan out; this will stop them from all driving to the same location.

Behavior E: A robot tank will pick a waypoint off a list—according to a variable specific to the robot's team—and will navigate to the waypoint. The variable will then be incremented so that the next bored robot picks a different destination.

Note that behaviors D and E both involve navigating around the map while avoiding walls. Thus, you need some path planning. This will cause you to subdivide these behaviors, but let's leave that out for now.

You now have a behavior priority tree with five behaviors identified (behaviors #1, #2, #3, D, and E). Next, you'll see behaviors #1, #2, and #3 implemented, and then you'll address the path planning for behaviors D and E.

9.2 Vision for Robot Tanks

If a robot tank can see an enemy, behaviors #1 and #2 require processing to determine the angle of the enemy tank. You want to have some realism in that a tank cannot see through the walls, so you'll add some tunnel vision to give them a limited field of view; this will allow other tanks to sneak up on them.

How are you going to achieve this robotic tank vision? You aren't going to try a full simulation and render an image from the tank's viewpoint and process this image for enemy tanks. However, this would be a good project for a computer vision researcher and may not be intractable if you identify the presence of tanks by color. Since you already have all the data for the robot tanks' positions, you can cut some corners and simulate the same effect.

In this section, you're not going to implement any behaviors; you're just going to add the *vision system*. Let's start by breaking down the vision system into more precise terms.

A robot tank A sees an enemy tank B if B's location in polar coordinates —centered on A—is within Θ of the direction A is facing (where Θ is half the field of view of tank A) and where there are no wall elements on the line segment between tank A and tank B.

The vision system is going to provide two outputs: a Boolean flag enemy_seen and a floating-point relative angle enemy_delta_angle. The angle tells you how many degrees to turn to face the enemy. The angle enemy_delta_angle is positive if the enemy tank is located clockwise from the friendly tank. Remember that you have defined clockwise as positive. If multiple enemy tanks are visible, enemy_delta_angle is the smallest angle of the angle to all enemies. After all, you want the tank to try to fire at the one it can hit first. If this angle is below a threshold, then the Boolean variable enemy_lined_up will be true; this tells you it's OK to fire a shell.

Here are the DEFINE statements related to tank properties. You're adding the ones for visibility:

YourARGame/Tank Wars Projects/twars_7_vision/twars_7_vision.cpp

```
#define SHOTS_PER_TANK 3
#define MISSILE_SPEED 8.0
//give tanks 120 degree field of view in front
#define TANK_FOV     120
#define HALF_TANK_FOV  TANK_FOV/2.0
//shoot if enemy is with 5 degrees of straight ahead
#define TANK_ALIGNED    5
```

Here are the new elements in the tank_s structure:

YourARGame/Tank Wars Projects/twars_7_vision/twars_7_vision.cpp

```
struct tank_s
{
    //current position
    float x,y,z,angle;
    //last position
    float last_x,last_y,last_z,last_angle;
    //translational and rotational velocity
    float velocity,dangle;
    //reset all movement requests
    bool move_cw,move_ccw,move_fast,move_slow,move_fire;
    //physics setting for this tank
    float max_rot_rate,max_speed;
    //status and actions
    //true=AI controlled, false=user controlled
    bool robot;
    int team;
    int damage;
    //true=active, false=destroyed
    bool status;
    //true for one time tick after collision with wall or missile
    bool crash;
    //missile info
    bool request_fire;
    //time in frames since tank last fired
    int reload_time;
    int time_to_reload;  //reload time setting
    //info on incoming missiles that recently hit tank
    bool recently_hit;  //true if tank has been hit
    float hit_angle;
    //vision system input
    bool enemy_seen;
    float enemy_delta_angle;
    //enemy tank is lined up, ready to fire a missile
    bool enemy_lined_up;
};
struct tank_s tank[NUM_TANKS];
```

Before you forget, initialize these booleans to false so that when you institute behaviors #1 and #2, the robot tanks don't misfire a missile as the game begins. As a conscientious tank commander, you want to avoid collateral damage.

YourARGame/Tank Wars Projects/twars_7_vision/twars_7_vision.cpp

```
for(int tank_num=0;tank_num<NUM_TANKS;tank_num++)  {
     tank[tank_num].dangle=0.0;
     //tank "performance" settings
     tank[tank_num].max_rot_rate=15.0; tank[tank_num].max_speed=5.0;
     //initial status and action settings
     //set all tanks to manual control
     tank[tank_num].robot=false;
     tank[tank_num].team=tank_num/5; tank[tank_num].status=true;
     tank[tank_num].crash=false; tank[tank_num].move_fire=false;
     tank[tank_num].damage=10;
     //reset all movement requests
     tank[tank_num].move_cw=false; tank[tank_num].move_ccw=false;
     tank[tank_num].move_fast=false; tank[tank_num].move_slow=false;
     tank[tank_num].request_fire=false;
     //missile related struct elements
     //time in frames since tank last fired
     tank[tank_num].reload_time=0;
     //reload time setting
     tank[tank_num].time_to_reload=4;
     //indicates if tank has recently been hit
     tank[tank_num].recently_hit=false;
     //robot tank AI
     tank[tank_num].enemy_seen=false;  tank[tank_num].enemy_lined_up=false;
   }
```

You're going to put all the AI code into a new function called game_engine_ai(), which you will call before game_engine_physics(). This new function is called from opengl_tick(); here is a code fragment with a single new line:

YourARGame/Tank Wars Projects/twars_7_vision/twars_7_vision.cpp

```
//update game
game_engine_ai();
game_engine_physics();

glutPostRedisplay();
```

And finally, here is the vision system implemented in game_engine_ai(). A double nested loop goes through all combinations of tanks. The outer loop goes through values of tank_num_a where A is the tank you're currently processing the vision for, and the inner loop goes through values of tank_num_b where B is the (potential) enemy tank.

```
YourARGame/Tank Wars Projects/twars_7_vision/twars_7_vision.cpp
```

```cpp
void game_engine_ai(void)
{
//vision for tanks
for(int tank_num_a=0;tank_num_a<NUM_TANKS;tank_num_a++)
    if(tank[tank_num_a].status)  {
        tank[tank_num_a].enemy_seen=false;  tank[tank_num_a].enemy_lined_up=false;
        tank[tank_num_a].enemy_delta_angle=HALF_TANK_FOV;
        for(int tank_num_b=0;tank_num_b<NUM_TANKS;tank_num_b++)
          if( (tank_num_a!=tank_num_b)&&(tank[tank_num_a].team!=tank[tank_num_b].team)
            //only consider alive tanks on different team
            &&(tank[tank_num_b].status) )  {
            float dx=tank[tank_num_b].x-tank[tank_num_a].x;
            float dy=tank[tank_num_b].y-tank[tank_num_a].y;
            float heading=get_angle(dx,dy);  //angle of B w.r.t A
            float heading_diff=heading-tank[tank_num_a].angle;
            if(heading_diff>180.0) heading_diff-=360.0;
            if(heading_diff<-180.0) heading_diff+=360.0;
            if(fabs(heading_diff)<HALF_TANK_FOV)  {
            //an enemy tank B does satisfy the angle criteria
            //see if tank B is in line of sight
            bool line_blocked=check_line_of_sight(tank[tank_num_a].x,tank[tank_num_a].y,
                tank[tank_num_b].x,tank[tank_num_b].y);
            if( (fabs(heading_diff)<fabs(tank[tank_num_a].enemy_delta_angle))
              &&(line_blocked==false))  {
              //enemy tank is visible, and is closest in angle so far
              //of all tanks checked
              tank[tank_num_a].enemy_delta_angle=heading_diff;
              tank[tank_num_a].enemy_seen=true;
              //see if tank B is within sights to fire missile
              if(fabs(heading_diff)<TANK_ALIGNED)
                tank[tank_num_a].enemy_lined_up=true;
                }
              }
            }
        }
}
```

In this code, you used a function called check_line_of_sight(x0, y0, x1, y1) to determine whether the line segment between tank A (assumed to be at x0, y0) and B (assumed to be at x1, y1) crosses a map square containing a wall.

This was put into a separate function because you're going to need this functionality later in your path planning.

YourARGame/Tank Wars Projects/twars_7_vision/twars_7_vision.cpp

```cpp
//see if a line segment crossed a "wall" square in the map
//check_line_of_sight() returns true if line segment does cross wall
bool check_line_of_sight(float x0, float y0, float x1, float y1)
{
    float dx=x1-x0;
    float dy=y1-y0;
    float distance=(float)sqrt(dx*dx+dy*dy);
    bool obstacle_in_way=false;
    float step_x=5.0*dx/distance,step_y=5.0*dy/distance;
    //send a text particle along trajectory to see if
    //it lands in a wall square
    float test_x=x0;
    float test_y=y0;
    for(float d=0.0;(d<=distance)&&(obstacle_in_way==false);d+=5.0)
    {
    int xm,ym;      //map coordinates
    //convert from world coordinates (in tank struct)
    //to map coordinates
    //using Eqn. 2 in chapter 9
    xm=(int)(0.1*test_x);
    ym=(int)(0.1*test_y);
    //check map image for wall square
    if(texmap[(xm+ym*MAP_WIDTH)*3]>50)
     obstacle_in_way=true;
    test_x+=step_x; test_y+=step_y;
    }
    return obstacle_in_way;
}
```

Since you are not yet implementing the behavior rules, you need some way to see whether your visibility code is working. To perform the test, you'll simply enlarge a tank depending on the Boolean flags enemy_seen and enemy_lined_up. If the former is true, the tank will be enlarged to 150%, and if the latter is true, it will be enlarged by 200%. Here is the code to do this temporary visualization:

YourARGame/Tank Wars Projects/twars_7_vision/twars_7_vision.cpp

```cpp
//--------adjust tank pose and render--------
//save modelview matrix for next iteration
glPushMatrix();
//convert from world coords to marker coords.
//Eqn. 1 in chapter 9
xa=0.5*tank[tank_num].x-80.0; ya=0.5*tank[tank_num].y-80.0;
glTranslatef(xa,ya,0.0);
glRotatef(tank[tank_num].angle,0,0,1);
```

```
//start temporary code for twars_7_vision to
//demonstrate vision engine
if(tank[tank_num].enemy_lined_up) glScalef(2.0,2.0,2.0);
else if(tank[tank_num].enemy_seen) glScalef(1.5,1.5,1.5);
//end temporary code for twars_7_vision to
//demonstrate vision engine

meshman_render_opengl(model_num,1,0);
glPopMatrix();
                    }
```

Figure 9.1, on the next page, shows the green tank enlarging to show that it has detected an enemy tank and is lined up with it (that is, ready to fire a missile). This causes the green tank to change from 100% to 150% and then to 200% of its normal size. The green tank starts at 100% in the top image; in the middle image, an enemy blue tank is in sight but not lined up, so the green tank is 150% of its normal size. In the bottom image, an enemy tank is visible and it's in the green tank's gun sights, so the green tank is 200% of its original size.

Here is the function get_angle(). You called this function in game_engine_ai() to turn an X and Y position into an angle (in degrees). This functionality will be needed several more times in the coming sections. As with other functions, the function is put at the top to avoid a function prototype.

```
YourARGame/Tank Wars Projects/twars_7_vision/twars_7_vision.cpp
```
```
float get_angle(double x,double y)
{
if(x!=0.0)
        {
        if(y>0.0) return atan2(y,x)*180.0/M_PI;
        else      return 360.0 + atan2(y,x)*180.0/M_PI;
        }
else
        {
        if(y<0.0) return 270.0;
        else      return 90.0;
        }
}
```

Now that you know it works, you'll remove the expanding tank visualization code in the next step.

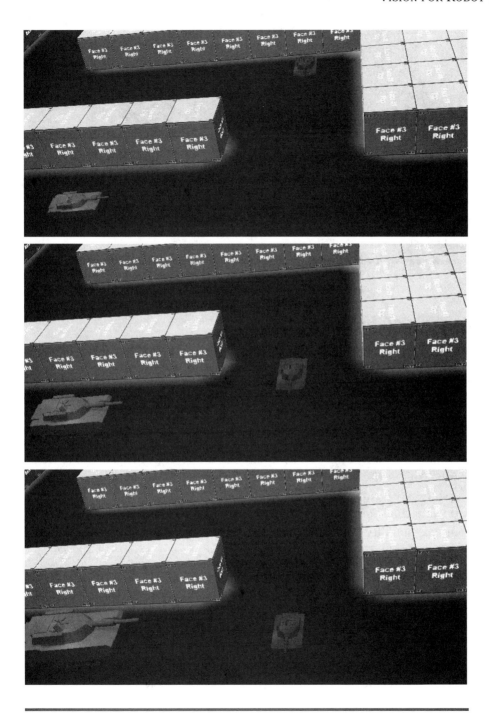

Figure 9.1: THE GREEN TANK CHANGES SIZE AS IT DETECTS AN ENEMY BLUE TANK.

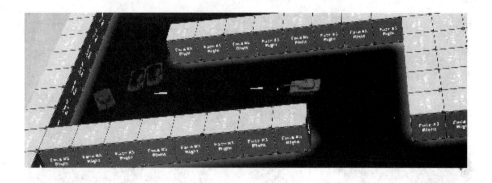

Figure 9.2: BEHAVIOR #1 IMPLEMENTED. THE GREEN ROBOT TANK FIRES SHELLS AT ENEMY TANKS.

9.3 Behavior #1: Firing a Missile

Here is behavior #1 again:

Behavior #1: if a robot tank sees an enemy tank and is lined up with it, it should launch a missile.

Figure 9.2 shows the green tank testing this fire behavior.

How do you implement behavior #1? Take a look at the next code fragment. This is the behavior section of code in game_engine_ai(), which runs after the game engine has determined what the robots tanks can *see*. Now that you have a clear plan and have already done the more complex visibility determination, it's only a couple lines to make behavior #1 happen:

```
YourARGame/Tank Wars Projects/twars_8_shoot/twars_8_shoot.cpp
//---- AI Behavior Priority System -----
for(int tank_num=0;tank_num<NUM_TANKS;tank_num++)
//AI only for alive robot tanks
   if((tank[tank_num].robot)&&(tank[tank_num].status)) {
      //check for conditions for behavior #1
      if(tank[tank_num].enemy_lined_up) {
         //behavior #1: If a robot tank sees an enemy tank
         //and is lined up with it, it should launch a missile.
         tank[tank_num].request_fire=true;
      }
   }
```

It may seem pedantic to not simply set the request_fire element directly inside your visibility code, but it clearly separates the stimulus from the response. This results in easier design and debugging, and it makes it easier to change things in the future.

To test your new behavior, select a tank and drive it in front of another. However, because of our testing of the tank[tank_num].robot flag (to see whether it's true), none of the tanks will fire because we have them all initialized to be manually controlled (that is, in main(), the .robot element of each tank structure was set to false). The following code must be added—both to the bottom of main() and after the existing code in opengl_key_down():

YourARGame/Tank Wars Projects/twars_8_shoot/twars_8_shoot.cpp

```
//make all tanks into robots except current manual tank
for(int tank_num=0;tank_num<NUM_TANKS;tank_num++)
  tank[tank_num].robot=true;
  tank[current_tank_num].robot=false;
```

9.4 Behavior #2: Rotating to Face the Enemy

Behavior #2: if a robot tank sees an enemy tank, it should rotate to line up with it.

Behavior #2 tells your robot tanks that if an enemy is seen—but not lined up—it should rotate to directly face the enemy. This will activate behavior #1, and the tank will fire a missile.

The angular speed dangle is set according to the direction and magnitude of the enemy_delta_angle reading. Using trial and error, a multiplier of 0.35 was chosen.

YourARGame/Tank Wars Projects/twars_9_face/twars_9_face.cpp

```
//---- AI Behavior Priority System -----
for(int tank_num=0;tank_num<NUM_TANKS;tank_num++)
//AI only for alive robot tanks
   if((tank[tank_num].robot)&&(tank[tank_num].status))  {
      //check for conditions for behavior #1
      if(tank[tank_num].enemy_lined_up)  {
         //behavior #1: If a robot tank sees an enemy tank
         //and is lined up with it, it should launch a missile.
         tank[tank_num].request_fire=true;
      }
      //check for conditions for behavior #2
      else if(tank[tank_num].enemy_seen)  {
         //behavior #2: "Behavior #2: If a robot tank
         //sees an enemy tank, it should rotate to line up with it.
         tank[tank_num].dangle=0.35*tank[tank_num].enemy_delta_angle;
      }
   }
```

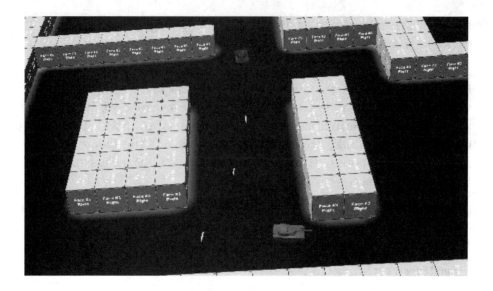

Figure 9.3: THE GREEN TANK DRIVES LEFT TO RIGHT WITH BLUE ROBOT FIRING.

Next, you will add the following code to the game_engine_ai() function. This will stop the robot tanks from rotating or driving too fast:

YourARGame/Tank Wars Projects/twars_9_face/twars_9_face.cpp

```
//make sure no robot tanks attempt to rotate or travel too fast
for(tank_num=0;tank_num<NUM_TANKS;tank_num++)
//AI only for alive robot tanks
   if((tank[tank_num].robot)&&(tank[tank_num].status))  {
      //keep velocity within limits
      if(tank[tank_num].velocity>tank[tank_num].max_speed)
         tank[tank_num].velocity=tank[tank_num].max_speed;
      if(tank[tank_num].velocity<-1.0*tank[tank_num].max_speed)
         tank[tank_num].velocity=-1.0*tank[tank_num].max_speed;
      //keep rotation speed within limits
      if(tank[tank_num].dangle>tank[tank_num].max_rot_rate)
         tank[tank_num].dangle=tank[tank_num].max_rot_rate;
      if(tank[tank_num].dangle<-1.0*tank[tank_num].max_rot_rate)
         tank[tank_num].dangle=-1.0*tank[tank_num].max_rot_rate;
   }
```

Figure 9.3 shows a green—manually controlled tank—driving left to right with a blue robot tank firing missiles.

9.5   Behavior #3: Responding to Attack

Behavior #3: If a robot tank gets hit by a missile, it will rotate to face the direction of the missile.

This code updates your behavior priority system by adding another "if else" loop:

```
YourARGame/Tank Wars Projects/twars_10_rotate/twars_10_rotate.cpp
```

```cpp
//---- AI Behavior Priority System -----
for(int tank_num=0;tank_num<NUM_TANKS;tank_num++)
//AI only for alive robot tanks
   if((tank[tank_num].robot)&&(tank[tank_num].status))  {
      //check for conditions for behavior #1
      if(tank[tank_num].enemy_lined_up)  {
         //behavior #1: If a robot tank sees an enemy tank
         //and is lined up with it, it should launch a missile.
         tank[tank_num].request_fire=true;
      }
      //check for conditions for behavior #2
      else if(tank[tank_num].enemy_seen)  {
         //behavior #2: If a robot tank sees an enemy tank,
         //             it should rotate to line up with it.
         tank[tank_num].dangle=0.35*tank[tank_num].enemy_delta_angle;
      }
      //check for conditions for behavior #3
      else if(tank[tank_num].recently_hit)  {
         //behavior #3: If a robot tank gets hit by a missile,
         //it will rotate to face the direction of where the
         //missile came from.
         float new_direction_to_face=tank[tank_num].hit_angle+180;
         float angle_to_attacker=new_direction_to_face-tank[tank_num].angle;
         while(angle_to_attacker>180.0)  angle_to_attacker-=360.0;
         while(angle_to_attacker<-180.0) angle_to_attacker+=360.0;
         tank[tank_num].dangle=0.35*angle_to_attacker;
      }
   }
```

9.6   Moving Tanks

Now it's time to add the behavior that defines where the tanks should move. Both behaviors D and E require that the tanks have the ability to travel from one point to another—even to points not in the current field of view. Consequently, you need the ability to tell a tank to find its way across the map by moving around the obstacles. In short, you need to institute some *path planning*.

Path planning is an area explored not only by game programmers but also by robotics researchers, and it also has parallels in circuit board design (that is, seeking to connect components). The path planning applications with which most people are familiar are the road navigation instructions you get from driving directions websites or from GPS navigation systems.

A common path planning algorithm is the *A* path planning* routine. A* (pronounced "A star") is a graph search algorithm that finds a path from a given initial node to a given goal node. The A* algorithm was first described in 1968 by Peter Hart, Nils Nilsson, and Bertram Raphael.

You will add A* path planning to your game so that the AI tanks can navigate around buildings as they make their way from one point on the map to another.

As with the other behaviors, you're going to create a simple path planning system. This is not necessarily the optimal solution, but it works and does not require too much abstract theory.

You're going to break the problem down into a process of finding a set of straight line segments that gives a solution from a start point to an endpoint. It will be a solution, but not necessarily the best solution.

We'll create a path_plan(xstart, ystart, xend, yend, tank_num) function that will return a set of intermediate line segments that will take us from the start point (xstart, ystart) to the endpoint (xend, yend) without crossing any wall map squares. At this point, it's time to rethink behaviors D and E. Here they are again:

Behavior D: helping behavior. A robot tank will drive to the last location where a teammate tank spotted an enemy.

Behavior E: patrolling behavior. A robot tank will pick a waypoint off a list (according to a pointer specific to the robot's team) and will navigate to the waypoint. The pointer will then be incremented so that the next bored robot picks a different destination.

Since you are solving the navigation problem by creating a list of waypoints, you should think about how this fits into your behavior priority scheme.

A tank that has invoked behavior E and is on its way to some destination for the patrolling behavior should break from this action if behavior D is invoked. After all, there is no point continuing to an arbitrary destination when your team already knows where an enemy is located.

How should you override the waypoint list? It probably wouldn't be good to do it every time a tank sees an enemy; that would lead to both a higher consumption of processing power (your path_plan() algorithm will take time to process), and it would also result in tanks indecisively twitching back and forth as they were pulled toward different battles.

A partial solution is to record whether the final destination is a patrolling landmark or the spotted location of an enemy. When path_plan() is called, you set a Boolean variable, coming_to_help, to true if you called path_plan() as part of behavior D, but not behavior E. So, at some time, a tank will decide whether to abort its current sightseeing mission and come to help. It will examine its coming_to_helptank_s structure element, and if it is false and somewhere in the map a team member tank sees an enemy, it will abandon its current waypoint stack and call path_plan() to the new destination.

To complete your solution, you need to decide when a tank should make the decision to change its travel plans. To stop the tank from the *twitching* behavior that we were worried about, you can do it whenever you have completed one leg of a waypoint list. A tank will thus ignore all pleas for help when it's busy driving in a straight line segment to a waypoint. Considering all of this, behaviors D and E need to be renamed.

Behavior #4: navigation. If it has any waypoints in its navigation list, a robot tank will navigate in a straight line to a waypoint.

Behavior #5: retasking. If a robot tank has just arrived at a waypoint, it will pull the next waypoint off the list if its coming_to_help variable is true. If coming_to_help is false and a team member currently sees an enemy, it will throw away the current waypoint list and plan a new path to the (X, Y) location of the friendly tank that spotted an enemy.

Behavior #6: patrolling: If a robot tank has no waypoints in its list, it will plan a path to one of a list of landmarks and set its coming_to_help Boolean variable to false.

These last three behaviors (#4, #5, and #6) are a slight departure from the first three in that behavior #5 is really a sub-behavior of behavior #4. Only if you are following the code for behavior #4 will you consider executing behavior #5, whereas behavior #6 stands alone.

Behaviors #4, #5, and #6 fit into the priority behavior structure as follows:

```
IF      (conditions for #1 are true) execute behavior #1
ELSE IF (conditions for #2 are true) execute behavior #2
ELSE IF (conditions for #3 are true) execute behavior #3
ELSE IF (conditions for #4 are true)
{
  execute behavior #4
  IF (tank arrives at waypoint)
  {
    IF (conditions for #5 are true) execute behavior #5
    ELSE    pop next waypoint off of list
  }
}
ELSE        execute behavior #6
```

Now that you have a framework, you're going to build it up piece by piece, and you'll test it as you go. First, in twars_11_travel.cpp, you're going to implement behavior #4 (following waypoints). You'll set up these waypoints manually, and then you'll actually create and test the path_plan() function (twars_12_path_plan.cpp). Following this, you'll code the two remaining behaviors (#5 and #6), and the game engine will be complete.

9.7 Behavior #4: Moving Agents: Getting from Point A to B

Path_plan(xstart, ystart, xend, yend, tank_num) will provide a list of points to target, each of which has a clear line one can navigate to from the last—without crossing a wall map square. You're not going to code path_plan() until the next section; right now, you're just going to test that you can execute behavior #4 and follow the output waypoint list of path_plan().

Behavior #4: navigation. If it has any waypoints in its navigation list, a robot tank will navigate in a straight line to a waypoint.

Next, let's set up the waypoints—the *planned travel*. For each tank, you'll add an array that will hold a list of waypoints and a variable that will define how many waypoints are valid.

YourARGame/Tank Wars Projects/twars_11_travel/twars_11_travel.cpp

```
struct tank_s
{
    //current position
    float x,y,z,angle;
    //last position
    float last_x,last_y,last_z,last_angle;
```

```
//translational and rotational velocity
float velocity,dangle;
//reset all movement requests
bool move_cw,move_ccw,move_fast,move_slow,move_fire;
//physics setting for this tank
float max_rot_rate,max_speed;
//status and actions
//true=AI controlled, false=user controlled
bool robot;
int team;
int damage;
//true=active, false=destroyed        bool status;
//true for one time tick after collision with wall or missile
bool crash;
//missile info
bool request_fire;
//time in frames since tank last fired
int reload_time;
int time_to_reload;  //reload time setting
//info on incoming missiles that recently hit tank
bool recently_hit;  //true if tank has been hit
float hit_angle;
//vision system input
bool enemy_seen;
float enemy_delta_angle;
//enemy tank is lined up, ready to fire a missile
bool enemy_lined_up;
//path planning for robot tanks
int num_waypoints;
float waypoint_x[MAX_NUM_WAYPOINTS];
float waypoint_y[MAX_NUM_WAYPOINTS];
};
struct tank_s tank[NUM_TANKS];
```

You'll also add a line to initialize num_waypoints to zero in the main()
initialization loop:

YourARGame/Tank Wars Projects/twars_11_travel/twars_11_travel.cpp

```
for(int tank_num=0;tank_num<NUM_TANKS;tank_num++)  {
tank[tank_num].dangle=0.0;
//tank "performance" settings
tank[tank_num].max_rot_rate=15.0; tank[tank_num].max_speed=5.0;
//initial status and action settings
//set all tanks to manually controlled
tank[tank_num].robot=false;
tank[tank_num].team=tank_num/5; tank[tank_num].status=true;
tank[tank_num].crash=false; tank[tank_num].move_fire=false;
tank[tank_num].damage=10;
//reset all movement requests
tank[tank_num].move_cw=false; tank[tank_num].move_ccw=false;
tank[tank_num].move_fast=false; tank[tank_num].move_slow=false;
tank[tank_num].request_fire=false;
```

```
//missile related struct elements
//time in frames since tank last fired
tank[tank_num].reload_time=0;
//reload time setting
tank[tank_num].time_to_reload=4;
//indicates if tank has recently been hit
tank[tank_num].recently_hit=false;
//robot tank AI
tank[tank_num].enemy_seen=false;
tank[tank_num].enemy_lined_up=false;
//path planning for robot tanks
tank[tank_num].num_waypoints=0;
}
//temporary code for testing navigation
//set tank #0 to robot
current_tank_num=-1;
tank[0].robot=true;
i=0;
tank[0].waypoint_x[i]=30.0; tank[0].waypoint_y[i]=120.0; i++;
tank[0].waypoint_x[i]=35.0; tank[0].waypoint_y[i]=155.0; i++;
tank[0].waypoint_x[i]=35.0; tank[0].waypoint_y[i]=240.0; i++;
tank[0].waypoint_x[i]=115.0; tank[0].waypoint_y[i]=275.0; i++;
tank[0].waypoint_x[i]=225.0; tank[0].waypoint_y[i]=275.0; i++;
tank[0].waypoint_x[i]=225.0; tank[0].waypoint_y[i]=175.0; i++;
tank[0].waypoint_x[i]=180.0; tank[0].waypoint_y[i]=100.0; i++;
tank[0].waypoint_x[i]=140.0; tank[0].waypoint_y[i]=100.0; i++;
tank[0].num_waypoints=i;
```

You will add some define statements at the top—including reducing NUM_TANKS to 1 so that you can experiment with your tank travel and path planning with just one tank. The others are angle, speed, and distance thresholds that are used in navigation.

> YourARGame/Tank Wars Projects/twars_11_travel/twars_11_travel.cpp

```
//#define NUM_TANKS 10
//just one tank for testing navigation
#define NUM_TANKS 1
#define MAX_NUM_WAYPOINTS 50
```

A tank will check its num_waypoints element, and if it's nonzero, it will turn and drive toward (waypoint_x[0], waypoint_y[0]). The tank will look at (waypoint_x[0], waypoint_y[0]) only if it arrives at the waypoint. At this point, it will bump the whole list down and decrement num_waypoints.

Here is the new code to be added to the main behavior priority code:

```
YourARGame/Tank Wars Projects/twars_11_travel/twars_11_travel.cpp
//---- AI Behavior Priority System -----
for(int tank_num=0;tank_num<NUM_TANKS;tank_num++)
//AI only for alive robot tanks
   if((tank[tank_num].robot)&&(tank[tank_num].status))  {
      //check for conditions for behavior #1
      if(tank[tank_num].enemy_lined_up)  {
         //behavior #1: If a robot tank sees an enemy tank
         //and is lined up with it, it should launch a missile.
         tank[tank_num].request_fire=true;
      }

      //check for conditions for behavior #2
      else if(tank[tank_num].enemy_seen)  {
         //behavior #2: If a robot tank sees an enemy tank,
         //            it should rotate to line up with it.
         tank[tank_num].dangle=0.35*tank[tank_num].enemy_delta_angle;
      }

      //check for conditions for behavior #3
      else if(tank[tank_num].recently_hit)  {
         //behavior #3: If a robot tank gets hit by a missile,
         //it will rotate to face the direction of where
         //the missile came from.
         float new_direction_to_face=tank[tank_num].hit_angle+180;
         float angle_to_attacker=new_direction_to_face-tank[tank_num].angle;
         while(angle_to_attacker>180.0)  angle_to_attacker-=360.0;
         while(angle_to_attacker<-180.0) angle_to_attacker+=360.0;
         tank[tank_num].dangle=0.35*angle_to_attacker;
      }

      //behavior #4: see if we have a path to travel on
      else if(tank[tank_num].num_waypoints>0)  {
         //navigate towards next destination
         float heading=get_angle(tank[tank_num].waypoint_x[0]-tank[tank_num].x,
                                 tank[tank_num].waypoint_y[0]-tank[tank_num].y);
         float heading_diff=heading-tank[tank_num].angle;
         if(heading_diff>180.0)  heading_diff-=360.0;
         if(heading_diff<-180.0) heading_diff+=360.0;

         //see if tank is facing close enough to the right direction
         if(fabs(heading_diff)<DRIVE_ANGLE_ERROR)  {
            tank[tank_num].dangle=0.0;
                        //stop rotating
            //drive towards next waypoint
            //measure distance (approximate with 'Manhattan'
            //distance to save sqrt)
            float distance=fabs(tank[tank_num].waypoint_x[0]-tank[tank_num].x+
                                tank[tank_num].waypoint_y[0]-tank[tank_num].y);
```

```
                          //see if we've arrived
                          if(distance<WAYPOINT_CLOSE_ENOUGH)  {
                              //----------- Add behavior #5 here --------------
                              //bump waypoints down one
                              for(int k=0;k<tank[tank_num].num_waypoints;k++)  {
                                  tank[tank_num].waypoint_x[k]=tank[tank_num].waypoint_x[k+1];
                                  tank[tank_num].waypoint_y[k]=tank[tank_num].waypoint_y[k+1];
                              }
                              tank[tank_num].num_waypoints--;
                              if(tank[tank_num].velocity>0.5)
                                  tank[tank_num].move_slow=true;  //slow down if still moving
                          }
                          else  {
                              //we haven't arrived, but are pointing in the right direction
                              //choose speed depending on distance
                              if(distance>DISTANCE_TO_SLOW_DOWN)
                              tank[tank_num].move_fast=true;  //accelerate
                              else  {
                                  //close to destination
                                  if(tank[tank_num].velocity<=0.0)
                                      //accelerate a bit if close but not there yet
                                      tank[tank_num].move_fast=true;
                                  if(tank[tank_num].velocity>1.6)
                                  //deaccelarate, getting close
                                      tank[tank_num].move_slow=true;
                              }
                          }
                      }
                      else  {
                          //rotate to face waypoint
                          tank[tank_num].dangle=0.35*heading_diff;
                      }
                  }
              }
          }
```

Note the comment Add behavior #5 here; this is where you'll plug in your helping behavior code where you consider aborting the remaining list in favor of going to help a team member.

Remember that it's a good idea to test every new piece of code as you add the lines. You created eight waypoints and initialized tank #0 with them in its list at start-up. Since there are no enemy tanks or incoming missiles to invoke behaviors #1–#3, it will proceed with behavior #4.

For this example, the waypoints were chosen by looking in an image viewer with map.ppm resized to 320 by 320 and inverted to have the origin in the bottom left (as in the map coordinate system). After the points were chosen, it was returned to its original vertically flipped mode.

The points were read off and entered in the following main() code:

```
YourARGame/Tank Wars Projects/twars_11_travel/twars_11_travel.cpp
for(int tank_num=0;tank_num<NUM_TANKS;tank_num++)  {
tank[tank_num].dangle=0.0;
//tank "performance" settings
tank[tank_num].max_rot_rate=15.0; tank[tank_num].max_speed=5.0;
//initial status and action settings
//set all tanks to manually controlled
tank[tank_num].robot=false;
tank[tank_num].team=tank_num/5; tank[tank_num].status=true;
tank[tank_num].crash=false; tank[tank_num].move_fire=false;
tank[tank_num].damage=10;
//reset all movement requests
tank[tank_num].move_cw=false; tank[tank_num].move_ccw=false;
tank[tank_num].move_fast=false; tank[tank_num].move_slow=false;
tank[tank_num].request_fire=false;
//missile related struct elements
//time in frames since tank last fired
tank[tank_num].reload_time=0;
//reload time setting
tank[tank_num].time_to_reload=4;
//indicates if tank has recently been hit
tank[tank_num].recently_hit=false;
//robot tank AI
tank[tank_num].enemy_seen=false;
tank[tank_num].enemy_lined_up=false;
//path planning for robot tanks
tank[tank_num].num_waypoints=0;
}
//temporary code for testing navigation
//set tank #0 to robot
current_tank_num=-1;
tank[0].robot=true;
i=0;
tank[0].waypoint_x[i]=30.0; tank[0].waypoint_y[i]=120.0; i++;
tank[0].waypoint_x[i]=35.0; tank[0].waypoint_y[i]=155.0; i++;
tank[0].waypoint_x[i]=35.0; tank[0].waypoint_y[i]=240.0; i++;
tank[0].waypoint_x[i]=115.0; tank[0].waypoint_y[i]=275.0; i++;
tank[0].waypoint_x[i]=225.0; tank[0].waypoint_y[i]=275.0; i++;
tank[0].waypoint_x[i]=225.0; tank[0].waypoint_y[i]=175.0; i++;
tank[0].waypoint_x[i]=180.0; tank[0].waypoint_y[i]=100.0; i++;
tank[0].waypoint_x[i]=140.0; tank[0].waypoint_y[i]=100.0; i++;
tank[0].num_waypoints=i;
```

Figure 9.4, on the following page, shows the planned path, and Figure 9.5, on page 255, shows the result. The glClear() command and camera quad–drawing code were removed to create the "time-lapse photography" effect, and the OpenGL image buffer is never cleared.

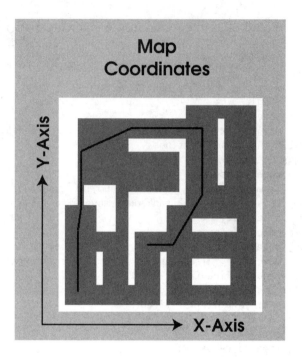

Figure 9.4: TEST OF TWARS_11_TRAVEL.CPP. A TANK AUTOMATICALLY NAVIGATING TO EIGHT WAYPOINTS.

9.8 Path Planning

A game or animation becomes a lot more impressive—and fun—if the elements are able to find their way around obstacles. We've defined our solution for navigation as navigating in straight line segments that are guaranteed not to collide with any walls. We have specified a challenging programming task: create a list of connecting straight line segments from a starting point to an endpoint such that none of them crosses through a map square occupied by wall. This is encapsulated in the function path_plan(xstart, ystart, xend, yend, tank_num). In video games, it is common for this function to be applied offline. However, we're going to use a simple enough algorithm that it will be done at run time.

Such a function is useful for many game and animation types—not just your Tank Wars game. For example, if we were writing a SimCity-style simulation, we may need your pizza delivery cars or fire engines to travel between points in the map.

Figure 9.5: THE glCLEAR() COMMAND AND THE CAMERA QUAD–DRAWING CODE WERE REMOVED.

Our path planning algorithm is going to use the map.ppm grid with a maze-finding algorithm. Obviously, this is going to take up some processing time—this is why our map.ppm file is a low-resolution (32 by 32) image. An alternative to a grid-based method with *occupied* and *free* squares for path planning is to consider all the obstacles as vectors— this way we would be free from a grid altogether. People have created path planning algorithms using a vector description and used them for things such as finding Delaunay triangulations and other theories from the field of computational geometry.

We're going to create a two-part system. The first part uses a maze-finding algorithm to find a solution, and the second part iteratively reduces the number of waypoints according to visibility criteria.

Let's dive right into the code for the path planning with the first part: using a *maze-finding* algorithm to find a route from our start point to an endpoint.

```cpp
#define MAP_SIZE MAP_WIDTH*MAP_WIDTH
#define MAX_MAZEFIND_STEPS 200
//comment out in running version
#define DEBUG_OUTPUT_MAZEFIND_PGM
//comment out in running version
#define DEBUG_OUTPUT_PATH_PLAN_PGM


void path_plan(float xstart, float ystart, float xend,
    float yend, int tank_num)
{
  int i,j;
  //working world map
  unsigned char temp_world[MAP_SIZE];
  FILE *maze_image;

  //maze finding variables
  int start_x,start_y,end_x,end_y,here_x,here_y,attempts,
    best_value;
  int off_x[4],off_y[4],maze_distance,best_dir,last_dir;
  int node_x[MAX_MAZEFIND_STEPS],node_y[MAX_MAZEFIND_STEPS],
    node_ptr,deletions;

  //encode directions with single index
  off_x[0]= 1; off_y[0]= 0;
  off_x[1]= 0; off_y[1]= 1;
  off_x[2]=-1; off_y[2]= 0;
  off_x[3]= 0; off_y[3]=-1;


  //------------ PATH PLAN STAGE 1 - MAZE FINDING ------

  //convert from world to map coordinates.
  //Eqn. 2 in chapter 9
  start_x=(int)(0.1*xstart);
  start_y=(int)(0.1*ystart);
  end_x=(int)(0.1*xend);
  end_y=(int)(0.1*yend);
  //check if start or end position is on a wall square
  if( (texmap[(start_x+start_y*MAP_WIDTH)*3]>50)
    ||(texmap[(end_x+end_y*MAP_WIDTH)*3]>50) )
    return;

  //create copy of world map
  for(i=0;i<MAP_SIZE;i++) {
    if(texmap[i*3]>50) *(temp_world+i)=2;
    else *(temp_world+i)=0;
  }
```

```
here_x=start_x;here_y=start_y;
node_ptr=0; last_dir=-1;
attempts=0;
while(((here_x!=end_x)||(here_y!=end_y))&&
    (attempts<MAX_MAZEFIND_STEPS-1))  {
    *(temp_world+here_x+here_y*MAP_WIDTH)=1;
    best_value=1000;
    for( i=0; i<4; i++ )  {
        if(*(temp_world+here_x+off_x[i]+(here_y+off_y[i])*MAP_WIDTH)==0)
    {
            maze_distance=abs(end_x-here_x-off_x[i])
                          +abs(end_y-here_y-off_y[i]);
            if(maze_distance<=best_value)
              {best_dir=i;best_value=maze_distance;}
        }
    }

    if(best_value==1000)  {
        // must be boxed in, now try best direction already been
        *(temp_world+here_x+here_y*MAP_WIDTH)=2;
        for(i=0;i<4;i++)  {
            if(*(temp_world+here_x+off_x[i]+(here_y+off_y[i])*MAP_WIDTH)==1)
    {
                maze_distance=abs(end_x-here_x-off_x[i])
                              +abs(end_y-here_y-off_y[i]);
                if(maze_distance<=best_value)
                    {best_dir=i;best_value=maze_distance;}
            }
        }
    }

    if(best_dir!=last_dir)  {
        node_x[node_ptr]=here_x;
        node_y[node_ptr]=here_y;
        if(node_ptr<100) node_ptr++;
        last_dir=best_dir;
    }

    if(*(temp_world+here_x+here_y*MAP_WIDTH)==0)
        *(temp_world+here_x+here_y*MAP_WIDTH)=1;
    here_x+=off_x[best_dir];
    here_y+=off_y[best_dir];
    attempts++;
}

if((here_x==end_x)&&(here_y==end_y))  {
    *(temp_world+here_x+here_y*MAP_WIDTH)=1;
    node_x[node_ptr]=here_x;
    node_y[node_ptr]=here_y;
    node_ptr++;
  }
```

```
#ifdef DEBUG_OUTPUT_MAZEFIND_PGM
//--temporary code for twars_12_path_plan.cpp--
//output greyscale PGM image showing result of
//maze-finding algorithm

  maze_image=(FILE*)fopen("debug_mazefind.pgm","wb");
  if(maze_image==NULL)
    {printf("ERROR: Couldn't open debug_mazefind.pgm
      for writing\n");exit(1);}
  fprintf(maze_image,"P5\n#twars_12_path_plan.cpp\n");
  fprintf(maze_image,"%d %d\n255\n",MAP_WIDTH,MAP_WIDTH);
  for(i=0;i<MAP_SIZE;i++) {
    if(temp_world[i]==0) fputc(0,maze_image);
    else if(temp_world[i]==1) fputc(100,maze_image);
    else fputc(255,maze_image);
  }
  fclose(maze_image);

#endif

if(attempts==MAX_MAZEFIND_STEPS-1) return;   //couldn't find path there
```

You can see in this code that we're copying your map image into a temporary map called temp_world. In this system, 0 corresponds to a free square, and 2 marks a wall. As our test point (here_x, here_y) navigates through the maze, it will leave a quasi-wall of one square behind it; this effect is similar to the light bikes in the classic Tron video game. Unlike Tron, though, we're allowed to go back on squares that were already visited.

The main action in the previous code sample happens in a while loop. We loop until either the test point makes it to the destination or we run out of iterations—the latter meaning the tank gives up. At each step, we evaluate one of four directions (north, west, south, east) and determine which brings us closest to our goal. We do this by examining the best_value variable). As we go along, we fill in our list of points (node_x[], node_y[]).

As always, we want to test each addition when creating a large program. How are we going to test this section? We can see that we are adding in some temporary code that writes out a binary PGM file (which shows the result of the path planning algorithm). Note that we can disable this code later by commenting out the #define DEBUG_OUTPUT_MAZEFIND_PGM statement. Remember that a PGM file is a grayscale version of a PPM file; it is simply a small header followed by an uncompressed stream of pixels—easy to use in programs.

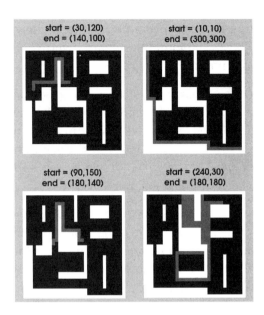

Figure 9.6: TESTING THE MAZE-FINDING PART OF PATH_PLAN()

With this debug code active, run it through a few tests by calling it in main(). Just after we load map.ppm (adding the code here saves time since we don't have to load all the 3D models, textures, and other elements). Notice how there are four calls to path_plan() with only one uncommented at a time. We are able to do this since we're writing out only one image and it always has the same name.

YourARGame/Tank Wars Projects/twars_12_path_plan/twars_12_path_plan.cpp

```
texmap=texture_read_ppm(MAP_BITMAP_NAME,&width,&height);
if (texmap!=NULL)
glTexImage2D(GL_TEXTURE_2D, 0, GL_RGB, width, height, 0,
  GL_RGB, GL_UNSIGNED_BYTE,texmap);
else {
 printf("Couldn't load <%s>\n",MAP_BITMAP_NAME);exit(1);}
 if((width!=MAP_WIDTH)||(height!=MAP_HEIGHT))
 {printf("ERROR: map width,height=%d,%d
    expecting %d,%d\n",width,height,MAP_WIDTH,MAP_HEIGHT);exit(1);}

/*
//--start temporary code for first part of twars_12_path_plan.cpp--
//    path_plan(30.0,120.0,140.0,100.0,0);
//    path_plan(10.0,10.0,300.0,300.0,0);
//    path_plan(90.0,150.0,180.0,140.0,0);
   path_plan(240.0,30.0,180.0,180.0,0);
   exit(1);
//--end temporary code for first part of twars_12_path_plan.cpp--
```

The result of testing these four planned paths is shown in Figure 9.6, on the preceding page. The map images are inverted to show how they look in an image manipulation program.

So far, path_plan() has created a list of waypoints (node_x[], node_y[]). These are not very efficient, especially those in the last path (see Figure 9.6, on the previous page). You will now improve your path planning with a second stage. In this stage, you will remove unnecessary points if there is a line of sight between the previous and subsequent points. This is the promised reuse of check_line_of_sight()!

Here is the new code (added to path_plan), which performs this reduction of waypoints. The actual code is quite small, but the debug visualization code to produce a PGM image that visualizes our path is larger. However, those who have done a lot of programming will tell you that debugging can take up a lot of your time, and it's worth it to be sure things work before you move on. Think of it like scaffolding that is taken down after a building is built. We have the option to deactivate this code by commenting out a define statement.

YourARGame/Tank Wars Projects/twars_12_path_plan/twars_12_path_plan.cpp

```
//------- PATH PLAN STAGE 2 - Remove Unnecessary Waypoints ----
    do {
        deletions=0;
        for(j=0;j<node_ptr-2;j++)  {
            //see if the second node from here is in line of sight. Convert
            //to point in center of map square (inverse of Eqn. 2)
            float xwa=10.0*node_x[j]+5.0;
            float ywa=10.0*node_y[j]+5.0;
            float xwb=10.0*node_x[j+2]+5.0;
            float ywb=10.0*node_y[j+2]+5.0;
            if(check_line_of_sight(xwa,ywa,xwb,ywb)==false)
            {
                deletions=1;
                //remove node j+1 and shift all down
                for(i=j+1;i<node_ptr;i++)  {
                    node_x[i]=node_x[i+1];
                    node_y[i]=node_y[i+1];
                    }
                node_ptr--;
            }
        }
    } while(deletions!=0);

    //check that our list is not too long for tank waypoints struct
    if(node_ptr>MAX_NUM_WAYPOINTS-1) return;  //cannot reduce
```

```
    for(i=1;i<node_ptr;i++)   {  //start from 1 not 0
    //for each waypoint, convert from map coords to world coords
    //put waypoint in middle of map square (+5)
    tank[tank_num].waypoint_x[i-1]=10.0*(float)node_x[i]+5.0;
    tank[tank_num].waypoint_y[i-1]=10.0*(float)node_y[i]+5.0;
    }
    tank[tank_num].num_waypoints=node_ptr-1;

#ifdef DEBUG_OUTPUT_PATH_PLAN_PGM
//--temporary code for twars_12_path_plan.cpp--
//output greyscale PGM image showing result of second stage
//of path planning
{
float x0,y0;
FILE *stage2file;
unsigned char *debug_stage2=(unsigned char*)malloc(MAP_SIZE*100);

if(debug_stage2==NULL)
    {printf("ERROR mallocing debug_stage2\n");exit(1);}

for(j=0;j<MAP_WIDTH*10;j++)
    for(i=0;i<MAP_WIDTH*10;i++)
        {
        int xm=i/10,ym=j/10;
        if(temp_world[xm+ym*MAP_WIDTH]==2)
            debug_stage2[i+j*MAP_WIDTH*10]=255;
        else
            debug_stage2[i+j*MAP_WIDTH*10]=180;
        }

//print out waypoints to console window
printf("%d waypoints\n",tank[tank_num].num_waypoints);
for(i=0;i<tank[tank_num].num_waypoints;i++)
    printf("Waypoint:%d   %f,%f\n",
      i,tank[tank_num].waypoint_x[i],tank[tank_num].waypoint_y[i]);

//draw lines connecting waypoints
x0=xstart; y0=ystart;
for(i=0;i<tank[tank_num].num_waypoints;i++)
    {
    float x1=tank[tank_num].waypoint_x[i];
    float y1=tank[tank_num].waypoint_y[i];
    float dx=(x1-x0)/500.0,dy=(y1-y0)/500.0;
    while(fabs(x1-x0)+fabs(y1-y0)>1.0)
        {
        debug_stage2[(int)x0+(int)y0*MAP_WIDTH*10]=0;
        x0+=dx; y0+=dy;
        }
    x0=x1; y0=y1;  //last point
    }
```

```
//write out as PGM file
stage2file=(FILE*)fopen("debug_path_plan.pgm","wb");
if(stage2file==NULL)
   {printf("ERROR: Couldn't open debug_path_plan.pgm
      for writing\n");exit(1);}
fprintf(maze_image, "P5\n#twars_12_path_plan.cpp\n");
fprintf(maze_image, "%d %d\n255\n",MAP_WIDTH*10,MAP_WIDTH*10);
fwrite(debug_stage2,MAP_SIZE*100,1,stage2file);
fclose(stage2file);
free(debug_stage2);
}
#endif
```

In Figure 9.7 and Figure 9.8, on the facing page, you can see the debug output results of using the previous four paths.

Now let's test it. We'll comment out the lines in the middle of main()— where path_plan() was called to generate the last two figures. Comment out the exit(1) statement with them, and add one path_plan() call at the end of main(). Also note that we're commenting out the manual waypoint assignments from twars_11.

YourARGame/Tank Wars Projects/twars_12_path_plan/twars_12_path_plan.cpp

```
//set tank #0 to robot
current_tank_num=-1;
tank[0].robot=true;

/*
   //manual waypoint creation for twars_11
   i=0;
   tank[0].waypoint_x[i]=30.0; tank[0].waypoint_y[i]=120.0; i++;
   tank[0].waypoint_x[i]=35.0; tank[0].waypoint_y[i]=155.0; i++;
   tank[0].waypoint_x[i]=35.0; tank[0].waypoint_y[i]=240.0; i++;
   tank[0].waypoint_x[i]=115.0; tank[0].waypoint_y[i]=275.0; i++;
   tank[0].waypoint_x[i]=225.0; tank[0].waypoint_y[i]=275.0; i++;
   tank[0].waypoint_x[i]=225.0; tank[0].waypoint_y[i]=175.0; i++;
   tank[0].waypoint_x[i]=180.0; tank[0].waypoint_y[i]=100.0; i++;
   tank[0].waypoint_x[i]=140.0; tank[0].waypoint_y[i]=100.0; i++;
   tank[0].num_waypoints=i;
*/
   path_plan(30.0,30.0,210.0,160.0,0);
```

If we call path_plan() with the wrong starting point, our tank will attempt to drive straight to the first waypoint and may crash into a wall. Due to a bug, this occurred during our testing, and it shows that the walls do stop the robot tanks—a benefit of having the AI separated from the game physics.

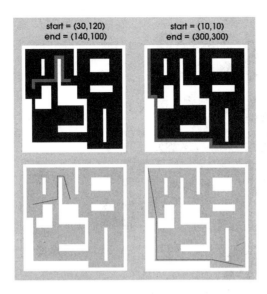

Figure 9.7: FIRST MAZE-FINDING STAGE (TOP) AND REDUCED WAYPOINT LIST (BOTTOM)

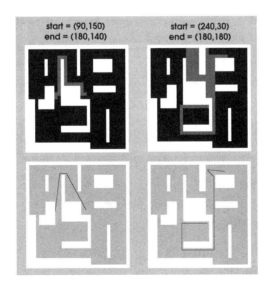

Figure 9.8: MORE PATH_PLAN() RESULTS

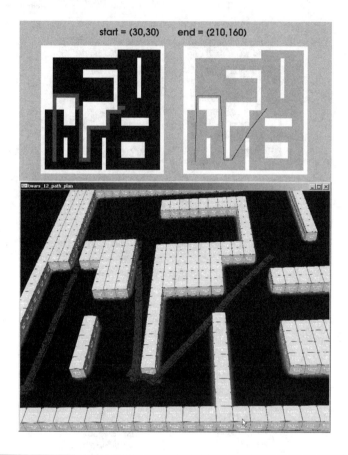

Figure 9.9: TESTING PATH_PLAN() WITH A ROBOT TANK

Figure 9.9 shows a time-lapse screenshot with the path planning PGMs added. Unlike the previous images in this section, the PGMs are vertically flipped to fit the world coordinate system.

For the next program, you'll comment out DEBUG_OUTPUT_MAZEFIND_PGM and DEBUG_OUTPUT_PATH_PLAN_PGM so that you're not writing out debug images every time you plan a path.

9.9 Behavior #6: Patrolling

Now that you have done all the path planning heavy lifting, you can implement the last two behaviors and complete the AI behavior for Tank Wars. You're going to go these in reverse order—you'll implement the last behavior first.

Behavior #6: patrolling. If a robot tank has no waypoints in its list, it will plan a path to a landmark and set its coming_to_help Boolean variable to false.

At this point, you need to create a list of landmark locations and add code to the behavior priority system to call path_plan() to one of these locations. You'll also need to manage an index of used landmarks so that the tanks fan out and search the whole world for enemies.

To do this, you'll add the patrol_landmark_num element to the tank_s structure, and the global variable array patrol_landmark_num—patrol_landmark_num[team_num] gives the next free landmark to target. The landmarks are stored in landmark_x[], _y[]. Every time a robot tank gets a landmark from the list using the index patrol_landmark_num[team_num], it increments the index (and possibly wraps around to zero) so that the next tank on the team goes to the next location.

YourARGame/Tank Wars Projects/twars_13_patrol/twars_13_patrol.cpp

```
struct tank_s
    {
    //current position
    float x,y,z,angle;
    //last position
    float last_x,last_y,last_z,last_angle;
    //translational and rotational velocity
    float velocity,dangle;
    //reset all movement requests
    bool move_cw,move_ccw,move_fast,move_slow,move_fire;
    //physics setting for this tank
    float max_rot_rate,max_speed;
    //status and actions
    //true=AI controlled, false=user controlled
    bool robot;
    int team;
    int damage;
    //true=active, false=destroyed
    bool status;
    //true for one time tick after collision with
    //wall or missile
    bool crash;
    //missile info
    bool request_fire;
    //time in frames since tank last fired
    int reload_time;
    int time_to_reload;  //reload time setting
    //info on incoming missiles that recently hit tank
    bool recently_hit;  //true if tank has been hit
    float hit_angle;
```

```
        //vision system input
        bool enemy_seen;
        float enemy_delta_angle;
        //enemy tank is lined up, ready to fire a missile
        bool enemy_lined_up;
        //path planning for robot tanks
        int num_waypoints;
        float waypoint_x[MAX_NUM_WAYPOINTS];
        float waypoint_y[MAX_NUM_WAYPOINTS];
        //true means that planned path is towards battle
        bool coming_to_help;
        int patrol_landmark_num;
        };
struct tank_s tank[NUM_TANKS];
int current_tank_num;

int patrol_landmark_num[64];   //assume worst case 64 teams
int num_landmarks;
```

You need to select some landmark areas to go to in the world:

```
YourARGame/Tank Wars Projects/twars_13_patrol/twars_13_patrol.cpp
```

```
landmark_x[0]=10.0;   landmark_y[0]=180.0;
landmark_x[1]=10.0;   landmark_y[1]=270.0;
landmark_x[2]=220.0;  landmark_y[2]=200.0;
landmark_x[3]=280.0;  landmark_y[3]=230.0;
landmark_x[4]=290.0;  landmark_y[4]=20.0;
landmark_x[5]=130.0;  landmark_y[5]=10.0;
landmark_x[6]=140.0;  landmark_y[6]=200.0;
landmark_x[7]=30.0;   landmark_y[7]=40.0;
landmark_x[8]=140.0;  landmark_y[8]=50.0;
landmark_x[9]=250.0;  landmark_y[9]=170.0;
num_landmarks=10;

patrol_landmark_num[0]=0;
patrol_landmark_num[1]=5;
```

Here is the implementation of behavior #6:

```
YourARGame/Tank Wars Projects/twars_13_patrol/twars_13_patrol.cpp
```

```
//---- AI Behavior Priority System -----
for(int tank_num=0;tank_num<NUM_TANKS;tank_num++)
//AI only for alive robot tanks
if((tank[tank_num].robot)&&(tank[tank_num].status))
{
//check for conditions for behavior #1
if(tank[tank_num].enemy_lined_up)  {
//behavior #1: If a robot tank sees an enemy tank
//and is lined up with it, it should launch a missile.
tank[tank_num].request_fire=true;
}
```

```
//check for conditions for behavior #2
else if(tank[tank_num].enemy_seen)  {
 //behavior #2: If a robot tank sees an enemy tank,
 //it should rotate to line up with it.
 tank[tank_num].dangle=0.35*tank[tank_num].enemy_delta_angle;
}
//check for conditions for behavior #3
else if(tank[tank_num].recently_hit)  {
 //behavior #3: If a robot tank gets hit by a missile,
 //it will rotate to face the direction of where the
 //missile came from.
 float new_direction_to_face=tank[tank_num].hit_angle+180;
 float angle_to_attacker=new_direction_to_face-tank[tank_num].angle;
 while(angle_to_attacker>180.0)  angle_to_attacker-=360.0;
 while(angle_to_attacker<-180.0) angle_to_attacker+=360.0;
 tank[tank_num].dangle=0.35*angle_to_attacker;
}


//behavior #4: see if we have a path to travel on
else if(tank[tank_num].num_waypoints>0)  {
//navigate towards next destination
float heading=get_angle(tank[tank_num].waypoint_x[0]-tank[tank_num].x,
 tank[tank_num].waypoint_y[0]-tank[tank_num].y);
 float heading_diff=heading-tank[tank_num].angle;
 if(heading_diff>180.0)  heading_diff-=360.0;
 if(heading_diff<-180.0) heading_diff+=360.0;
 //see if tank is facing close enough to the right direction
 if(fabs(heading_diff)<DRIVE_ANGLE_ERROR)  {
tank[tank_num].dangle=0.0;      //stop rotating
//drive towards next waypoint
//measure distance (approximate with 'Manhattan' distance to save sqrt)
 float distance=fabs(tank[tank_num].waypoint_x[0]-tank[tank_num].x+
   tank[tank_num].waypoint_y[0]-tank[tank_num].y);
   //see if we've arrived
   if(distance<WAYPOINT_CLOSE_ENOUGH)  {

   //------------ Add behavior #5 here --------------
   //bump waypoints down one
   for(int k=0;k<tank[tank_num].num_waypoints;k++)  {
    tank[tank_num].waypoint_x[k]=tank[tank_num].waypoint_x[k+1];
    tank[tank_num].waypoint_y[k]=tank[tank_num].waypoint_y[k+1];
    }
    tank[tank_num].num_waypoints--;
    if(tank[tank_num].velocity>0.5)
    tank[tank_num].move_slow=true;  //slow down if still moving
    }
    else  {
    //we haven't arrived, but are pointing in the right direction
    //choose speed depending on distance
     if(distance>DISTANCE_TO_SLOW_DOWN)
      tank[tank_num].move_fast=true;  //accelerate
```

```
    else   {       //close to destination
     if(tank[tank_num].velocity<=0.0)
      //accelerate a bit if close but not there yet
      tank[tank_num].move_fast=true;
     if(tank[tank_num].velocity>1.6)
       //deaccelarate, getting close
       tank[tank_num].move_slow=true;
       }
      }
    }
    else   {       //rotate to face waypoint
     tank[tank_num].dangle=0.35*heading_diff;
    }
   }
//behavior #6: idle tanks pick a waypoint and navigate towards it
else  {
int landmark=patrol_landmark_num[tank[tank_num].team];
path_plan(tank[tank_num].x,tank[tank_num].y,
 landmark_x[landmark],landmark_y[landmark],tank_num);
 //increment next landmark pointer
 patrol_landmark_num[tank[tank_num].team]++;
 if(patrol_landmark_num[tank[tank_num].team]>=num_landmarks)
 patrol_landmark_num[tank[tank_num].team]=0;
 //allow behavior #5 to override
 tank[tank_num].coming_to_help=false;
 }
}


//make sure no robot tanks attempt to rotate or travel too fast
for(tank_num=0;tank_num<NUM_TANKS;tank_num++)
//AI only for alive robot tanks
   if((tank[tank_num].robot)&&(tank[tank_num].status))  {
      //keep velocity within limits
      if(tank[tank_num].velocity>tank[tank_num].max_speed)
        tank[tank_num].velocity=tank[tank_num].max_speed;
      if(tank[tank_num].velocity<-1.0*tank[tank_num].max_speed)
        tank[tank_num].velocity=-1.0*tank[tank_num].max_speed;
      //keep rotation speed within limits
      if(tank[tank_num].dangle>tank[tank_num].max_rot_rate)
        tank[tank_num].dangle=tank[tank_num].max_rot_rate;
      if(tank[tank_num].dangle<-1.0*tank[tank_num].max_rot_rate)
        tank[tank_num].dangle=-1.0*tank[tank_num].max_rot_rate;
   }
```

To test this code, change NUM_TANKS to 5, and let the game run with just the five blue tanks from team 0. No enemies will be found, and only behaviors #4 and #6 will be invoked (see Figure 9.10, on the facing page). A time-lapse mode was set again by not clearing the image or rendering the camera image (see the TIME_LAPSE_DEMO compile-time flag in twars_13).

Figure 9.10: With no enemies, tanks go into behavior #6: patrolling.

9.10 Behavior #5: Helping

You have just one more behavior to add before your game engine AI is complete!

Behavior #5: retasking. If a robot tank has just arrived at a waypoint, it will pull the next waypoint off the list if its coming_to_help variable is true, or if coming_to_help is false and a team member currently sees an enemy, it will throw away the current waypoint list and plan a new path to the (X, Y) location of the sighted enemy.

Since you have set it up before, you need only to place a bit of code into your behavior priority system, and you're done:

```
YourARGame/Tank Wars Projects/twars_14_help/twars_14_help.cpp

//---- AI Behavior Priority System -----
for(int tank_num=0;tank_num<NUM_TANKS;tank_num++)

//AI only for alive robot tanks
if((tank[tank_num].robot)&&(tank[tank_num].status))  {

 //check for conditions for behavior #1
 if(tank[tank_num].enemy_lined_up)  {
 //behavior #1: If a robot tank sees an enemy tank
 //and is lined up with it, it should launch a missile.
 tank[tank_num].request_fire=true;
 }

 //check for conditions for behavior #2
else if(tank[tank_num].enemy_seen)  {
 //behavior #2: If a robot tank sees an enemy tank,
 //it should rotate to line up with it.
 tank[tank_num].dangle=0.35*tank[tank_num].enemy_delta_angle;
 }
 //check for conditions for behavior #3
else if(tank[tank_num].recently_hit)  {
 //behavior #3: If a robot tank gets hit by a missile,
 //it will rotate to face the direction of
 //where the missile came from.
 float new_direction_to_face=tank[tank_num].hit_angle+180;
 float angle_to_attacker=new_direction_to_face-tank[tank_num].angle;
 while(angle_to_attacker>180.0)  angle_to_attacker-=360.0;
 while(angle_to_attacker<-180.0) angle_to_attacker+=360.0;
 tank[tank_num].dangle=0.35*angle_to_attacker;
      }
 //behavior #4: see if we have a path to travel on
 else if(tank[tank_num].num_waypoints>0)  {
 //navigate towards next destination
 float heading=get_angle(tank[tank_num].waypoint_x[0]-tank[tank_num].x,
   tank[tank_num].waypoint_y[0]-tank[tank_num].y);
 float heading_diff=heading-tank[tank_num].angle;
 if(heading_diff>180.0)  heading_diff-=360.0;
 if(heading_diff<-180.0) heading_diff+=360.0;
 //see if tank is facing close enough to the right direction
 if(fabs(heading_diff)<DRIVE_ANGLE_ERROR)  {
 tank[tank_num].dangle=0.0;      //stop rotating
 //drive towards next waypoint
 //measure distance (approximate with
 //'Manhattan' distance to save sqrt)
 float distance=fabs(tank[tank_num].waypoint_x[0]-tank[tank_num].x+
   tank[tank_num].waypoint_y[0]-tank[tank_num].y);
```

```
//see if we've arrived
if(distance<WAYPOINT_CLOSE_ENOUGH)  {

//------------ Add behavior #5 here --------------
if(tank[tank_num].coming_to_help==false)
{
//consider aborting current path if any other
//team members see an enemy
for(int i=0;i<NUM_TANKS;i++)
if((tank[i].status)&&(tank[i].enemy_seen))  {
//tank i sees an enemy, go over to tank i's location
path_plan(tank[tank_num].x,tank[tank_num].y,
 tank[i].x,tank[i].y,tank_num);
 tank[tank_num].coming_to_help=true;
 }
 }
//bump waypoints down one
for(int k=0;k<tank[tank_num].num_waypoints;k++)  {
 tank[tank_num].waypoint_x[k]=tank[tank_num].waypoint_x[k+1];
 tank[tank_num].waypoint_y[k]=tank[tank_num].waypoint_y[k+1];
}
 tank[tank_num].num_waypoints--;
 if(tank[tank_num].velocity>0.5)
 tank[tank_num].move_slow=true;  //slow down if still moving
 }
 else  {
//we haven't arrived, but are pointing in the right direction
//choose speed depending on distance
 if(distance>DISTANCE_TO_SLOW_DOWN)
 tank[tank_num].move_fast=true;  //accelerate
 else  {
//close to destination
 if(tank[tank_num].velocity<=0.0)
//accelerate a bit if close but not there yet
 tank[tank_num].move_fast=true;
 if(tank[tank_num].velocity>1.6)
//deaccelarate, getting close
 tank[tank_num].move_slow=true;
 }
 }
}
else  {
 //rotate to face waypoint
 tank[tank_num].dangle=0.35*heading_diff;
 }
 }
//behavior #6: idle tanks pick a waypoint and navigate towards it
else  {
 int landmark=patrol_landmark_num[tank[tank_num].team];
 path_plan(tank[tank_num].x,tank[tank_num].y,
   landmark_x[landmark],landmark_y[landmark],tank_num);
```

```
//increment next landmark pointer
patrol_landmark_num[tank[tank_num].team]++;
if(patrol_landmark_num[tank[tank_num].team]>=num_landmarks)
  patrol_landmark_num[tank[tank_num].team]=0;
//allow behavior #5 to override
tank[tank_num].coming_to_help=false;
}}

//make sure no robot tanks attempt to rotate or travel too fast
for(tank_num=0;tank_num<NUM_TANKS;tank_num++)
//AI only for alive robot tanks
  if((tank[tank_num].robot)&&(tank[tank_num].status))  {
    //keep velocity within limits
    if(tank[tank_num].velocity>tank[tank_num].max_speed)
      tank[tank_num].velocity=tank[tank_num].max_speed;
    if(tank[tank_num].velocity<-1.0*tank[tank_num].max_speed)
      tank[tank_num].velocity=-1.0*tank[tank_num].max_speed;
    //keep rotation speed within limits
    if(tank[tank_num].dangle>tank[tank_num].max_rot_rate)
      tank[tank_num].dangle=tank[tank_num].max_rot_rate;
    if(tank[tank_num].dangle<-1.0*tank[tank_num].max_rot_rate)
      tank[tank_num].dangle=-1.0*tank[tank_num].max_rot_rate;
  }
```

This new behavior is shown in Figure 9.11, on the next page. One unlucky green tank is put in the world with five enemy blue tanks. After the first blue tank finds it, several others navigate to the blue tank's location. The green tank is put into manual mode, so it stays still for the test. When one tank sees an enemy tank, other team members, who are completing a waypoint change course, will to come help.

9.11 Complete Tank Wars

Now let's pull out the stops and see our full game in action! The define statement NUM_TANKS is set back to 10, and all tanks are set to be robot tanks. The battle then ensues, and we can enjoy the action (see Figure 9.12, on page 274, and Figure 9.13, on page 275).

9.12 Conclusions to Tank Wars

You are now the proud owner/programmer of an AR game. It could use some improvement, but it contains many useful elements that can be applied to many AR games or animations. The basic alignment of real and virtual cameras is done with the ARTag library, 3D models are loaded into memory from OBJ files using the Mesh Manager, a path

Figure 9.11: TEAM MEMBERS COME TO HELP.

planning algorithm was provided, and the behavior priority system was outlined. Behaviors were built up based on stimuli provided from path planning and simulated visibility.

Where can you go from here, and what would be some satisfying programming exercises to help you learn some of the material from this chapter?

Here are some possibilities:

- Remove the aggressive first three behaviors of tanks firing missiles at each other, and instead make a simulated simple city in which vehicles simply drive around on errands.
- Make an action strategy game where you use a handheld pointer pattern (such as used in the ARTag program ARTag Cad) and the artag_project_between_objects() function to direct your tanks from one area to another.
- Create a larger pattern, such as the table.gif/table.cf pattern, and create a larger world. Expand the size of the map image, and increase the number of tanks to have dozens of combatants.

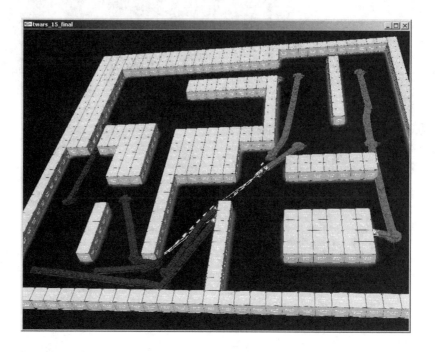

Figure 9.12: ALL BEHAVIORS CODED AND ALL TANKS IN PLAY

- Add a runaway behavior and make a different model type (such as a military truck) flee when it gets hit with a missile—it could be a modified form of the tank structure.
- Improve behavior #4. You may notice that the tanks sometimes run into walls. Some tweaking could help the tanks follow their waypoints more easily.
- Change the game so that tanks cannot drive through each other.
- Try to design behaviors to get tanks out of traffic jams.
- Change the map so that you can load an arbitrary rectangular map instead of our fixed 32 by 32 map.

9.13 Expanding Tank Wars

To give you something more to play with, we have provided our extension of Tank Wars in the book download—the executable is twars. This version of the game has more elaborate behaviors added to the robot tank AI, such as traffic jam avoidance. The Tank Wars examples are

Figure 9.13: ANOTHER VIEW OF THE BATTLE

actually simplified versions of this twars program. You will find the twars project and a compiled version in code\YourARGame.

If you want to try adding some new scenery, there is a twars directory that contains some OBJ models for buildings and a ground texture (see Figure 9.14, on the following page). However, these models are not as interesting as they could be. Try making your city look even better by using your own—more detailed—models (see Figure 9.15, on the next page, and Figure 9.16, on page 277).

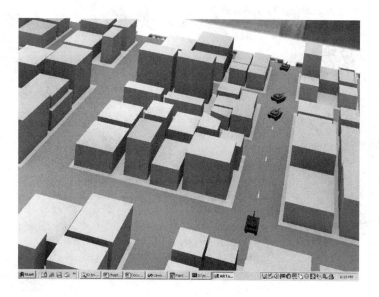

Figure 9.14: TWARS WITH PLAIN BUILDINGS

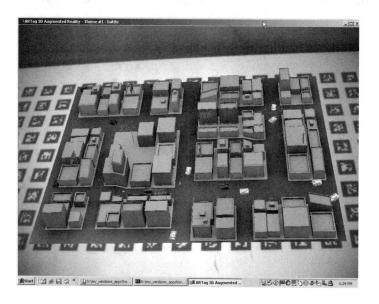

Figure 9.15: TWARS WITH DETAILED BUILDING MODELS

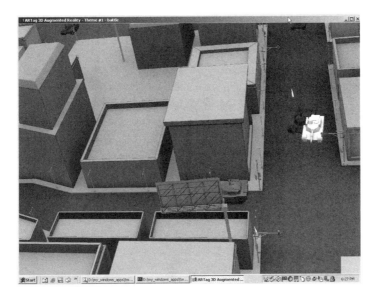

Figure 9.16: TOP VIEW OF TWARS WITH DETAILED BUILDING MODELS

How Does ARTag Work?

In past chapters you've been introduced to AR, seen some ARTag demos, and learned some of the theory behind image formation. This appendix will help you understand how an AR marker system works. Of course, this background information is not specifically necessary to create AR applications—it is here to satisfy your curiosity.

A.1 The ARTag Marker System

AR marker systems are designed to find correspondences between an image point (u,v) in pixel coordinates and a point in the real world's 3D space (x,y,z). The correspondences are used to find the pose (position and orientation) of the real camera so the virtual camera can be set to match. To find these correspondences, marker systems employ passive computer vision to locate specially designed marker patterns in images. Figure A.1, on the next page, shows examples of some the markers used with the ARTag system.

Figure A.2, on the following page, shows ARTag markers being detected in an image. In this example, the markers are arranged in arrays. It is possible to use single markers, but using arrays of markers allows for more reliable detection and less jitter-prone projection matrix determination. In other words, using multiple markers will allow you to nail down where an augmentation should appear because you can use more points of reference within the image.

Why is ARTag a great AR system? Here are some reasons:

- It runs in near real-time.
- It reliably finds markers in images.

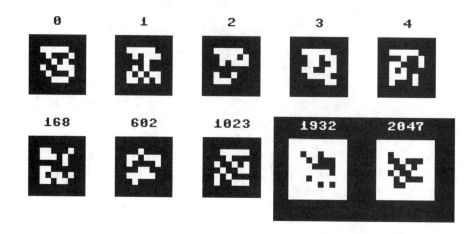

Figure A.1: EXAMPLE ARTAG MARKERS

Figure A.2: ARTAG MARKERS BEING DETECTED IN AN IMAGE

- ARTag markers can be partially blocked and will still be detected.
- The markers use reliable digital coding techniques, so the odds of falsely detecting an ARTag marker or confusing one for another is very slim.
- ARTag has a large "library" of markers (2002), so we can use them on many objects without running out.
- The system can handle varied lighting situations. This means we don't need to carefully control the lighting.
- ARTag can be used in arrays (the preferred choice). The ARTag library combines the pose information from many markers and calculates the overall OpenGL matrix for us.
- ARTag is platform agnostic. Samples are provided for Linux, Windows, and Mac OS X.

ARTag markers are white and black—this aids detection since the ARTag software has to find the difference between only two levels. Each marker is a 10 by 10 unit grid, composed of a two-unit-wide border and a 6 by 6 grid of *interior cells*. The border can either be black on white—the most common case—or be white on black. The marker design was chosen to optimize several factors such as how big the markers need to be in the image and how reliably they're detected. The 6 by 6 grid size and the cool *space invader* patterns are the result of this optimization. The patterns are designed to be as different from one another as possible so as to avoid being detected with the wrong ID.

First, the border is found. The outline from the square markers are seen as *quadrilateral* outlines in the image. From the four corners, a homography is found that allows perspectively correct sampling of the interior cells. Once the digital symbols (each being a 1 or 0) are acquired, a 36-bit code is created—one bit for each of the units in the 6 by 6 grid. Then, using robust digital communication methods, the 36-bit code is turned into a 10-bit ID. This is done to fix errors and to reject codes that don't correspond to a legitimate ARTag marker. A 16-bit checksum is used to reduce the probability of a false detection. Since there are no special features in the marker denoting direction, four rotated copies of the 36-bit code are tried. The markers are unique to rotation, so rotating one will not falsely appear as another.

The processing of ARTag markers can therefore be viewed as a two-stage process; the first is locating the unique feature, and the second is the verification and identification stage. The unique feature is the quadrilateral outline, and the second stage is the digital sampling and symbol processing of every outline found in the first stage.

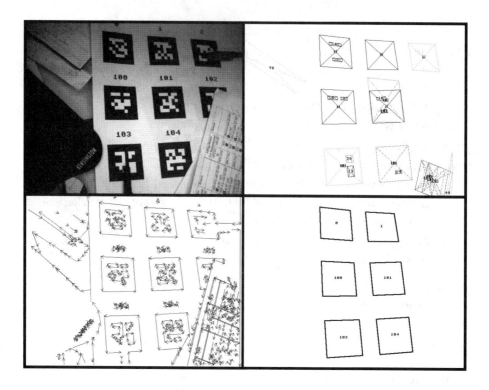

Figure A.3: DIGITAL SYMBOL PROCESSING OF ARTAG INTERIOR CODES

The first processing stage finds the unique quadrilateral features. Line segments are found in the image by looking for edges, as shown in Figure A.3. These segments are joined to form hypothetical quadrilateral shapes. The line segments are found by a randomized search of *edgels* (edge pixels). Note that the borders can be broken, such as those blocked by the two pens or the paper that is cutting off the corner of marker 104.

Using edgels, and line segments formed at borders, allows markers to be found across an image with uneven lighting. This contrasts with another marker system called ARToolkit. ARToolkit relies on a single grayscale threshold to split black from white. An example where both marker systems are subjected to identical lighting is shown in Figure A.4, on the facing page. In this example, ARToolkit can find some markers only because of its reliance on this threshold value. The ability for a marker system to work in various lighting situations is referred to as its *lighting immunity*.

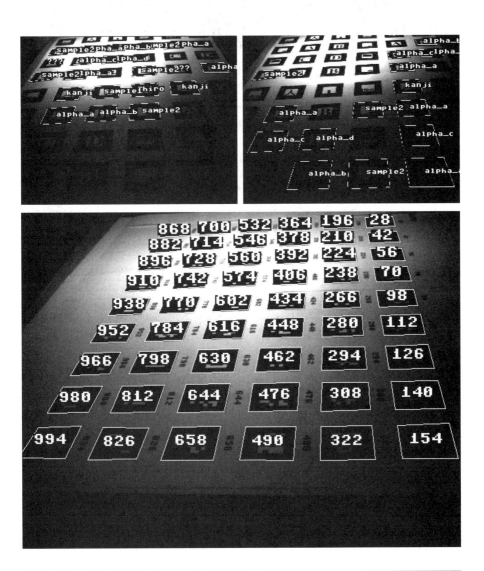

Figure A.4: COMPARISON OF ARTAG'S AND ARTOOLKIT'S IMMUNITY TO POOR LIGHTING

Figure A.5: ARTAG CAN STILL DETECT MARKERS DESPITE PARTIAL OCCLUSION.

Finding partially blocked markers, which is known as *occlusion immunity*, allows more markers to be found in an image. To do this, ARTag uses line segments and *heals* broken sides and corners. How this compares to ARToolkit, which cannot detect partially blocked markers, is shown in Figure A.5.

Figure A.6, on the facing page, shows how using line segments and healing broken sides also helps ARTag find markers that are lying partially outside the image border.

The digital processing steps, starting with the marker (after the 1 and 0 symbols are read from inside the quadrilateral), are shown in Figure A.7, on the next page. All four rotation positions are tried in the Forward Error Correction (FEC) stage. This finds and repairs error bits and processes the checksum test.

A.2 When to Use ARTag

This is a summary of possible situations where you could effectively use ARTag:

- You are creating a video see-through AR application (that is, the user sees a real-time video stream that consists of the real world, as seen from a video camera, plus virtual content added in).

- You do not have, or do not want to use, specialized 3D position measuring systems (for example, ultrasonic, LED, or magnetic systems).

- It is possible to place ARTag markers in the real-world scene.

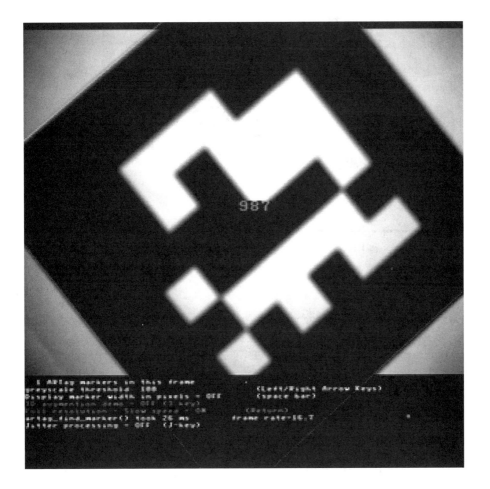

Figure A.6: ARTAG MARKER DETECTED DESPITE ALL ITS CORNERS BEING OUTSIDE THE IMAGE

Figure A.7: DIGITAL SYMBOL PROCESSING OF ARTAG INTERIOR CODES

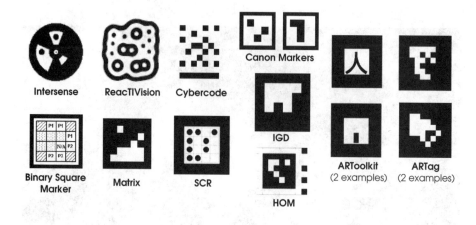

Figure A.8: FIDUCIAL MARKER SYSTEMS

Finding correspondences between points in the video image, and their known 2D or 3D locations in space, allows for the pose (or simply a projection matrix) to be found. This allows for successful overlay of virtual content. Finding these correspondences reliably is the key to making AR work.

A.3 Fiducial Marker Systems

ARTag is not the only fiducial marker system available. A few examples of marker systems—including ARTag—are shown in Figure A.8.

Figure A.9, on the next page, shows a circular fiducial system used by many in the field of photogrammetry (a measurement from photographs). Most of these are research prototypes and aren't available for public use (for example, Binary Square Marker, Matrix, and Reactivision). Others, such as the Intersense circular fiducial, the Canon Markers, and the SCR and IGD markers from the European ARVIKA project, are proprietary and not available for your own AR programs. The HOM marker, also known as the Hoffman marker, is used in photogrammetry for measuring physical objects such as walls and pipes within buildings with a digital camera. The marker must be seen by many pixels and is not suitable for real-time pose determination.

The public fiducial marker systems that are the most usable are ARTag, ARToolkit, and a digitally-improved version of ARToolkit that goes by

Figure A.9: CIRCULAR FIDUCIAL MARKERS—AN INNER DOT IS SUR-
ROUNDED BY BROKEN RING SEGMENTS THAT ENCODE IDENTITY

the name of ARToolkit Plus. ARToolkit was developed by Hirokazu Kato
at the Human Interface Technology Laboratory (HITLab) at the University of Washington. ARTookit is an older fiducial marker system that
inspired ARtag. Some ARToolkit markers are shown in Figure A.10,
on the following page. The BBC and Invisible Train examples shown in
Chapter 1 use ARToolkit Plus.

Both ARToolkit and ARToolkit Plus use a method called *binary thresholding* to find the quadrilateral unique feature outline. In this method, a
grayscale value is required, and all pixels are labeled either as black or
as white—depending on whether their grayscale value is above or below
this threshold. Black pixels are then grouped into connected components, and the border is analyzed to see whether it is a quadrilateral.
The interior of the ARTookit marker is then compared to a stored pattern. The set of patterns is preloaded from a file for every marker that
the system should detect. Figure A.11, on the next page, shows these
stages of detection for ARToolkit. Figure A.12, on the following page,
shows some pattern files that include the internal pattern that is compared to the interior of quadrilaterals found in the image. Each marker
has twelve prototypes stored in the file. For each of three markers, the
marker itself is shown on the left, and the data in the pattern file is
shown on the right.

ARToolkit was a tremendous invention. Many research projects and
graduate studies theses have been written about it, and it is still used
in many AR projects.

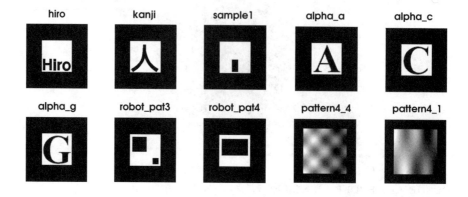

Figure A.10: ARTOOLKIT MARKERS

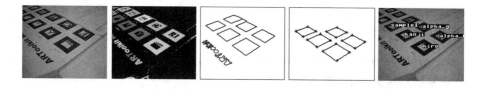

Figure A.11: STAGES OF PROCESSING FOR ARTOOLKIT MARKERS

Figure A.12: VISUALIZATION OF PATTERN FILES FOR ARTOOLKIT

ARTag improves upon the performance of ARToolkit simply by virtue of having been created when more processing power was available. ARToolkit was created in an era of slower computers—there are many ingenious optimizations and clever algorithms to perform the binary thresholding in real time on slower machines. Therefore, ARToolkit's processing does not require as much processing power as ARTag. ARTag became feasible for real-time performance only a few years later. ARToolkit also has more human-readable interior patterns. In other words, it's softer on the eyes than ARTag.

However, it does have some drawbacks, mainly that of lighting sensitivity and the number of false positive detections and *intermarker confusion* events that occur. Intermarker confusion occurs when one marker is falsely mistaken for another. Note that this is different from a false positive, which is when a marker is *detected* but doesn't actually exist. False positives usually occur when there happens to be a quadrilateral shape in the environment.

ARToolkit Plus is a recent improvement over ARToolkit, inspired by the improved performance that the binary coding in ARTag achieves. It was created by Daniel Wagner at the Technical University of Vienna. ARToolkit Plus uses the same quadrilateral search code as ARToolkit but adds some digital encoding for the second stage. However, the digital coding is not as advanced as ARTag, and it can return a higher intermarker confusion rate. In addition, it can't recover from error symbols as well as ARTag. Still, for applications requiring high speed, you may want to consider ARToolkit Plus as an alternative to ARTag. If you have any doubts, there are several publications in computer vision and augmented reality comparing the various systems.

A.4 Comparing Fiducial Marker Systems

How should one compare different marker systems?

Here are fiducial marker performance criteria/metrics:

- False positive rate: how often is a marker erroneously reported?
- False negative rate: how often is a marker missed?
- Intermarker confusion rate: how often is one marker mistaken for another?
- Lighting immunity: working under harsh uncontrolled lighting.

- Occlusion immunity: does the marker have to be completely visible for successful detection?
- Perspective/affine projection support.
- *Planarity restriction*: can the system handle markers on flat or curved/warped surfaces?
- Library size: how many unique markers can be handled?
- Minimum and maximum image size: range of distances for detection.
- Is *photometric calibration* required?
- Performance: processing requirements.

All of the four-sided fiducial marker types satisfy the perspective projection criteria (that is, their interiors can be extracted correctly from the four quadrilateral corners). ARToolkit, to some degree, needs photometric calibration (light response of cameras and marker material), which is usually done by capturing sample marker prototypes for the pattern files using the same lighting and camera that will be employed in the final application. ARToolkit and ARToolkit Plus boast better speed than ARTag, but at the cost of the first five criteria listed.

Because of ARTag's digital checksum, it provides a lower false positive rate. False markers are rarely detected, and the intermarker confusion rate is also low—because of the digital coding used. ARTag also has a lower false negative rate. This is because of detection despite broken borders and also because of ARTag's digital error correction. When comparing the first three criteria between fiducial marker systems that use black-and-white digital encoding, the number of data bits generally gives you an idea of how low these various error rates can be. Most of the marker systems that use black and white digital cells (square regions in the interior) have a 4 by 4 grid; this allows only 16 bits that have to encode rotation, some ID bits, and preferably some checksum and/or error correcting codes. ARTag dedicates 16 bits just to the checksum for preventing false positives, so ARTag will perform better.

A.5 ARTag Markers Using Arrays

Throughout this book, you have seen ARTag markers used in planar arrays. Arrays are used because no single marker has to be relied upon to find the projection matrix. The use of multiple markers also improves the system performance since the odds of not seeing any markers is greatly reduced.

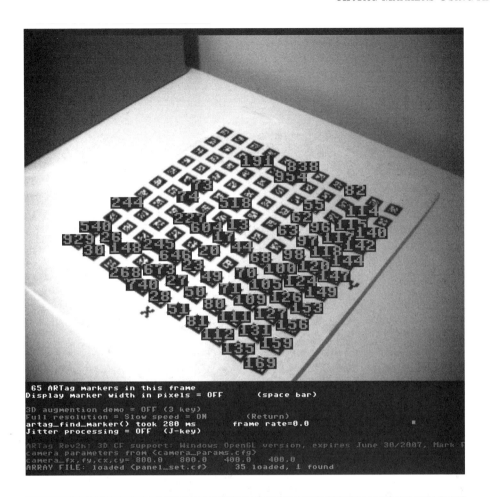

The following text appears within the figure:

```
65 ARTag markers in this frame
Display marker width in pixels = OFF        (space bar)

3D augmentation demo = OFF (3 key)
Full resolution = Slow speed = ON          (Return)
artag_find_marker() took 280 ms      frame rate=0.0
Jitter processing = OFF  (J-key)

ARTag Rev2h: 3D CF support: Windows OpenGL version, expires June 30/2007, Mark F
camera parameters from <camera_params.cfg>
camera_fx,fy,cx,cy= 800.0   800.0   400.0   400.0
ARRAY FILE: loaded <panel_set.cf>      35 loaded, 1 found
```

Figure A.13: INDIVIDUAL ARTAG MARKERS DETECTED IN AN ARRAY

Also, the projection matrix can be calculated to a higher precision that provides less augmentation jitter if the correspondence points are spread across the image.

A screenshot from artag_viewer_image.exe, which is an executable in the behind_the_scenes directory in the ARTag SDK download, is shown in Figure A.13. The figure shows individual markers being detected.

Figure A.14, on the following page, shows markers combined to form the projection matrix, which can then be used to render 3D augmentations for AR. ARTag markers provide correspondences that allow the camera-object pose—in the form of a projection matrix—to be found with low jitter. The X, Y, and Z axes are labeled, and a grid shows the X-Y plane.

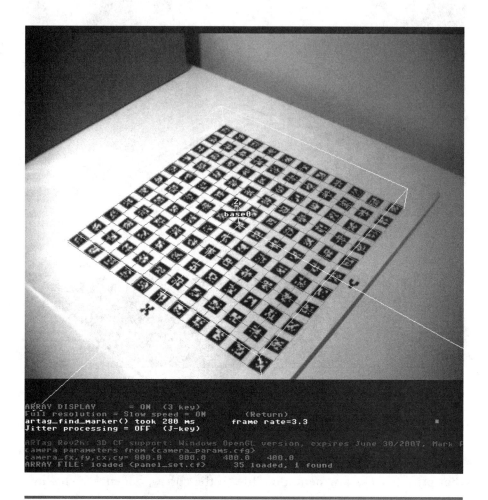

Figure A.14: THE MARKERS PROVIDE CORRESPONDENCES THAT ALLOW THE CAMERA-OBJECT POSE.

A.6 Further Reading on ARTag

You can read more about ARTag, its applications, and comparisons to other marker systems in the following papers:

- Mark Fiala. "ARTag, a Fiducial Mark System Using Digital Techniques." *CVPR 2005* (*Proc. IEEE Computer Vision and Pattern Recognition*). Vol 2, pages 590–596. July 2005.

- Mark Fiala. "ARTag Revision 1, A Fiducial Marker System Using Digital Techniques." NRC publication NRC 47419, NRC/ERB-1117. November 24, 2004.

- Mark Fiala. "ARTag, an Improved Marker System Based on AR-Toolkit." NRC publication NRC 47166, NRC/ERB-1111. July 28, 2004.

- Mark Fiala. "Magic Lens Augmented Reality: Table-top and Augmentorium." SIGGRAPH 2007, poster. Aug. 5–9, 2007.

- M. Kostandov, J. Schwertfeger, O. Jenkings, R. Jianu, M. Buller, D. Hartmann, M Loper, A. Tsoli, M. Vondrak, W. Zhou, Mark Fiala, Robot Gaming. "Learning Using Augmented Reality." SIGGRAPH 2007, poster. Aug. 5–9, 2007.

- Mark Fiala. "Magic Mirror and Hand-held and Wearable Augmentations." VR 2007 (IEEE Virtual Reality 2007). March 2007.

- Mark Fiala, Chang Shu. "Self-Identifying Patterns for Plane-Based Camera Calibration." Machine Vision and Applications Journal (MVA)—accepted, to be printed.

- Mark Fiala, Chang Shu. "3D Model Creation using Self-Identifying Markers and SIFT Keypoints." HAVE 2006 (IEEE Intl. Workshop on Haptic Audio Visual Environments and their Applications). November 2006.

- Mark Fiala. "3D Input Using Hand-held Objects and Computer Vision." HAVE 2006 (IEEE Intl. Workshop on Haptic Audio Visual Environments and their Applications). November 2006.

- Mark Fiala. "Dark Matter Method for Correct Augmented Reality Occlusion Relationships." HAVE 2006 (IEEE Intl. Workshop on Haptic Audio Visual Environments and their Applications). November 2006.

- Mark Fiala. "Automatic Projector Calibration Using Self-Identifying Patterns." CVPR/Procams 2005 (PROCAMS workshop in conjunction with IEEE Computer Society International Conference on Computer Vision and Pattern Recognition). NRC 48207. June 20–26, 2005.

- Mark Fiala. "ARTag Fiducial Marker System Applied to Vision Based Spacecraft Docking." Robvis/IROS, IEEE Robot Vision for Space Applications Workshop held in conjunction with IEEE/RSJ International Conference on Intelligent Robots and Systems (IROS 2005). NRC 48243. August 2–6 2005.

- Mark Fiala, Chang Shu. "Background Subtraction Using Self-Identifying Patterns." CRV 2005 (Second Canadian Conference on Computer and Robot Vision). May 2005.

- Mark Fiala. "Comparing ARTag and ARToolkit Plus Fiducial Marker Systems." HAVE 2005 (IEEE Intl. Workshop on Haptic Audio Visual Environments and their Applications). October 2005.

- Mark Fiala, "Fiducial Marker Systems for Augmented Reality: Comparisons Between ARTag and ARToolkit." MIRAGE 2005 (IEEE Intl. Computer Vision/Computer Graphics Collaboration for Model-based Imaging, Rendering, Image Analysis and Graphics Effects), INRIA Rocquencourt, France. March 2005.

Appendix B

Troubleshooting

B.1 General Issues

Q: The AR demos will not work on my computer. How can I check what's wrong?

A: Chapter 2 gives details about setting up AR on your machine.

Q: When I try to run image_test.exe, all I see is a gray gradient.

A: Make sure that camera_image.pgm is in the same directory as image_test.exe.

B.2 Webcam Issues

Q: No image appears when I run the AR demos. What's happening?

A: Are you using a USB 2.0 webcam? The exercises in this book were tested only with USB 2.0 webcams. If you are using a USB 2.0 camera, did you test your webcam with other software before trying the AR demos? If not, verify that your camera will display real-time video.

B.3 ARTag Issues

Q: No AR elements appear when I place an ARTag marker in front of the camera. What is wrong?

A: Check that you are using the right ARTag markers for the demo that you are running. If you have written your own AR application, make sure you're loading and searching for the correct ARTag pattern. Also, are your ARTag markers close enough to the camera? To be recognized,

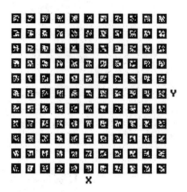

Figure B.1: THESE MARKERS ARE TOO SMALL.

the individual ARTag markers should be at least 20 to 30 pixels in the camera image. Markers that are too small or that are missing the white border may not be recognized by the ARTag software (see Figure B.1).

This means that if you're printing out a number of markers, each one must be the right size (see Figure B.2, on the facing page). If the markers are large enough, even a portion of the pattern could be enough for it to be recognized (see Figure B.3, on page 298).

Only a few of the markers in the *base0* array need to be visible for the ARTag software to detect the object. But if you use a detail from *base0*, make sure to use the markers in the middle of the image. If you use the ones on the far sides, you may not be able to see the augmentation because it is drawn relative to the object and it may be out of the visible range.

Q: I'm trying to associate a model (or image) with an individual ARTag marker, but the model (or image) isn't appearing properly.

A: You cannot repeat markers, so make sure you're not loading additional array patterns in setup_artag_3d. Most of the IDs 1-16 are inside panel_set.cf, many are inside *base0*, and the toolbar patterns use markers in the 600s.

ARTag first finds markers, then it goes through and checks which markers match arrays loaded in setup_artag_3d. Then ARTag uses the markers that belong to arrays to find the projection matrix of those arrays—whatever markers are left over can be associated in the individual markers section.

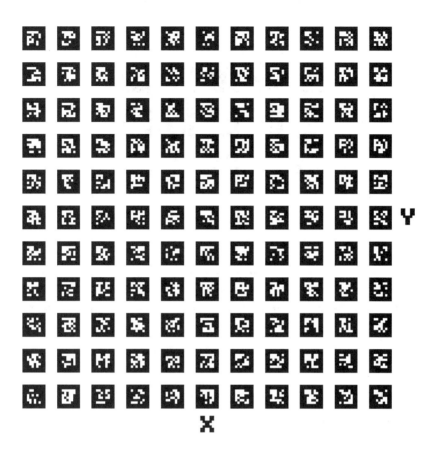

Figure B.2: THIS ARTAG PATTERN WILL BE FOUND.

Q: When I try to use ARTag, my models jump around on their own.

A: There are a few ways to deal with models that are jittery. The best way is to calibrate your camera and use more markers. For example, use an array such as *base0*. Also, make sure your markers are flat. You might want to actually mount the markers on something stiff—regular paper will not work as well as something that is properly mounted.

Figure B.3: THIS DETAIL OF AN ARTAG PATTERN WILL BE FOUND.

B.4 ARTag Development Issues

Q: I get build errors when I try to compile an ARTag program.

A: Check whether your issue is discussed in Chapter 6.

Q: When I try to compile an ARTag project in Visual Studio 2005, I get the build error "Fatal error cannot open 'LIBC'."

A: This is a common migration issue from Visual Studio 2003. To remove the error, navigate to Configuration Properties > Linker > Input, and set Ignore specific library to "libc." In earlier versions of Visual Studios libc.lib was already added.

Q: I'm seeing an error similar to this: "Fatal error C1083: Cannot open include file: 'glut.h': No such file or directory."

A: The OpenGL extension library GLUT is required to run ARTag programs. You will need to get the files for GLUT: glut.h, glut32.lib, and glut32.dll. Either copy them into your project or configure your compiler to find them.

Q: When I try to build an ARTag project, it fails with this error, "Cannot open include file: 'pgrflycapture.lib': No such file or directory."

A: This Point Grey Research Dragonfly camera file should be included only if you are using a Dragonfly camera. To remove the error, go to Project > Properties > Configuration Properties > Linker, and remove pgrflycapture.lib from the list of Additional Dependencies.

Q: When building my project, I see a linking error about "External symbols" being "already defined." It looks like this: "LIBCMTD.lib(hooks.obj) : error LNK2005: 'void __cdecl terminate(void)'."

A: You are probably using a project that was created in an earlier version of Visual Studio. From http://msdn2.microsoft.com/en-us/library/6db3z985.aspx:

"When you open a .NET Class Library or ASP.NET Web Service project created in a previous version of Visual C++, /Zl will be added to the Command Line property page for the compiler in the project setting dialog box, but msvcrt.lib and msvcmrt.lib will not be added to the linker's Additional Dependencies property. This will result in a linker error (LNK2001) when you build the project. To resolve the error, add msvcrt.lib and msvcmrt.lib to the linker's Additional Dependencies property or delete /Zl from the compiler's Command Line property page."

To solve this problem, go to Project > Properties > Configuration Properties > Linker, and add msvcrt.lib and msvcmrt.lib to the list of Additional Dependencies.

Q: I want to write code that can be ported to multiple systems, but when I create a Visual Studio project, I'm required to include stdfax.h, which is a Windows-specific file.

A: If you choose Empty Project (when you create a new Visual Studio project), you don't need to add the stdfax files, and hence the .cpp files can be used unchanged. If you have already created the project, you can try to remove the dependency by excluding stdfax.h and stdfax.cpp from the project and then changing Project > Properties > Create/Use Precompiled Header to Not Using Precompiled Header. This should allow you to build the project without the dependency.

Q: When I try to run an ARTag demo, I get the following error: "The variable 'width' is being used without being defined."

A: This error occurs when the ARTag software cannot load your camera or no camera is connected.

Q: I'm having trouble debugging ARTag projects in Visual Studio.

A: Refer to the "Debugging in Visual Studio 2005" section of Chapter 6.

B.5   Linux Issues

Q: Why does my OpenGL program work in Windows but produce a blank white texture in Linux?

A: You may need to keep your texture files to a maximum of 256 by 256 pixels or find the settings in your system to raise this limit. Often an OpenGL program will work in Windows but produce a blank white texture in Linux until the texture size is reduced.

B.6   OpenCV Issues

Q: When I try to compile the AR samples, I get an error from camera_cvcam_windows.c.

If you get errors that appear in camera_cvcam_windows.c, you may have the wrong version of OpenCV installed on your machine. Search the Web, and find the most recent version built for your operating system.

Acknowledgments

Stephen: First of all, thanks to Dr. Mark for adding this project to his schedule and explaining the finer points of AR to his writer friend. Thanks to Andy Hunt and Dave Thomas for making the project a reality. Thanks also go to editor Daniel Steinberg for helping us get over the hurdles. And, as always, thanks to my agent Neil Salkind (from the Studio B literary agency).

Mark: Much thanks to Stephen for his work over the many months of this project and help finding an audience outside academic publications. Gerhard Roth is appreciated for his introduction to and mentorship in the world of AR. And we both have to thank all the reviewers listed next, especially Christian Langis whose reviews, comments, and diligent bug fixes almost filled a book by themselves.

Mark and Stephen would especially like to thank the following technical reviewers for lending their expertise to the book:

- Christian Langis
- Cosmin Smeu-Cinteza
- Shahzad Malik
- Steven Ness
- Gerhard Roth
- Andy Dunn
- Herb Schilling
- Bruce Stewart
- Mike Laing

Glossary

AR: See *Augmented reality (AR)*.

ARTag: A system of augmented reality marker tags that was developed by Dr. Mark Fiala at the National Research Council of Canada labs. ARTag is a digitally coded fiducial marker system for augmented reality. ARTag differs from previous marker systems in that the tags have been digitally produced and the markers have been verified to be the optimum symbols for reducing false positives and the negative effect of occlusion.

Augmented reality (AR): Supplementing a user's perception of the world by combining computer generated elements with the real world. The most common AR systems use displays to augment a user's vision. Virtual reality is different from AR because, in virtual reality systems, the user's experience is entirely virtual.

HMD: See *Head-mounted display*.

Head-mounted display: A computer display that is worn on the head. HMDs are becoming more popular and will surely play a large role in the future of visual augmented reality.

Homography: According to Wikipedia, "a relation between two figures, such that any given point in one figure corresponds to one and only one point in the other, and vice versa.... In the field of computer vision, a homography is defined in two-dimensional space as a mapping between a point on a ground plane as seen from one camera to the same point on the ground plane as seen from a second camera." (Source: http://en. wikipedia.org/wiki/Homography)

Occlusion: When a real-world object interferes with an AR marker tag, for example, putting your hand on top of an AR marker tag such that the marker is blocked from the view of the AR camera. Occlusion can result in unrecognized markers.

Optical see-through: An AR see-through display that allows the user to actually see the real-world while AR elements are overlaid on top.

Marker tracking: Technology that uses predetermined patterns to place virtual elements in a digital image. One example of an AR marker system is ARTag. To use ARTag, the patterns are printed and then placed where the user wants the virtual elements to appear.

Markerless tracking: AR technology that uses a system other than marker tags for including AR elements in a digital image. One method for creating markerless AR technology is to use light-emitting diodes.

Registration: Tracking the position and orientation of a user's head. This allows an AR system to use graphics software to overlay virtual elements that are aligned with the user's view of reality.

Triangle strips: Triangle strips are an OpenGL primitive type that allows you to save memory and processing by having to specify only one vertex for every triangle.

Video see-through: An AR see-through display that presents AR elements overlaid on a real-time video image of the world.

VR: See *Virtual reality*.

Virtual reality: Creating an entirely computer-generated environment. Virtual reality is different from augmented reality because AR adds virtual elements to the real world.

Z-buffer: A memory buffer used to increase performance in computer graphics. The z-buffer stores the depth of each pixel so that pixels that are underneath something else are not displayed.

Index

U

V

W

Web 2.0

Welcome to the Web, version 2.0. You need some help to tame the wild technologies out there. Start with *Prototype and script.aculo.us*, a book about two libraries that will make your JavaScript life much easier.

See how to reach the largest possible web audience with *The Accessible Web*.

Prototype and script.aculo.us

Tired of getting swamped in the nitty-gritty of cross-browser, Web 2.0–grade JavaScript? Get back in the game with Prototype and script.aculo.us, two extremely popular JavaScript libraries that make it a walk in the park. Be it Ajax, drag and drop, autocompletion, advanced visual effects, or many other great features, all you need is write one or two lines of script that look so good they could almost pass for Ruby code!

Prototype and script.aculo.us: You never knew JavaScript could do this!
Christophe Porteneuve
(330 pages) ISBN: 1-934356-01-8. $34.95
http://pragprog.com/titles/cppsu

The Accessible Web

The 2000 U.S. Census revealed that 12% of the population is severely disabled. Sometime in the next two decades, one in five Americans will be older than 65. Section 508 of the Americans with Disabilities Act requires your website to provide *equivalent access* to all potential users. But beyond the law, it is both good manners and good business to make your site accessible to everyone. This book shows you how to design sites that excel for all audiences.

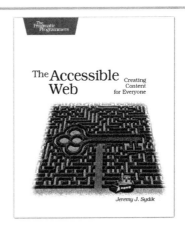

The Accessible Web
Jeremy Sydik
(304 pages) ISBN: 1-934356-02-6. $34.95
http://pragprog.com/titles/jsaccess

Enterprise Ready

Your application is feature complete, but is it ready for the real world? See how to design and deploy production-ready software and *Release It!*.

Did you know Ruby could glue together all sorts of enterprise technologies? See how in *Enterprise Integration with Ruby.*

Release It!

Whether it's in Java, .NET, or Ruby on Rails, getting your application ready to ship is only half the battle. Did you design your system to survive a sudden rush of visitors from Digg or Slashdot? Or an influx of real-world customers from 100 different countries? Are you ready for a world filled with flaky networks, tangled databases, and impatient users?

If you're a developer and don't want to be on call at 3 a.m. for the rest of your life, this book will help.

Design and Deploy Production-Ready Software
Michael T. Nygard
(368 pages) ISBN: 0-9787392-1-3. $34.95
http://pragprog.com/titles/mnee

Enterprise Integration with Ruby

See how to use the power of Ruby to integrate all the applications in your environment. Learn how to
• use relational databases directly and via mapping layers such as ActiveRecord • harness the power of directory services • create, validate, and read XML documents for easy information interchange
• use both high- and low-level protocols to knit applications together

Enterprise Integration with Ruby
Maik Schmidt
(360 pages) ISBN: 0-9766940-6-9. $32.95
http://pragprog.com/titles/fr_eir

Pragmatic Projects

See what an agile project is supposed to feel like in the award-winning *Practices of an Agile Developer*.

Have you ever noticed that project retrospectives feel too little, too late? What you need to do is start having *Agile Retrospectives*.

Practices of an Agile Developer

Agility is all about using feedback to respond to change. Learn how to apply the principles of agility throughout the software development process
• establish and maintain an agile working environment • deliver what users really want
• use personal agile techniques for better coding and debugging • use effective collaborative techniques for better teamwork • move to an agile approach

Practices of an Agile Developer: Working in the Real World
Venkat Subramaniam and Andy Hunt
(189 pages) ISBN: 0-9745140-8-X. $29.95
http://pragprog.com/titles/pad

Agile Retrospectives

Mine the experience of your software development team continually throughout the life of the project. Rather than waiting until the end of the project—as with a traditional retrospective, when it's too late to help—agile retrospectives help you adjust to change *today*.

The tools and recipes in this book will help you uncover and solve hidden (and not-so-hidden) problems with your technology, your methodology, and those difficult "people issues" on your team.

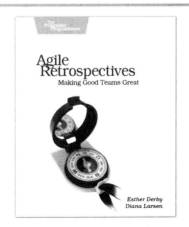

Agile Retrospectives: Making Good Teams Great
Esther Derby and Diana Larsen
(170 pages) ISBN: 0-9776166-4-9. $29.95
http://pragprog.com/titles/dlret

Ruby and Rails

Interested in learning Ruby, or in learning how to use a scripting language the right way? Start with *Everyday Scripting with Ruby: For Teams, Testers, and You*.

If you know Java, and are curious about Ruby on Rails, you don't have to start from scratch. Read *Rails for Java Developers*, and you can catch up to the industry leaders by learning this exciting new technology.

Everyday Scripting with Ruby

Don't waste that computer on your desk. Offload your daily drudgery to where it belongs, and free yourself to do what you should be doing: thinking. All you need is a scripting language (free!), this book (cheap!), and the dedication to work through the examples and exercises. Learn the basics of the Ruby scripting language and see how to create scripts in a steady, controlled way using test-driven design.

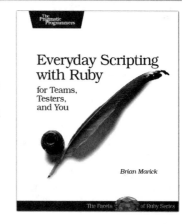

Everyday Scripting with Ruby: For Teams, Testers, and You
Brian Marick
(320 pages) ISBN: 0-9776166-1-4. $29.95
http://pragprog.com/titles/bmsft

Rails for Java Developers

Enterprise Java developers already have most of the skills needed to create Rails applications. They just need a guide which shows how their Java knowledge maps to the Rails world. That's what this book does. It covers: • the Ruby language • building MVC applications • unit and functional testing • security • project automation • configuration • web services This book is the fast track for Java programmers who are learning or evaluating Ruby on Rails.

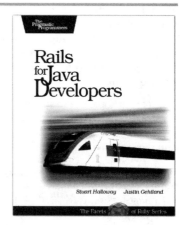

Rails for Java Developers
Stuart Halloway and Justin Gehtland
(300 pages) ISBN: 0-9776166-9-X. $34.95
http://pragprog.com/titles/fr_r4j

Erlang and More

New challenges call for new solutions. The coming multicore crunch makes parallel programming a necessity, not a luxury. Learn how to do it right with *Programming Erlang*.

And whatever language you use, you'll need a good text editor, too. On the Mac, we recommend TextMate.

Programming Erlang

Learn how to write truly concurrent programs—programs that run on dozens or even hundreds of local and remote processors. See how to write high-reliability applications—even in the face of network and hardware failure—using the Erlang programming language.

Programming Erlang: Software for a Concurrent World
Joe Armstrong
(536 pages) ISBN: 1-934356-00-X. $36.95
http://pragprog.com/titles/jaerlang

TextMate

If you're coding Ruby or Rails on a Mac, then you owe it to yourself to get the TextMate editor. And, once you're using TextMate, you owe it to yourself to pick up this book. It's packed with information that will help you automate all your editing tasks, saving you time to concentrate on the important stuff. Use snippets to insert boilerplate code and refactorings to move stuff around. Learn how to write your own extensions to customize it to the way you work.

TextMate: Power Editing for the Mac
James Edward Gray II
(200 pages) ISBN: 0-9787392-3-X. $29.95
http://pragprog.com/titles/textmate

The Pragmatic Bookshelf

The Pragmatic Bookshelf features books written by developers for developers. The titles continue the well-known Pragmatic Programmer style and continue to garner awards and rave reviews. As development gets more and more difficult, the Pragmatic Programmers will be there with more titles and products to help you stay on top of your game.

Visit Us Online

Augmented Reality's Home Page
http://pragprog.com/titles/cfar
Source code from this book, errata, and other resources. Come give us feedback, too!

Register for Updates
http://pragprog.com/updates
Be notified when updates and new books become available.

Join the Community
http://pragprog.com/community
Read our weblogs, join our online discussions, participate in our mailing list, interact with our wiki, and benefit from the experience of other Pragmatic Programmers.

New and Noteworthy
http://pragprog.com/news
Check out the latest pragmatic developments in the news.

Save on the PDF

Save on the PDF version of this book. Owning the paper version of this book entitles you to purchase the PDF version at a terrific discount. The PDF is great for carrying around on your laptop. It's hyperlinked, has color, and is fully searchable.

Buy it now at pragprog.com/coupon.

Contact Us

Phone Orders:	1-800-699-PROG (+1 919 847 3884)
Online Orders:	www.pragprog.com/catalog
Customer Service:	orders@pragprog.com
Non-English Versions:	translations@pragprog.com
Pragmatic Teaching:	academic@pragprog.com
Author Proposals:	proposals@pragprog.com